KEEPERS
OF THE
CASTLE

Real Estate Executives on
Leadership and Management

WILLIAM J. FERGUSON

Urban Land
Institute

ABOUT THE URBAN LAND INSTITUTE

The mission of the Urban Land Institute is to provide leadership in the responsible use of land and in creating and sustaining thriving communities worldwide. ULI is committed to

- Bringing together leaders from across the fields of real estate and land use policy to exchange best practices and serve community needs;
- Fostering collaboration within and beyond ULI's membership through mentoring, dialogue, and problem solving;
- Exploring issues of urbanization, conservation, regeneration, land use, capital formation, and sustainable development;
- Advancing land use policies and design practices that respect the uniqueness of both built and natural environments;
- Sharing knowledge through education, applied research, publishing, and electronic media; and
- Sustaining a diverse global network of local practice and advisory efforts that address current and future challenges.

Established in 1936, the Institute today has more than 34,000 members worldwide, representing the entire spectrum of the land use and development disciplines. ULI relies heavily on the experience of its members. It is through member involvement and information resources that ULI has been able to set standards of excellence in development practice. The Institute has long been recognized as one of the world's most respected and widely quoted sources of objective information on urban planning, growth, and development.

PROJECT STAFF

Dean Schwanke
Senior Vice President,
Publications

James A. Mulligan
Managing Editor

Lise Lingo, Publications Professionals LLC
Manuscript Editor

Betsy VanBuskirk
Creative Director/Book Designer

Craig Chapman
Director, Publishing Operations

Library of Congress Cataloging-in-Publication Data
Ferguson, William J.
  Keepers of the castle : real estate executives on leadership and management / William J. Ferguson.
     p. cm.
  ISBN 978-0-87420-101-7
1. Real estate business—United States—Management. 2. Executives—United States—Interviews. I. Title.
  HD1381.5.U5F47 2009
  333.33068′4—dc22
                                    2009006584

Urban Land Institute
1025 Thomas Jefferson Street, N.W.
Washington, D.C. 20007-5201

ULI Catalog Number: K05

10 9 8 7 6 5 4 3 2 1
Printed in the United States of America.

DEDICATION

A tribute to one of the real estate industry's great leaders, Robert C. Larson.

This leadership research is dedicated to Bob Larson, who has touched many lives and influenced many people. He is the personification of leadership in the truest sense—on the one hand, following his instincts and always doing what he feels is right, while on the other, taking time to be there for anyone who needs him.

One of this book's chapter headings, "Pray for forgiveness, not for permission," is a quote from my interview with Bob. It epitomizes his leadership credo. One example is illustrative. When he became chairman of United Dominion Realty Trust, he recognized that he needed a new chief executive officer to replace the founder, successfully recruited Tom Toomey, and moved the headquarters to Denver from Richmond, Virginia, because it afforded a location to put a world-class management team in place and better operate a national business. The change constituted a large risk, but ultimately offered a tremendous reward.

Another example is Bob becoming chairman of Lazard Real Estate Partners, where he not only assuaged many unhappy investors, but also mentored a management team, including Matt Lustig, that has become one of the premier real estate advisory/principal investment firms in the real estate sector.

Bob's other accomplishments are too numerous to mention, but each reflects his unique leadership talents. Among his leadership roles are trustee of the Urban Land Institute and past chairman of the ULI Foundation; member and chairman emeritus of the advisory board of the Wharton Real Estate Center at the University of Pennsylvania; 26 years with The Taubman Company, culminating in his appointment as chief executive officer; interim president and chief executive officer of Cranbrook, one of the finest independent secondary schools in the country; and independent member of the Thrift Depositor Protection Oversight Board under presidents George H.W. Bush and Bill Clinton. Bob's public board service—ranging from Inter-Continental Hotels Group to Six Continents plc and Bass plc, plus numerous civic organizations where he has assumed a leadership role—is simply too broad to acknowledge here.

Bob Larson is a special person who, more than anyone else in the real estate industry, has proved that leadership is alive and well. All of us whom he has touched are eternally grateful and will never forget his leadership lessons.

William J. Ferguson

ACKNOWLEDGMENTS

Each person who has helped me with this book deserves a paragraph on his or her contribution, but I can only thank them here briefly. First, I would like to thank Jonathan Miller, who has been extraordinarily helpful to me in drafting much of the industry background and historical perspective throughout the book. I would also like to acknowledge my co–managing partner, Michael Herzberg, who has taught me so much about our industry and with whom I have tirelessly partnered in advising our clients on a host of strategic, operating, and human capital issues. I also want to extend my appreciation to a number of others who have worked with me at FPL Advisory Group, especially Kim Chantelois, in moving the publishing process along. And finally, I want to acknowledge Rachelle Levitt and the entire team at ULI for partnering with me most effectively.

And last but not least, I want to acknowledge my wife, Andrea Redmond, who has generously spared me the time, on weekends and at late hours of the night, to spend hundreds of hours drafting the interviews and writing the book. She has always been tremendously unselfish with our time together.

William J. Ferguson

PREFACE

Since the draft of this book was finished, the U.S. real estate markets changed dramatically—for the worse. Many homeowners suddenly faced substantial hardship, while many financial institutions and bond holders have recognized significant losses due to borrower foreclosures and the revaluation of securities that were backed by subprime residential mortgage bonds and other property-related collateral. The resulting pullback in debt availability for borrowers and the reduced market liquidity initially helped precipitate a substantial decline in housing values. The housing crisis, credit crunch, rising energy prices, and a related economic slowdown promise to affect commercial real estate markets as well, although reasonably sound supply/demand fundamentals should help cushion any downturn. In the meantime, real estate leaders have learned another "hard knocks" lesson in how businesses linked to a global credit market must prepare for unforeseen events and move capital prudently.

Economic dislocation self-corrects inevitably, with the usual dose of cyclical pain typically meted out more severely to borrowers who over-leveraged and investors who cut corners on their underwriting and analysis. Astute leaders understand that a steady hand coupled with long-term vision builds organizations that can endure the downs of multifaceted business cycles successfully and profitably take advantage of ensuing opportunities in recovery.

As the collective wisdom of the real estate leaders in this book underscores, the mainstreaming and institutionalization of property-related businesses appears largely irreversible. Future leaders must be able to do more than staff executive teams and manage increasingly complex organizations with financial acumen and interpersonal savvy. They must also understand local markets and bricks-and-mortar principles, while having a firm grasp of national and global economic trends. Leadership matters more than ever in a rapidly evolving business landscape. And tomorrow's leaders will require ever greater skills and innate abilities to ensure success for themselves and their businesses.

CONTENTS

INTRODUCTION

INSTITUTIONALIZING
ENTREPRENEURSHIP

This book examines the transformation of America's largest industry—
real estate—and identifies the attributes necessary for chief executives
and other leaders who are guiding their businesses through profound
change. Over the past three decades real estate companies have morphed
from mostly private, local businesses run by mercurial entrepreneurs into
more institutionalized, publicly traded entities—often with global operations. The skill sets required for managing these organizations have necessarily expanded and grown steadily more complex.

The nation's skylines and expansive suburbs have been sculpted
largely by shrewd developers with the vision and energy to create something out of nothing. From vacant or underused land, these lone cowboys
fashioned office buildings and shopping centers, apartments and warehouses,
as well as hotels and single-family-home subdivisions, using bricks-and-
mortar acumen, financing from banks or insurance companies, and a dose
of marketing chutzpah to attract tenants and buyers. Today, their collective
work product comprises a staggering $20 trillion in assets spread across
the country. The industry generates 70 percent of all local tax revenues and

employs 10 million people. Its size, strengths, and influence get lost next to the more glamorous technology sector, which expanded into telecommunications and entertainment from its foundation in semiconductors, computer software, and hardware. Likewise, real estate has moved well beyond its agency and deal-shop roots.

Indeed, Wall Street bankers and the players in the nation's financial markets have sought to tap the investment opportunities represented in the nation's substantial property marketplace. Institutional players covet vast asset pools of office, retail, and industrial properties: they pursue predictable, income-oriented returns with the opportunity for realizing appreciation. Financial intermediaries, meanwhile, envision transaction structures and brokerage fees that could fatten profit lines. Spurred by the dislocation precipitated by the early 1990s real estate depression, Wall Street firms recapitalized many flailing private real estate companies into public entities. Wall Street's influence helped advance several ownership and management changes that had been underway since pension funds began investing in real estate two decades earlier:

- Financial companies and institutional intermediaries now package commercial real estate into multibillion-dollar portfolios for investment by pension funds, endowments, foundations, foreign investors, and high-net-worth individuals.
- Publicly traded REIT (real estate investment trust) companies in recent years have been stock-picker favorites and familiar choices in 401(k) plans.
- Fixed-income managers structured real estate debt into diversified mortgage instruments (RMBS and CMBS—residential mortgage–backed securities and commercial mortgage–backed securities), sliced and diced in offerings that resemble the range of rated and unrated corporate bonds.
- Rating agencies, stock analysts, and securities regulators now scrutinize transactions and company business, encouraging transparency and providing oversight.

As a result, in the early to mid-2000s global capital poured into U.S. real estate debt and equity through various new securities market channels, providing welcome stores of liquidity to cushion markets and fund projects. But the discipline and disclosures required of public companies naturally clash with the deeply rooted entrepreneurial traditions in the real estate industry. Company managers must grapple with risk management parameters, investor and client relations, Sarbanes-Oxley, and a raft of other financial reporting requirements. Effective leaders realize they must complement their tried-and-true, kick-the-bricks instincts with MBA skills, financial proficiency, and a managerial temperament. In fact, institutionalizing entrepreneurship has become the paradigm for real estate leadership in today's globalizing economy. The challenge of doing so requires companies to install effective management platforms that can nurture and preserve entrepreneurial vision and avoid the chokehold of bureaucracy.

The remarkable evolution of the real estate industry provides a unique research laboratory for understanding how leadership styles and management models must change in the face of the rapidly altering competitive landscape. Over three years, we interviewed industry leaders to better understand their leadership attributes and the cultures they have created. Not surprisingly, much of what we discovered about leadership in real estate organizations applies across the broader spectrum of American business. Our research suggests that corporate failures can often be linked to high egos in chief executives, and that competitive cultures can transform themselves by implementing thin bureaucracies, flat hierarchies, and a risk orientation among senior management. Today's successful chief executive officers typically embody a values-oriented leadership style that incorporates integrity, humility, empathy, enthusiasm, and self-awareness. Good listeners, they are willing to learn from others. They take responsibility for failure and credit others for corporate success. Usually fierce competitors, these leaders demonstrate an unwillingness to lose but stay focused on sustained, long-term results, not the quick fix.

In our research, we found that most leaders, irrespective of their industry niche, follow six essential leadership principles:

- **Afford a Place to Dock:** Build cultures to nurture employees and in turn nourish company growth.
- **Pray for Forgiveness, Not Permission:** Encourage proactive management rather than tentative, "avoid mistakes" decision making.
- **Hire Hard, Manage Easy:** Set a high bar when hiring people and give executives sufficient autonomy.
- **Learn What Not to Do:** Set clear objectives and maintain a focus.
- **Build a Legacy, Not a Reputation:** Emphasize winning teams, not superstar status.
- **Share a Sense of Vulnerability:** Acknowledge that leaders don't have all the answers or make all the right decisions.

In short, these leadership principles presented themselves as the core elements of a paradigm that is crucial to the successful institutionalization of a real estate enterprise—and one that offers lessons for every business.

For this project, I interviewed more than 150 real estate executives, each of whom has been at the forefront of one of the most significant and sudden industry transformations in the history of business. These leaders were selected as the "best and brightest" by their peers, grouped in committees across six industry sectors—commercial mortgage financing, commercial real estate ownership/brokerage, residential mortgage finance, homebuilding, lodging and hospitality, and housing for seniors. These committees comprised investment bankers, research analysts, money managers, and industry consultants, as well as current and retired chief executives. Committee members chose the ten outstanding leaders in their sectors on the basis of certain characteristics, and within each committee, these lists were compiled and winnowed to produce 25 prospects. Each person was interviewed for about 90 minutes. In this book, in addition to culling and analyzing the wealth of insights and information from these meetings, I have included key passages from each executive to impart the flavor and passion of the lessons they have learned.

For more than 25 years, I have recruited senior-level executives and board members for all sectors of the real estate industry, including the majority of the industry's newly appointed CEOs. In addition, I have assisted real estate corporations with succession planning, board performance assessment, culture transitions, and CEO coaching. I have made it my business to develop a good feel for leadership qualities: my "nose" for leadership is the reason many real estate leaders listen to me. With my partner, Michael Herzberg, I established FPL Advisory Group in 1989 to help clients in the commercial and residential real estate world think through the strategic, human capital, and financial considerations of running a business. Our early clients were largely entrepreneurial deal shops. Since then, leading firms in the industry have developed into sophisticated, global corporations with an organizational mindset.

Despite that experience, I didn't know what to expect at the outset of this research. Leadership in the real estate industry is often identified with the sector's entrepreneurial origins. Television shows and films exaggerate and embroider the stock character of the real estate mogul—the bold opportunist with a glamorous but sometimes fatal mix of arrogance, intolerance, and unchecked ego. As likely to inspire as to repulse or amuse, Hollywood's archetypal barons often teeter between spectacular accomplishment and colossal failure.

Of course, what I discovered in the real world was quite different. The real estate leaders interviewed for this book acknowledge the need for entrepreneurial spirit and vision: willingness to take risks, inherent dissatisfaction with the status quo, openness to doing things differently, and willingness to push to accomplish what others said couldn't be done. Yet every one also recognizes the need to institutionalize the management of their enterprises. They understand that the size and probable growth of their organizations demands values-based leadership as well as a focus on creating and building organizations that care for, nurture, and educate their people.

There were numerous reasons for writing this book. Studying the leadership attributes of these chief executives is an important step in recognizing and defining real estate's emerging role as America's largest industry. Acknowledging the important contribution of these great people was also a driving force. And as more and more research suggests that leadership stems from experience rather than genetic temperament, it is my hope that these leadership lessons can be passed on to the emerging generation of America's business leaders. We asked each interviewee to address the following questions:

- What are the common attributes among high-performing companies in your sector?
- What differentiates your organization as an employer of choice?
- How do you prioritize your time in running your business?
- Describe your greatest leadership moment.
- What are your concerns about the overall industry and your specific sector?
- What leadership attributes are important for the success of the next generation of leaders?

The effort to institutionalize entrepreneurship presents a fascinating context for evaluating how to manage any business, especially in expanding, fast-changing industries. Effective real estate leaders not only show vision and have the capacity to take chances, but also carefully develop teams and corporate infrastructure to meet the expectations of investors, clients, and customers. Ultimately, entrepreneurial drive needs to inspire leaders in a broadening industry that is ever further removed from its roots.

CHAPTER ONE

AMERICA'S
LARGEST INDUSTRY

The real estate industry's magnitude and impact on the global ecomony is truly staggering. According to an analysis by the *Economist*, the assets of the world's developed economies are composed of

- ⊶ Residential property: $48 trillion;
- ⊶ Commercial property: $14 trillion;
- ⊶ Equities: $20 trillion;
- ⊶ Government bonds: $20 trillion; and
- ⊶ Corporate bonds: $13 trillion.

Of a total of $115 trillion, real estate (residential and commercial property) accounts for $62 trillion, or 54 percent of the assets of developed economies.

In the United States, the real estate industry serves as a barometer of economic health. It is the engine providing space for expanding businesses and a growing population, expected to increase by 100 million over the next 30 years. When property markets short-circuit, shock waves follow. In fact, an unsustainable housing boom and mortgage lending spree led the country into deep recession during 2008 and 2009, deflating property values and the industry's near-term prospects. In the run-up to the recent economic bust, real estate generated nearly one-third, or $2.9 trillion, of the nation's gross domestic product (GDP) and provided jobs for more than 10 million Americans, equivalent to all the workers in New York state.

Real estate is the source of more than 70 percent of local tax revenues, which pay for schools, roads, police, and other essential services. America's commercial real estate is worth approximately $5.5 trillion and includes 4 billion square feet of office space, 13 billion square feet of industrial property, almost 6 billion square feet of shopping center space, 4.5 million hotel rooms, and 33 million square feet of rental apartment space. Some 47,000 shopping centers account for $1.98 trillion in sales and generate $84.3 billion in state sales taxes. Spending by U.S. and international travelers averages $1.4 billion a day, and one of every eight Americans is directly or indirectly employed in the lodging and tourism industries. Residential real estate is an even bigger market: the value of single-family (owner-occupied) housing totals $15.2 trillion, while homeowner equity totals $8 trillion, representing approximately 32 percent of household wealth. Clearly, real estate is one of the most important asset classes in the U.S. and global economies.

The CEOs and other business leaders interviewed for this book operate in a broad universe of real estate–related businesses divided into six primary sectors:

- Commercial mortgage finance
- Commercial real estate ownership/brokerage
- Residential mortgage finance
- Homebuilding
- Lodging/hospitality and gaming
- Housing for seniors.

Economic, demographic and structural changes buffet these industry sectors, creating uncertainty, opportunity, and risk. Today's real estate leaders not only face the exigencies of overcoming recessionary fallout, they also will struggle to cope with transformed public markets, deleveraging priorities, and managing increasingly complicated global businesses. In charting strategy and new directions, they will become more mindful than ever before of the pitfalls to the status quo. Economic turbulence may raise special challenges for reducing balance sheet debt and reenergizing tenant demand. But real estate veterans have become inured to industry cyclicality, which rarely keeps markets in desired supply/demand equilibrium for long.

Commercial Mortgage Finance

From the end of World War II until well into the 1980s, the nation's commercial real estate was financed primarily by banks, insurance companies, and savings and loan operations in private market transactions. Real estate was mostly a buy-and-hold, long-term investment, cloaked in conference room negotiations. It was very much the province of local entrepreneurs backed by their favored lenders. Developers typically built and held properties in their own accounts, collecting a steady flow of tenant rents while gradually building up their equity stakes as they paid down debt. Likewise, many large companies owned their own headquarters. Even the big retail chains developed suburban shopping centers to showcase their flagship department stores as they moved out of the city cores.

Banks and the savings and loans dominated construction lending and the small to medium-size whole loan market. The major life insurers, meanwhile, were primary lenders in the institutional markets for downtown office buildings, regional malls, warehouse complexes, and hotels. A complicated transaction involved putting a secondary mortgage behind a first loan position, which was secured by property equity. As skylines sprouted and metropolitan areas expanded toward the horizon, commercial real estate was largely a very private, get-rich-slow business without a "buy, sell quick" mentality or highly structured financing. Although insurers and pension funds began investing in equity real estate during the 1970s, the once simple world of mortgage lending began changing in the late 1980s as commercial real estate markets engaged in an overdevelopment binge and Wall Street investment banks became more actively involved in brokering and structuring transactions. The advent of residential mortgage securities led to attempts to create collateralized commercial mortgage bonds. When commercial markets collapsed in oversupply during the economic downturn in 1990 and 1991 and the savings and loan crisis ensued, commercial real estate finance was on the cusp of a radical makeover.

The federal government established the Resolution Trust Corporation (RTC) to clean up the massive mess of failed loans from savings and loans, while banks and insurers were forced into wholesale workouts of underperforming investments with a slew of bankrupt and nearly insolvent borrowers. Regulators constrained new lending by the reeling bankers and penalized struggling insurers with larger reserve requirements. While these traditional lenders took to the sidelines, licking their expensive wounds, the RTC began securitizing pools of nonperforming loans. Wall Street houses, meanwhile, opportunistically established conduits to fill holes in the lending market left by the demise of the savings and loans and provided desperately needed capital liquidity. The formation of CMBS markets was well underway, precipitating nothing short of revolutionary change.

Insurers became more niche lenders. Banks still originated the largest share of new loans. But both banks and insurers began using the securities markets to pool portfolios into bond issues and remove loans from balance sheets, spreading their risk and enabling the redeployment of capital. By 2006, about three-quarters of bank and insurer originations were securitized. Although their fast-growing origination volume still lagged that of the commercial banks, conduit lenders and loan securitizers vaulted into the most influential position in the finance markets.

The New World Order. Conduit lenders and loan securitizers vaulted into the most influential position in the finance markets, although their fast-growing origination volume still lagged that of commercial banks. CMBS effectively morphed into the primary regulator of real estate markets and opened the property sector to huge global sources of fixed income capital. Investors from all over the world bought mortgage-backed bonds marketed by Wall Street firms, based on credit agency ratings. Buyers of B-piece and unrated tranches—the high-risk, higher-return segments—were touted as self regulators, kicking out loans from offerings that did not meet their requirements. Banks and insurers readily took advantage of burgeoning CMBS markets and securitized pools of their loan originations to reduce balance sheet risk and enable stepped-up lending activity.

In hindsight, securitization channeled vast capital flows into real estate markets and created unprecedented market liquidity, but it also led to unsustainable risk tolerances by lenders and other investors. Mortgage bankers—both residential and commercial—focused more on increasing loan volumes and related fee revenues than on diligent underwriting. Transaction activity escalated, speculation increased, and property values spiked. Buyers of properties took advantage of low interest rates, adjustable rate loans, and schemes that required little or no equity down. In turn, financial institutions offloaded bulging loan portfolios from their books into increasingly complicated bond offerings, which were highly leveraged. Ratings agencies gave their imprimaturs to these offerings without much scrutiny of the underlying real estate, relying on the diversification of collateral— by geography, property sector, maturity, and type of financing. Residential loans were lumped with commercial loans, subprime residential mortgages were tranched alongside shopping center and office loans. Even careful bond buyers would have trouble identifying exactly what portfolios comprised. Mostly they relied on the ratings and the reputations of Wall Street underwriters for security.

Meltdown. The spiral in lax lending, higher property prices, and more securitization offerings ended in a precipitous meltdown: U.S. homebuying slackened over sticker shock, and borrowers with subprime residential loans began defaulting as mortgage payments reset upward and property values began to decline. Risk premiums returned with a vengeance, not only to mortgage securities markets but also throughout the credit system, gridlocking lenders and forcing writedowns in investor portfolios. The ensuing credit crisis may take years to play out. For now, discipline has returned to the credit markets—conservative loan to equity value ratios, low debt-service coverages, and recourse financing. The CMBS industry hopes for a second chance, and borrowers who overleveraged and overpaid for properties risk major losses. The real estate industry faces yet another cyclical downturn.

Commercial Real Estate Ownership/Services

Until the early 1970s, most large commercial real estate properties were owned by corporations for their headquarters and operations centers or by local entrepreneurs—typically developers and often family groups such as the Rudins and Fisher Brothers in New York, Trammell Crow in Dallas, Oliver Carr in Washington, or Walter Shorenstein in San Francisco. Major local owners usually formed strong relationships with national life insurance companies or money center banks to finance their projects and holdings.

America's cities had started a heady expansion as the baby boomers entered the work force in droves. Suburbs had mushroomed and Sunbelt cities like Atlanta and Dallas had expanded in the wake of interstate development, new airports, and readily available air conditioning. Gleaming glass and steel skyscrapers, multilevel enclosed shopping malls, and campus-style office parks had sprung up throughout burgeoning metropolitan areas from coast to coast.

While development took off nationally, the federal government mandated that pension funds diversify their assets beyond stocks and bonds when Congress passed the Employee Retirement Income Security Act (ERISA) in 1972. The large life insurance companies, meanwhile, figured out that they could make more money by partnering as equity owners with their developer borrowers. As lenders, they realized no upside, while risking a downside if an investment soured in foreclosure. Why not get a piece of the developer action? Institutional money from plan sponsors and insurers began to flow into real estate from pooled equity investment funds, managed by insurers and some banks, as well as from insurance company general accounts.

Syndicators, meanwhile, emerged to entice affluent individuals into real estate partnerships that could take advantage of favorable tax laws for passive investors. Foreign institutions led by the Japanese also acquired portfolios of trophy office buildings in primary cities. By the mid-1980s, commercial real estate ownership was increasingly dominated by institutional owners and various syndicators. Developers welcomed the flood of capital—often their partnerships gave them sizeable equity stakes and attractive project fees for little or no financial investment. Cranes sprouted everywhere and many markets suddenly and disastrously became overbuilt. When Congress passed the 1986 Tax Reform Act, many syndications cratered—their tax write-offs evaporated, and investments in low-occupancy markets were under water.

Although national space brokers issued market vacancy reports on a quarterly basis, a dearth of real-time information on tenant movements, rental rates, defaults, and foreclosures lulled the industry into complacency despite softening markets. Bank and insurance regulators had limited data from which to raise alarms, and stock analysts and rating agencies had no reason to cover real estate, a mostly private and institutional investment enterprise. Building continued into the teeth of the early 1990s recession, where oversupply met a severe dropoff in tenant demand. Commercial real estate ownership entered its darkest hour since the Great Depression.

The Recapitalization of the Asset Class. The ensuing capital gridlock and a wave of owner bankruptcies, defaults, foreclosures, and workouts ushered in a new era that has transformed real estate from an arcane, privately owned asset class into a more transparent, global business. Ownership, which had evolved from entrepreneurial developers to institutions, became dominated by the public markets. Just as investment bankers devised CMBS conduits to help resurrect the real estate debt markets, Wall Street opportunistically moved to resuscitate large property owners and their companies by raising money through REITs, stock vehicles that own income-producing real estate, distributing 95 percent of their taxable net income as annual dividends to shareholders.

REIT structures had been around since 1960 but had never gained traction among stock pickers or private owners. Running public companies

meant dealing with officious stockholders, managing boards, and comply-
ing with costly federal regulations. Why would an"anything goes"real estate entrepreneur go public and give up so much control when institutional
money had been so readily available?

Forsaken by banks and insurance partners, owners struggled, despite
largely intact businesses. In order to survive, they were only too willing to give
up some control of their development and management companies by turning them into public entities. Wall Street sold investors on the REIT concept—
a classic buy-low opportunity with significant dividend opportunities as
property cash flows improved with the economic recovery. Starting from only
$10 billion in equity market share in 1992, REITs came to comprise almost
$300 billion by 2005, far surpassing the equity stakes of both pensions and in-
surers. Many smaller REIT companies have merged or been acquired by larger
companies, creating dominant owners in various property categories—office,
apartment, shopping centers, regional malls, warehouses, mobile homes, and
self-storage facilities.

The New Breed of Players. Individuals—whether developers or new
forms of non-tax-oriented partnership syndications—continue to own the
largest share of the nation's total commercial properties. A changing array
of foreign investors—wealthy individuals, institutions, and more recently
sovereign wealth funds—also play a significant role, especially in the ownership of larger properties. Germans, Australians, Irish, Canadians, Middle
Easterners, Japanese, and more recently Chinese investors all view the United
States as a safe asset haven. But the emergence of public real estate markets
has had the most telling impact, not only allowing average investors to own
property shares but also establishing a network of industry analysts who track
trends and marshal data on supply and demand. Although REIT information
and CMBS oversight proved insufficient to avoid the subprime meltdown
and overbuilding in housing and condominium markets, the commercial
real estate supply side appeared more disciplined. Unlike the early 1990s, the
recent commercial correction is mostly demand driven, as tenants retrench in
the recession and overleveraged investors cannot meet debt service based on

earlier optimistic cash flow projections. Markets cannot get overbuilt easily without analysts sending up red flags and vulnerable stocks taking hits, sending signals to all investors, owners, and lenders.

REITs, meanwhile, led the way in helping globalize equity real estate investment. The larger companies have the potential to grow into multinationals with cross-border assets. Once world economies regain their traction, American developers will likely resume exporting their skills and expertise to expanding overseas markets. Multinational tenants—large international financial institutions, consumer companies, retailers, and manufacturers—should continue to work with global leasing and management firms to select space on different continents. REIT markets have been established in Europe and Pacific Rim countries (Japan, Australia, Singapore), opening international flows into property stocks. Prime tenants—large international banks, financial institutions, retailers, and manufacturers—work with global leasing and management firms to select space on different continents.

Brokers, leasing companies, and construction firms have significantly expanded from local and regional businesses into national and international organizations, to serve corporate and institutional clients that extended their global operations. Since the mid-1990s many smaller firms have consolidated into larger organizations, seeking efficiencies and the advantages of economies of scale deriving from greater brand awareness, better market research, and vanguard information technology. Larger construction firms have leveraged greater buying power from vendors and subcontractors while providing consistent and tailored standards for their space-using clients across different markets in different countries. While some niche players can find success in tenant representation or property management and leasing, today's most successful brokerage firms are multidisciplined giants that can buy, sell, lease, and manage properties as well as offer investment advisory services in some cases. A broad range of services can help cushion companies against downturns in cyclical transaction markets, but they require a set of nimble management skills.

Investment bankers, who traditionally had brokered large real estate transactions and structured REIT offerings, also dramatically extended their reach by funneling client capital into opportunity funds. These financial megacompanies harnessed their well-established ties to owner clients to source deals while accessing substantial capital flows from their various institutional, financial, and retail brokerage relationships. Their ability to command capital from an array of global sources, control transactions, and structure deals made investment bankers increasingly formidable players in the equity markets. Wall Street firms also led the charge in taking REITs private, breaking up portfolios, and later turning some of these companies back into public entities. While the large Wall Street footprint in the transaction markets provided greater liquidity and heightened overall buying and selling activity during the latest real estate up cycle, the resulting frenzy left many owners and investors highly vulnerable to global credit market distress and resulted in precarious deal structures.

At its core, real estate ownership remains a very local business governed by submarket demand, location, and structural viability. But today's owners require knowledge of many national and international markets that comprise extensive portfolios. They need the essential bricks-and-mortar expertise involved in property development and management. But they also must have the temperament to deal with shareholders or other capital clients and the tools to manage public entities and deal with various regulators. No longer do they manage just a collection of real estate assets. Today's real estate leaders must be equipped to operate highly complex business entities throughout the world.

Residential Mortgage Finance

In the United States, the federal government has been the financial linchpin supporting levels of homeownership that are unprecedented compared with virtually anywhere else in the world. By 2007 almost 70 percent of Americans lived in homes they owned, enabled by ample funds and manageable mortgage rates from commercial banks, Internet lenders, savings and loans, and credit unions. Through a series of government programs and government-sponsored entities a huge secondary mortgage market was created, allowing originators to sell their loan portfolios into securities markets and replenish their funds for new loans. Theoretically, this market has great benefits: lender balance sheets are improved, risk is spread out, and—most important for borrowers and the housing markets—financing costs are reduced. By 2007, between 55 and 60 percent of loans originated in the United States passed into the secondary mortgage market through mortgage- or asset-backed securities. The total mortgage-backed securities market exceeded $6 trillion, having grown larger than the U.S. Treasury note and bond markets. And it was poised to fall.

The U.S. government established the Federal Housing Administration and the Federal National Mortgage Association (Fannie Mae) in the 1930s, to provide insured mortgage loans for low-income borrowers and operate a secondary market for residential loans. The U.S. Department of Veterans Affairs (VA) loan program (begun in 1947) extended favorable mortgage terms to hundreds of thousands of returning World War II veterans and their families, jump-starting the development of many suburbs in the 1950s. Ginnie Mae, the Government National Mortgage Association, was formed in 1968 to help low-income borrowers and offer mortgage-backed securities guaranteed by the U.S. Treasury. Fannie Mae was turned into a private corporation that year, joined by the Federal Home Loan Mortgage Corporation (Freddie Mac) in 1970. Both Fannie and Freddie are government-sponsored entities (GSEs) that have special authority to borrow from the U.S. Treasury. Both were placed into conservatorship by their regulator, the Federal Housing Finance Agency, in 2008.

The New Paradigm. The two GSEs paved the way for establishing the mortgage-backed securities markets in the 1970s. Fannie and Freddie purchase mortgages from banks and other originators, assemble the loans into pools, and sell securities into the bond markets, whose payouts come from the cash flows derived from the mortgages. These bonds are known as passthroughs. In the early 1980s, Wall Street bankers created collateralized mortgage obligations, more sophisticated instruments that segment the mortgage-backed securities into tranches with different risks and returns. Fannie and Freddie also are the primary financing sources for affordable housing—low- and middle-income rental apartments. These loans are made to developers through designated underwriters—established banks, mortgage bankers, and brokers—and are also packaged into securities.

Although banks retain a large percentage of loans on their books, the mortgage-backed securities markets revolutionized housing finance. Selling mortgages off lenders' balance sheets and into securitized investments funneled money back to lenders and allowed them to lend those funds to other borrowers, creating more mortgages than a bank could extend based simply on the funds on deposit. The securities markets, connected to global capital sources, could channel significantly more money into the U.S. housing market than otherwise would be available, and the public could benefit from greater financial resources to buy homes. Bond investors could gain low-risk income—supported though not guaranteed by the government—and often attractive spreads relative to comparable bonds. The GSEs are required by the government to finance affordable housing options, thereby encouraging the development of more apartment units for low- and middle-income Americans.

Not only could the mortgage securities markets and the GSE conduits provide more long-term funding at lower cost, but their participation also led to the unbundling of mortgage functions—origination, funding, servicing, and accepting mortgage risk. Banks still undertook originations and held onto servicing, but the conduits took on the credit risk and the bond investors assumed the interest rate risk. Consequently, the industry became more segmented, specialized, and institutionalized, with larger national bankers originating more loans, using technology and economies of scale to drive volumes. The larger bankers remained full-service institutions, staying close to borrowers by continuing to service their loans. They also outsourced loans from other lenders and conduits.

The Internet allowed borrowers to comparison shop for better terms and rates and move beyond their local banks, which were consolidating into national networks anyway. Price shopping boosted competition among lenders and spurred the introduction of various higher-risk, adjustable rate, no principal down, balloon mortgage products, which catered to borrowers who were financially stretched in economic downturns.

With all these changes, the challenges for many residential mortgage bankers were to maintain high underwriting standards as they became more disconnected from local markets and their borrowers, use technology to manage their costs, and use the securities markets to their best advantage in laying off loans and strengthening balance sheets. As the 2007–2008 residential mortgage debacle highlighted, many banks failed on all counts. Competition among lenders to increase mortgage volumes trumped sound underwriting and lending discipline. Many borrowers with poor credit were able to obtain loans, which quickly left them exposed to impossible payment hurdles once property values began to decline. Better-credit borrowers also overextended themselves in refinancings or with equity lines of credit.

A Market Destined to Recover. Accounting scandals, high-level executive resignations over compensation abuses, and government takeovers have sullied Fannie and Freddie in the wake of the housing crisis, but have not derailed them from their central roles in supporting housing finance and ultimately bankrolling homebuilders. In efforts to restore some liquidity to mortgage markets, Congress even extended their reach into larger loan categories. But GSE underwriting failures will result in increased regulation and oversight of lending practices by Congress and the Federal Reserve. Those institutions will constrict the future flow of funds and better harness the mortgage markets.

Burned bond investors will be slow to return to the mortgage-backed securities markets without greater assurance of credit quality and government oversight. Rating agencies will need to revamp their processes and

analyses to regain market confidence. Progress by other nations in emu-
lating U.S. CMBS and RMBS markets has been stopped in its tracks by
America's setbacks. Lessons learned from the U.S. experience reinforce the
need for proper regulatory infrastructure to manage the loan process and
provide satisfactory transparency to assess credit risk. In addition, many
countries need basic procedures for registration and clearing titles as well
as for implementing foreclosures and evictions. Lending standards and
government participation vary from country to country. In many developing areas, the regulatory environment is still lacking but can be expected to
improve with time.

Ultimately, growth prospects in global residential mortgage securities
markets could be exponential. But the residential mortgage business, like
other real estate activities, remains grounded in local markets—their economic trends, supply and demand constraints, social conditions, and government
practices. Recent market losses certainly reminded U.S. mortgage bankers
that no substitute exists for properly analyzing borrower credit and assessing
prospects for area stability and growth. And interest rates will always play a
critical role. Lower rates will enable greater borrowing and increase lender
volumes. Higher rates will diminish activity. For mortgage bankers, rate volatility will always be the greatest challenge to their business health.

Homebuilding

Homebuilding is a bedrock American industry, one of the nation's most
important businesses. Spending on housing represents about 16 cents of
every dollar, and housing wealth accounts for almost $8 trillion in accu-
mulated capital. Unprecedented housing appreciation between 1995 and
2006 transformed people's homes from nests into nest eggs, encouraging
increases in homeownership rates to nearly 70 percent. Low interest rates,
rapidly escalating prices, and lax underwriting whipped up a frenzy of unsustainable buying and refinancing activity. The federal government helped
propel homebuying through tax breaks on mortgage interest expenses and

deductions for local property taxes as well as by creating a secondary mortgage market to make more capital available to borrowers.

Cyclicality. The nosedive in house prices in the mid-2000s underscores how highly cyclical and growth related homebuilding remains. Analysts are not shy about characterizing the business as highly volatile, subject to sometimes heady booms and severe busts. Homes are the biggest of big-ticket expenditures. Most buyers require financing and how much buyers can afford typically depends on their income relative to the expected mortgage interest and principal payments, as well as insurance and other expenses. Periods of low interest rates like the early 2000s increase affordability and higher interest rates can dampen sales and pricing. Of course, economic upswings—typically featuring low unemployment and rising wages—as well as recessions, which depress income levels, affect homebuilders very directly.

Population and income growth are essential to stimulate greater housing demand and raise price points. It is a simple equation—more people will require more housing, and the U.S. population is expected to expand by 100 million people by 2040. Market strength can vary dramatically from region to region and even from community to community. In the United States, coastal areas near major cities have experienced the greatest increases in appreciation and house costs, because of difficult barriers to entry and diminishing land availability. High incomes offset slower population growth in some Northeast markets, but more expensive land and a slower entitlement process can impinge on builder profits on pricier homes. South and Southwest suburban agglomerations have enjoyed the greatest population growth and homebuilding activity—relatively cheap, easily available land reduces costs, keeping volumes high and profits up. Many Midwest states suffer from stagnating population growth and declining job prospects as manufacturing has plummeted. Some Rustbelt areas suffer from sluggish or sinking home values, substantially diminishing homebuilding prospects. These trends are expected to continue as people gravitate to warmer climes and as coastal areas and as wealth and global business activity concentrate in the large, 24-hour cities.

The Players. Like their products, homebuilders come in all shapes and sizes—at their recent peak in 2006 about 20,000 operated in the United States. Many are small, local firms that construct houses on contract for individual landowners. Local subdivision developers and regional homebuilders construct on speculation and are well positioned to acquire and control land in their backyards. Increasingly, though, large national firms dominate the market activity. In 2006, national builders were responsible for about 20 percent of new building volume, according to estimates. Over time, this percentage could grow to more than 50 percent with the anticipated consolidation of various regional and middle market companies, which cannot compete as effectively on their own.

While local builders have advantages in knowing the often arcane political and zoning landscapes in their regions, national builders can marshal substantially more capital and purchasing power to assemble land tracts, buy construction materials, and secure talent to navigate the intricacies of the local planning process. These firms are typically public companies that are positioned to make land acquisitions in joint ventures with institutional investors. Their capital strength provides additional staying power for gaining necessary approvals, as many cities and towns make the entitlement process more costly and complicated. Since the federal government provides less funding for highway and infrastructure building than in the past, localities are forcing developers to pay higher tabs for new roads, sewers, and water mains. Again, the larger homebuilders are better capitalized to meet the demands. Competition for building materials in developing countries—particularly China and India—could keep commodity prices high for years to come. Bulk purchasing agreements with suppliers give the larger companies a decided edge.

A New Landscape. The homebuilding markets continue to evolve and become more sophisticated. Greenfield development is meeting increasing resistance in many areas, as local governments attempt to rein in sprawl and environmentalists gain traction in their campaigns for preserving parks and wetlands. Suburban-edge, single-family subdivisions and large-scale homes may continue to get built, but at declining rates—especially if gasoline and heating and air-conditioning bills continue to escalate and traffic congestion worsens. Homebuilders will need to shift gears to exploit opportunities to redevelop infill areas that are attractive to buyers who are looking to decrease car commutes and find greater convenience living near retail and office centers. Town center projects and new urbanist communities are gaining in popularity. They feature mixed-use development in pedestrian-friendly communities with varied housing alternatives—single family, townhouse, and apartment condominiums. Many of these projects are more complex and capital intensive, requiring the skill sets of national builders.

More successful homebuilders will be better at identifying and exploiting niches in their markets. Expanding numbers of affluent baby boomers will continue to ignite development of luxury second homes in resort areas near coasts and in mountains as well as in rural areas within two- to three-hour drives from major cities. Rising numbers of second-generation Hispanic and Asian immigrants will also create an expanding market opportunity for starter homes with designs that cater to extended families, as well as community parks that have amenities like soccer fields as well as baseball diamonds. Larger homebuilders will selectively export their capabilities into international markets. These initiatives will usually involve local partners who can manage the local regulatory maze and set development strategies, including effective marketing plans, tailored to local preference and custom.

The housing depression of the mid-2000s has taken its toll on many homebuilding companies that were caught with inventories of new product and land, which have declined in value. Smaller players especially have been forced from the business or sent to the sidelines while the markets correct. Like other real estate sectors, homebuilding is consolidating, becoming more national in scope with larger players controlling more of the business. Scale and access to capital have become more critical to achieving growth and greater profitability as the regulatory environment becomes more challenging. But over time homebuilders' greatest test remains antici-

pating cyclical swings that can make housing starts mushroom or suddenly
curtail market demand. Understanding the economy and interest rate
moves is still the homebuilder's highest hurdle.

Lodging, Hospitality, and Gaming Industry

Hotels have always been viewed as a specialized sector, requiring unique
business skills and capabilities. Lodging and hospitality requires sophisticated marketing and branding, furnishing and upkeep, and food service,
as well as 24-hour care and attention to a client base that is constantly
turning over. Managing staff, facilities, and systems for a full-service hotel
is a complex, integrated business that requires a high degree of training and
supervision.

Lodging is not only the most management-intensive real estate
sector; it is also the most volatile and is extremely vulnerable to economic
downturns and event risk. Recessions, bad weather, terror warnings, sharply
higher fuel costs, or flu epidemics can curtail cash flows precipitously and
suddenly. In good times, room rates can be escalated on a nightly basis; but
in bad times, bookings can evaporate and the absence of long-term leases
offers no financial cushion to offset high overhead costs.

The hotel industry is highly segmented, ranging from sumptuous resorts and luxury urban brands like Ritz-Carlton and Four Seasons to funky
boutique concepts like W; full-service business hotels like Marriott, Hyatt,
and Hilton; suite hotels with more limited services like Courtyard and
Doubletree; and various downscale suburban hotel and motel categories
ranging from the venerable Holiday Inn to Motel 6. Matching brands and
service to locations and clientele are often keys to success. Large hospitality companies offer brands across different segments to capture travelers at
various price points. By consolidating multiple brand categories under their
control, operating companies can spread costs for managing information
technology, finance, human resources, and bulk purchasing.

The Players. Ownership takes various forms but is ultimately highly dependent on operations and management. Large, publicly traded owner-operators have proven most adept at establishing reservation systems, marketing programs, and customer loyalty discounts, as well as securing purchasing concessions. For large, high-profile properties in larger markets, operators typically franchise their flags to hotel owner/investors, providing operating teams, marketing programs, and reservation links. In these markets operators also will enter into joint venture ownership with investors, who take a slice of the property equity as well as the management fees, typically calculated using generous revenue formulas.

Institutional investors have proven skittish about hotel ownership. Pension funds and insurance companies have had mixed experiences with mastering the management-intensive businesses, getting entangled with union employee issues and dealing with high rehabilitation and capital expenditures. Gaming properties typically have too many regulatory and public relations issues to warrant any interest from institutional investors. Joint ventures with those operators can limit flexibility to change brands, and management fees have traditionally favored operators.

Investors increasingly view hotel ownership as a cyclical timing play, buying in the early stages of economic recovery and selling before the next slump. So-called value-add and opportunity investment funds tend to be the most active traders. The big lodging companies concentrate their ownership in prime markets and in flagship properties. In fact, a mere eight lodging companies own 100 or more hotels in the United States, and just 14 own between 50 and 100.

In order to overcome the vicissitudes of the hotel cycle, the large owner-operators must use leverage carefully and plan for rehabilitation and redevelopment judiciously. On the leverage front, owners have been largely successful, reducing debt service costs substantially since the industry's last full-blown recession in the early 1990s. With more stabilized balance sheets, these companies were much better able to withstand the short-term dislocation caused in the period after the attacks of September 11, in the fall of 2001 and early 2002, when travel was drastically curtailed by both businesses and tourists.

The hotel sector has been prone to overdevelopment, especially in the low-end, limited-service segments where buildings can be slapped up easily at interstate highway exits or in fast-growing suburbs. Historically, institutional owners have steered clear of these markets and the large owner/operators focus on franchising, not owning directly. Hotels in these more downscale categories are owned by a myriad of local or regional entrepreneurs and businesspeople, who buy into franchises. The operators strive to ensure that their franchisees meet uniform brand service standards, locking in fees for using the name, accessing reservation systems, training personnel, and purchasing all the familiar branded items from soap and signage to blankets and furniture.

A Future of Globalization. Among real estate categories, hotels were the first to expand internationally. U.S. brands appeared in major overseas markets decades ago, and European and Asian lodging companies operate in U.S. gateway cities. Familiar names give some comfort to offshore travelers and offer a natural marketing opportunity back home. Further globalization and consolidation of operators appear inevitable as regional economies become more interdependent and international travel for both business and leisure expands.

Hotel companies will continue to succeed by meeting guest expectations for service and comfort and by making the increasingly harried conditions of travel easier and more hassle free. Personalized attention and better service delivery will become increasingly important. Discount programs for frequent travelers, knowing room preferences, providing ease of check-in and check-out, wireless Internet service, and complimentary snacks help create an experience in a highly competitive industry where clean and comfortable rooms are a requirement. The lodging business is one real estate category in which location and bricks and mortar can take a business only so far. Service and marketing really make the difference.

Housing for Seniors

Changing demographics and lifestyle patterns over the past 50 years have
combined with longer life spans to set the stage for substantial growth in
seniors' housing. In the 1940s and 1950s many elderly Americans lived with
their children or other family members, who were forced to pool resources
to support them. Social Security and corporate pensions were just gaining their footing, and Medicare would not be enacted until the mid-1960s.
Many senior citizens could not afford to live on their own. Average life ex-
pectancies increased steadily from under 65 at the time Social Security was
established during the Depression to nearly 80 today. Until the late 1970s,
seniors' housing consisted mostly of nursing homes, usually the last stop for
seriously ill or incapacitated elderly people. These facilities were health-care
oriented, often government supported, with varying standards of care, some
scandalously deficient.

An Evolving Model of the Industry's Service Providers. Today
older Americans are generally more active and healthier than in the past,
a result of significant medical advances, new drugs, and fitness regimens.
They also are far more financially independent and secure than in previous
generations, thanks to government safety nets and generous employer-
defined benefit plans. Better health and fiscal autonomy have led to more
living options for aging Americans, as the real estate industry looks to capitalize on the vanguard of the baby boomers, leading its vast demographic
wave beyond age 60.

In fact, in the late 1990s eager developers overbuilt markets, getting
ahead of the wave. Investors and lenders took losses, although the sector
found equilibrium in subsequent years. It was not until 2001 that the first
3.2 million baby boomers turned 55, the age at which residents can legally
live in age-restricted housing. By 2025 there will be 65 million Americans
ranging in age from 61 to 79, or 25 percent of the population over the age of
16. Increasing numbers will consider various forms of senior-oriented residences, precipitating a boom in seniors' housing boom over the next decade.

Seniors' housing today extends well beyond nursing homes, including various components of the housing, hospitality, and health care industries. The size and diversity of the aging population warrants a range of lifestyle considerations and price points. At present, six housing segments track life stages, accommodating the graying generation into retirement and beyond as they become less self reliant and more infirm:

Active adult communities: These communities consist of for-sale single-family homes, townhouses, cluster homes, or condominiums with no specialized services, restricted to adults who are 55 or older. Many are connected to resorts or golf clubs, or are located in suburban communities near where buyers have been living. Empty nesters move into smaller spaces that are easier to maintain than conventional single-family homes. Lawns are mowed by the homeowners association. Grandchildren can visit, but community environments are tailored to a quieter, hassle-free lifestyle.

Seniors' apartments: These multifamily rentals include kitchens and are restricted to adults at least 55 years old. The buildings may have community rooms and offer social programs but not common dining facilities.

Independent living communities: These age-restricted rental apartments provide central dining and access to housekeeping and linen service as well as social and recreational activities. They do not offer health care or nursing attendants.

Assisted living residences: These state-regulated rental properties provide the same services as independent living communities but also offer supportive care in daily living—including managing medication, bathing, dressing, toileting, and ambulating—as well as dining facilities. They also may have some skilled-nursing beds or wings for patients who have Alzheimer's disease.

Nursing homes: These facilities are licensed daily-rate or rental properties that provide skilled nursing for residents who require 24-hour care. They may stand alone or be connected to assisted living residences.

Congregate care retirement communities: Also known as life care communities, these age-restricted properties offer independent living, assisted living, and skilled nursing on one campus. Residents can shift in and out of units as required by their medical condition. They pay sizeable entry and ongoing maintenance fees to ensure that their changing needs can be attended to in a single facility.

The different seniors' housing segments present varying challenges for owners, investors, and operators. Active adult communities are, in effect, for-sale homes for seniors. Developers sell the units and move on, typically leaving future management of the communities to a homeowners association. Seniors' apartments are a multifamily equivalent with specialized features and some service extras tailored to an older, healthy tenant base. In both formats buyers or tenants live independently and do not require any care or attention. Successful developers know how to construct properties that have efficient layouts and recreational features that attract senior residents. Their marketing teams are experienced in executing sales strategies, appealing to more active older adults. Ongoing management of seniors' apartments has requirements that are similar to those of other multifamily housing—maintaining common areas, providing janitorial services, and leasing.

Independent living communities take on hospitality features, offering meal plans in dining rooms as well as maid service. These facilities require specialized operators who can provide hotel services that are customized for full-time residents who are generally still healthy but older and less active. Owners and investors have learned through hard experience that capable operators are essential for success.

Assisted living facilities and nursing homes are complicated businesses, requiring highly skilled nursing and medical capabilities. Operators face myriad government regulations, inspections, and reviews. Not only do owners provide residences and service lodging; they also are licensed health care givers, obligated to meet high standards for ensuring the comfort and well-being of their residents. For these reasons, institutional real estate owners have been more reluctant to invest directly in health care properties, although there has been heightened interest in buying shares of health care companies, including REITs that provide these services and own these facilities.

Operating Expertise Key to Success. Undoubtedly, demand will grow substantially for all forms of seniors' housing and tested owners and operators of these properties will be positioned to reap significant cash flows. Especially in the case of health care facilities, success will depend on having a considerably more ambitious skill set than real estate investment, development, and management. Owners will need or have operating partners with proven hospitality, nursing, and geriatric expertise.

CHAPTER TWO

LEADERSHIP IMPERATIVES AND ATTRIBUTES FOR LEADERSHIP SUCCESS

In order to manage profitably in the ever-changing real estate landscape, business initiatives need to be reevaluated constantly. As organizations have become increasingly sophisticated and more complex, business decisions need to be implemented expeditiously. Thoughtful leadership is required today more than ever.

Industry Trends

The real estate industry will continue to experience evolutionary change driven by clients and investors as well as the need to manage profitable enterprises. Consolidation permits firms to create economies of scale. Globalization occurs as investors and clients seek to expand their reach in growing world markets. And securitization allows property owners access to capital and to public and private debt as well as to equity, which is critical to managing business through industry cycles.

Inevitable industry declines—brought on by supply-demand imbalances or economic turmoil—always present leadership challenges. Savvy executives somehow have a sixth sense, anticipating market tops and reining in expansion. The severe 2008–2009 recession short-circuited transaction activity, gridlocked credit markets, and brought the industry to a standstill. Ravaging homebuilders first and spreading into retail, hotels, and other commercial sector groups, the tailspin forced senior executives into difficult cost-cutting and downsizing modes in some cases to enable survival. Starved for credit, companies tried to husband capital to take advantage of eventual opportunities in recovery—buying weakened competitors, acquiring discounted assets, and luring top talent. Vision typically sets great leaders apart, and visibility is never good coming out of downturns. Companies that can go on the offensive early—buying at market lows, adding to expertise, and widening geographic footprints—can propel growth through entire "up" cycles.

Managing Change. Under any circumstances, the playing field constantly changes. Some variation of expansion, consolidation, and globalization will continue to capture the attention of real estate leaders as they juggle operating strategies to contend with prevailing economic conditions and inevitable cycles. In the new world order, the industry gravitates away from smaller, local private firms—typically family-owned businesses—to larger, public companies, many of which operate internationally, seeking capital efficiencies and the benefits of scale. Greater size allows companies to control assets, operate at a lower cost of capital, and serve tenants and customers across many markets as they expand their businesses into the promising global marketplace. In many CEO suites, on-the-ground property operations or development deals sometimes take a back seat to forging operating platforms in Asia and Europe or structuring corporate bond offerings.

Going Public (and Private). Over the past two decades, public ownership and mortgage securitization mainstreamed real estate, connecting property markets into global capital channels. The unprecedented liquidity had a price, helping instigate a transaction frenzy and price spiral, which suddenly reversed in the ensuing credit market crisis. In theory, public ownership and securitized mortgages should have produced greater transparency and forced fiscal discipline among management teams. In fact, most commercial real estate markets kept relative control over development activity, a marked change from the late 1980s when markets overbuilt. But CMBS analysts' oversight and rating agencies' scrutiny came up short in assessing and tracking mortgage collateral. Borrowers eagerly overleveraged as lenders offloaded poorly underwritten loans into securitized offerings, bought by far-flung bond investors who depended on credit ratings. Despite vaporized liquidity, the securitization pipeline will flow again, albeit restrained by a heavy dose of regulation, increased reserve requirements, and underwriting discipline.

Public REITs have taken managements on a volatile ride since emerging from the early 1990s market debacle. Some cash-poor private owners had no choice but to go public back then and were rewarded with sharply rising stock prices in the mid-1990s recovery. After a momentary steep drop in the 1998 credit crisis, REITs were stock market leaders until the 2007–2008 bear market, when they tumbled badly. A pattern should continue of smaller REIT companies consolidating into larger competitors or going private depending on the availability of credit. The costs and regulatory requirements for operating in public markets can hamstring managers of small-cap companies. CEOs of public REITs must tend to time-consuming investor relations and discourse with ratings agencies. The work entailed in anticipating and preparing for quarterly reporting sessions often dictates a REIT's choice of financial and communication strategies. But that will not stop well-positioned private companies from accessing public markets when timing permits. The back and forth of private to public will continue.

Heading Overseas. Real estate's global thrust follows broader economic precedents and technological advances, which foster global trade and intercontinental enterprise. Because many mature U.S. metropolitan areas have been picked over by buyers and can sustain only limited new development, investors will continue to seek opportunities in emerging markets; office buildings, shopping centers, and hotels sprout in places that are primed for business expansion. China and India receive the most attention, but other countries along the Pacific Rim show strong prospects over time. Major hotel brands—Marriott, Hilton, and Starwood—will continue to grow largely by increasing market share through international opportunities. Some homebuilders look to markets outside the United States, while real estate investment managers lure dollars into offshore funds. Investment bankers eventually will resume exporting REIT and CMBS structures into overseas markets, creating prospects for acquiring international funds and for nurturing new capital sources.

While the severity of the 2008–2009 recession offers pause, offshore capital has never shied away from the perceived stability of the United States' safe haven. Canadian and European (U.K., German, and Dutch) investors have been mainstays. Asian and Middle Eastern investors should continue to be significant players, and Australians and mainland Chinese have become major forces.

Some CEOS interviewed for this book, particularly in the lodging and commercial property sectors, urged a deliberate approach to global expansions. Real estate ownership and management, at base, remains a local business, relying on familiarity with local customs, laws, nuances, and commercial practices. American companies need to form effective partnerships or assemble teams of local talent to navigate foreign markets. In particular, rampant corruption and lack of transparency can hamper or short-circuit forays into developing markets. What works well in the United States may not work abroad, even in European Union countries.

Enduring Cycles. As transitions from private to public and from domestic to global operations can reconfigure the industry, real estate leaders' greatest challenge remains coping with constantly changing property markets in a fundamentally cyclical business. Interest rate fluctuations, economic tides, consumer confidence levels, and demographic shifts ripple through the marketplace, requiring constant attention and analysis even during the most prosperous times.

Cyclicality ultimately means different things to different industry sectors. The supply and demand cycles for homebuilders do not necessarily track those for warehouse or office owners. Lease terms enable varying strategies in each sector. Hotels can change room rates nightly, depending on demand, while office landlords try to lock in long-term leases at market highs to ride out the inevitable cyclical softening or worse.

Any number of scenarios can play out just from the interplay of interest rates and economic growth. Low interest rates make cheap capital available and fuel deal making, and high interest rates constrict capital availability and, inevitably, slow development and constrain transaction volumes. The economy always has its say, as well. Employment and wage growth often indicate the health of apartment, retail, and office REITs. But a bullish stock market often spells trouble for REIT stocks, as investors turn their backs on income-oriented investments and buy into high-growth stories. Recessions hit lodging properties immediately because businesses and tourists eliminate trips on a moment's notice, as they did following the attacks of September 11. But apartment, retail, and office owners still collect rents on leases.

For a short time in the early 2000s boom, some prominent industry players made the argument that inexpensive capital had removed cyclicality from the real estate business. The ensuing credit crisis obliterated that notion. Even wizened leaders have been reminded to resist complacency and anticipate the risk of cyclical change as investors were crushed across the board.

Facing Consolidation. The rigors of real estate business cycles, amplified by the increasingly global environment and the influence of public markets, push firms in every sector toward consolidation. For many companies, bigger is better. As the industry plays in global markets, size matters. Smaller, less well-capitalized firms are more vulnerable to interest rate swings. Specialized companies need to rethink their silo identities. Regional firms consider going national, and national companies ponder acquiring regional players and expanding internationally. Effective use of technology becomes more crucial in tying disparate organizations together as well as ensuring productivity efficiencies, which bolster advantages of scale.

The commercial mortgage market debacle and business slowdown triggered a consolidation wave. Real estate ownership companies will follow the same pattern. In the wake of the housing nosedive, surviving big firms will absorb middle-market companies—especially regionally focused builders or those specializing in entry-level, mid-level, or high-end homes. Ultimately, a majority of the housing market will be controlled by big builders. Hospitality brands also will expand and push for greater national reach, which provides a competitive edge in reservations systems, marketing, training, and purchasing. Smaller senior care operators, too, will have trouble surviving competitive pressures without merging into larger firms.

In general, silo business models—originating mortgages or managing commercial properties, for example—are endangered one-stop shops. Larger companies can work more seamlessly to satisfy client requirements for all financing and for managing their debt and equity needs. Firms will continue to consolidate not only geographically, but also vertically, attempting to offer wider-ranging services in order to be competitive and reduce their exposure to cyclical volatility. At a minimum, residential mortgage banks will need to provide both originations and servicing. The servicing component allows these firms to stay close to their customers, especially as they refinance, and provides steady cash flows in the event of declining origination volumes. On the equity side, the strongest companies will be those that are able to acquire, develop, manage, lease, and sell assets in all property categories across the pricing spectrum.

Public operating companies will face shareholder pressures for greater operational efficiencies. Particularly, companies in the building and service ends of the industry will be pushed to manage costs aggressively while increasing revenues. Their ability to execute lower-cost, higher-quality, and higher-volume strategies will determine their stock market viability.

Leadership Imperatives

To profit from new strategies in the shifting real estate landscape, change needs to be well considered and implemented expeditiously throughout ever more complex and sophisticated organizations. The composite leader

identified by our interviewees seems like a kind of business superman—
"balanced and well-rounded" with "mental agility, nimbleness," and
"significant bandwidth"—but those requirements indicate the depth and
complexity of today's real estate industry, as well as its dynamism. The men
and women who are leaders need to develop a clear vision that engages
employees and customers and can be executed successfully, both organi-
zationally and operationally. Institutionalizing entrepreneurship requires
empowering executives while providing the tools and management controls
to ensure efficiencies and proper governance.

Essentially, today's successful leaders must build a framework that
reinforces a compelling company culture, sets out an understandable road
map for doing business, and communicates effectively. No leader can go
it alone—he or she needs to hire a complementary team and enable it to
carry out the vision and strategy. Our research highlights the "must have"
principles for taking command and setting the proper course.

Establish a Strong Culture and Values by Example. All employees
need to be in synch with how a company works and how they should relate
to each other in order to drive success. Company culture becomes ingrained
on the basis of executive behaviors and standards that are pushed down by
example through the entire organization. The universal values often touted
by companies are integrity, honesty, responsiveness, respect, and delivering
on expectations. But if leaders do not return phone calls or e-mail messages
and appear to take liberties with the company's values, company culture
suffers. Employees who live up to company values and embody the culture
need to be rewarded and recognized by company leaders. Others need to be
weeded out.

Communicate a Clear Vision of Organizational Direction. Taking a company public or creating a one-stop shop out of a group of silo
businesses requires communicating a clear vision of company goals and
business strategy that can be understood readily by employees, customers,
and shareholders. Leaders need to recognize that if a scheme cannot be
explained, it probably cannot be implemented. Behaviors and policies may

need modification or strengthening, if operating in the regulated environment of public companies. Business heads, meanwhile, should be motivated to anticipate broader client development opportunities and engage actively in cross-selling other units' products and services.

Build a Management Team. Managing and leading well in a large organization means surrounding oneself with good people. Team-building skills are essential. In hiring for and promoting to senior leadership ranks, chief executives should look for executives who exhibit fairness, integrity, and low ego. The best real estate leadership flows from a passion for developing and engaging people, for developing essential relationships with colleagues and employees. Team building orients decisions around "what's best for the team" rather than what is best for an individual or a particular business unit.

Allow Autonomy through Effective Delegation. While steering ever larger organizations that ultimately are responsible to shareholders and regulators, the leaders of tomorrow's real estate companies must keep their firms growing by encouraging visionary, deal-making opportunism. Effective delegation, greater autonomy, and access to top management all encourage a more entrepreneurial environment. Senior leaders below the CEO want the latitude to run a business and make mistakes while earning victories. This is the only way to develop and retain talent, providing for qualified successors.

Enable Flexibility. No matter how big or successful, firms always need to be able to shift and redeploy quickly when competition or economic conditions dictate. Leadership needs to be able to react to change quickly in a volatile industry, where rate shifts can change the business landscape overnight. Regulatory changes, increasing globalization, and new technological paradigms also contribute to an environment that requires considerable flexibility. If interest rates rise dramatically, for example, a mortgage finance company must staff up with business development people to source transactions from troubled lenders. If rates remain low and stable, then producers need to be added to complement the existing underwriting, closing, and asset management staff. Flatter organizations can offer greater flexibility and can be more prone to action. Responsibilities tend to overlap both geographically and functionally but leaders have greater access to all levels, which can be good for building teams and empowering business heads.

Integrate Operations and Finance. Real estate leaders realize that they need more than knowledge of bricks-and-mortar issues to grow their businesses. Executives who run large, sophisticated companies that operate in public markets require certain indispensable financial skills to interface effectively with Wall Street bankers and analysts. However, that financial acumen must be complemented by integrating the operating side of the business. Investments must be made and harvested, and a portfolio must be managed proactively to drive cash flow and increase value.

Stay Close to Clients. Real estate is fundamentally a relationship-based people business involving buyers, sellers, tenants, brokers, and lenders doing deals with each other. Success is predicated to some degree upon whom you know, trust, and respect. As firms grow bigger and more complex, managers must guard against losing touch in key relationships, particularly with clients and customers. Leaders need to keep channels of communication open to listen to and hear what clients want and need. Residential mortgage lenders, hospitality brand managers, and seniors' housing providers must keep tabs on hundreds of thousands of customers and average consumers, understanding what they want. Top residential mortgage bankers and online lenders have found innovative ways to reduce or eliminate fees, while others tout their almost instantaneous processing. Ultimately, some lenders will need only a database and a workflow engine to process mortgage loans. In the hospitality and senior care sectors, club floors, morning newspapers, loyalty programs, and adult communities with championship golf courses are but a few examples of the constant innovation necessary to stay ahead.

Think Globally. The march toward business globalization means that real estate company management teams must be oriented toward developing global strategies and seeking lines of business overseas. Effective teams must be able to operate across borders with an understanding of how to maneuver around cultural and national differences. Nurturing partnerships and relationships with experienced local players in growth economies around the world will become more essential to enable company expansion.

Attributes for Leadership Success. But following through on leadership imperatives can take CEOs only so far. Personal leadership attributes and qualities that drive successful implementation and enduring achievement are often intangible: engendering respect, energizing the team, and capturing opportunity, for example.

The leaders of America's largest industry are like other business leaders, only more so. Along with the disciplined, team-oriented leadership traits found among chief executives of other high-performing corporations in any industry, real estate leaders embody the deal-making, entrepreneurial spirit that lies at their industry's foundation. This unique synergy has enabled America's real estate CEOs to create an economic sector so dominant and diversified that it begs for a new categorization and offers valuable new lessons in business leadership.

The 150 CEOs, chairmen, and other senior managers whose thoughts are contained in this book collectively form an unprecedented, composite portrait of leadership in the real estate industry. Beyond validating the findings of broader business studies about successful leadership, the study reported here provides a new model for executive success, one specific to the emerging, transforming, diversifying economic sector known as real estate. It also provides prescriptions for the industry's next generation of leadership.

The CEOs and chairmen profiled here may be stewards of some of the industry's largest corporations, but it is because they are entrepreneurs—deal makers who put relationships first—that their organizations and their industry have been so successful. Entrepreneurial spirit shapes their vision and their companies: looking at markets in a new way, creating business opportunities where no one else can see them, taking risks, and learning from mistakes. But these men and women also understand that their organizations require a stable management platform for harnessing diversified growth, building an enduring enterprise, and incubating the next generation of leadership. They look to marry entrepreneurial and management attributes in corporations that can remain nimble, responsive, and opportunistic. Their encompassing mission can be summed up in the seeming paradox of institutionalizing entrepreneurship.

Although the institutionalization of entrepreneurship has made sustained success possible for many real estate organizations, most of the CEOs interviewed for this book expressed concern about keeping the entrepreneurial spirit alive while managing larger, more complex organizations as they hurtle through the current wave of consolidation, globalization, and greater regulation.

The composite portrait of real estate leadership drawn in these chapters deconstructs the volatile, high-ego stereotypes that personify the real estate entrepreneur for many Americans. Broader business studies have detailed how many business failures are tied to egocentric leaders who blur the lines between personal and corporate interests or who are intolerant of the perspectives of others. In *Why Smart Executives Fail*, author Sidney Finkelstein highlights what happens when leaders who think they have all the answers rely on fixed notions from past experience: ultimately they fail to cope with change. The dots often connect between high-visibility corporate bankruptcies and high-ego CEOs.

By contrast, the leaders chosen for this study draw much of their success from values-oriented leadership—a style based on qualities such as integrity, humility, empathy, self-awareness, and enthusiasm. They tend to be good listeners who are open to new ideas and are willing to understand their failures. We frequently encountered modesty and understatement, as well as a penchant to attribute company success to others while accepting full responsibility for failures. These leaders' extraordinarily high standards and their near-fanatical focus on sustained results are tempered with patience. Recognizing both their strengths and their weaknesses, successful CEOs tend to surround themselves with management teams that complement their skill sets. Not surprisingly, we found that values-oriented management at the top tends to create open and balanced corporate cultures, which helps build morale and fosters entrepreneurial behavior.

Effective real estate leaders not only show vision and have the capacity to take chances, but also carefully develop teams and corporate infrastructure to meet the expectations of investors, clients, and customers. Institutionalizing entrepreneurship presents a fascinating context for evaluating how to manage any business, especially in expanding, fast-changing industries.

CHAPTER THREE

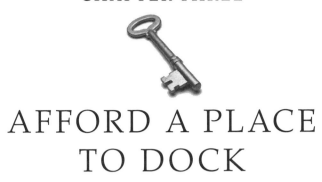

AFFORD A PLACE
TO DOCK

High-performing organizations tend to attract the best people, because they become places where people can build careers and make money in relative balance with their family responsibilities and personal lives. Besides competitive compensation and benefits, these companies provide mentoring and training in team-oriented cultures characterized by openness and respect. Leaders willingly invest in technology, infrastructure, and resources to give employees the tools they need to enhance performance and personal growth. In return, they can expect employee commitment and determination to meet established performance objectives.

Priming the Pump

Many real estate businesses revolve around investment transactions or sales forces: origination units serve as engines for growing the business, by providing deals or attracting capital for investment. The individuals on these teams are typically provided incentives for production volume, and the more successful organizations orient producers as coworkers and collaborators rather than competitors. Dan Smith, who ran the commercial mortgage debt business in North America for GE Capital, explains, "Our people understand they need to perform up to expectations, but the culture does not pit them against one another." Developing clients across regions or organizations often involves group sales efforts. Cross-selling products and services means eliminating tunnel vision in producers. Overall, company performance targets need to take priority over individual achievement. Mark Patterson, formerly of Merrill Lynch, reminded his transaction group constantly that "competition is in the marketplace and cannot be in our ranks."

More than Compensation

Companies should offer both professional and personal growth opportunities for employees. Larry Hirsch, retired chairman and CEO of Centex Homes, believes that "the only way to sustain long-term growth in a company is to spend a tremendous amount of time and money in developing people and investing in infrastructure." Greg Hauser, who ran the real estate business for Principal Financial Group, says, "Compensation is critically important, [but] … people must feel bonded together in running and building a business. Especially as companies get larger, people can't be lost in the shuffle—they need to be appreciated and given the opportunity to grow." Work-family balance can be difficult to achieve in today's highly competitive markets, but where face time is less critical for some workers, technology allows people to cut down on commuting and spend more hours with spouse and children. High-speed Internet connections and telecommunications permit the welcome accommodation of working from home on some days. "Balance in life is critical to success," says Ed Mace, former CEO of Rock Resorts. "You need to look at business more like a marathon than a sprint. Often situations demand urgent actions, but over time leaders need to exercise patience."

Sense of Belonging

Effective leaders create a sense of belonging through shared success in business performance. Partnership-styled cultures, in particular, offer executives—especially origination team members—a place to dock within a company. "You want to create an environment where team members rely on one another and trust each other," says Mike Rose of Gaylord Entertainment, one of the leading hospitality companies. "A partnership dynamic requires each partner to have accountability for the whole."

Creating a Winning Culture

So this "affording a place to dock" involves a lot of notions. It is about a place where people can go to work and feel like they are provided incentives to push and contribute, and do that on a collaborative basis with their fellow employees. At the end of the day, companies make more money (as do individuals), if their clients are well cared for, as well as when the companies' best interests are given priorities. One has only to think about how employees can help drive revenue, control costs, and hence generate better profitability.

Success in building a company where people generally enjoy coming to work has many facets. Yet, let's not make this too pollyanna-ish. Remember, there's a reason they call it "work." But many concepts touched upon in the following interviews are relevant in this regard. First of all, there is acknowledgment that these cultures have to be built—they don't happen naturally. Dan Baty of Emeritus points this out quite clearly. The concept of creating a learning environment where people can grow and develop is extraordinarily important. Part of doing so is developing people's leadership skills so that they can advance in the organization, as Peter Donovan at CB Richard Ellis points out. A company with a homegrown culture, as Larry Hirsch articulates, encourages people to think they will always have a place if they perform. Simply spending time with your people and hearing what they have to say is an important part of building a culture; just review Richard Kincaid's thoughts. Companies that encourage people to work hard and also respect balance in one's life tend to be good career choices.

"Having a diverse workforce," as Tom O'Neill, former CEO of Parsons Brinckerhoff Inc., points out, "allows people to learn from one another and appreciate different perspectives." The concept of blaming failure on the company, not the individual, is an interesting one. As Bill Pettit of Merrill Gardens says, "companies succeed and fail together" and no one is either exalted or blamed. And yet, when people misbehave, the issues need to be addressed directly, rather than just putting a bandage on the problem. Everyone is accountable, from the CEO down to the newest hire.

There are two additional points worth making here. One of the critical factors in creating a winning culture is a pride in the organization that makes people feel like they are working for a winner. Mark Patterson, formerly of Merrill Lynch, hammers this point home. And yet as trite as it sounds, having fun is a part of any successful culture. When John Gates was running CenterPoint Properties, for example, his organization delivered results but it was also a fun place to work.

The leaders quoted throughout this chapter pushed the importance of creating a culture that nurtures its people. Motivated people deliver satisfied clients and financial performance.

_____

DAN BATY
CHAIRMAN AND CEO
EMERITUS CORPORATION

> *"My partners and I reached the conclusion that culture doesn't create itself. It has to be built."*

Emeritus Corporation, headquartered in Seattle, is one of the leading assisted living companies. It owns or manages 180 communities in 35 states. One of its founders, Dan Baty has served as its CEO since 1993. Baty also serves as chairman of the board of Holiday Retirement Corporation, an independent living company that he wholly owns. Emeritus is publicly traded on the NYSE.

As a CEO, I spend most of my time determining where the business needs to go over the next three years. I visit our properties to get perspective on what's happening so we can position ourselves effectively. That also gives me an opportunity to be a cheerleader for the organization. I am a delegator and expect my people to make good decisions relative to how the business should be managed. This frees me up to spend a lot of time walking around and talking to people. We want people who are comfortable working in a delegated environment and who are excited about making decisions.

We learned a very important lesson about culture in 2004. The company was four years old and growing rapidly. My partners and I reached the conclusion that a culture doesn't create itself. It has to be built. We had five people running the business who didn't personify the culture important to us, and we recognized that the entire senior management team needed replacing. While traumatic for the company, it was the right thing to do. I took a leadership role—not only communicating to the incumbents but also recruiting new executives. But I had to do more. My partners and I recognized we had to be culture carriers. Whenever we gave a speech or presentation, or drafted any type of company correspondence, we constantly emphasized and repeated our values and principles. We made sure that our middle management team stayed motivated, constantly communicating to them through the senior team changes. Tough duty, but at the end of the day it was worth it.

STEPHEN F. BOLLENBACH
FORMER CO-CHAIRMAN AND CEO
HILTON HOTELS CORPORATION

"We view ours as a safe environment for people to work and grow in."

Hilton Hotels is one of the largest hoteliers in the world, with operations in more than 80 countries. Serving as CEO from 1996 to 2008, Steve Bollenbach oversaw the complete transformation of the company, reuniting the Hilton and Hilton

International brands as well as acquiring Bally Entertainment and Promus Hotel Corporation.

We have been successful at Hilton because we run a flat organization—the vast majority of key business decisions get made by business unit leaders. We believe in empowering people and promoting from within. We view ours as a safe environment for people to work and grow in, and we haven't lost a key person in the last ten years.

After 9/11, the management team decided to run the business as usual. We didn't go to the government for subsidies nor did we fire anyone, although we asked some of our people to work fewer hours. Our competitors let people go, which can create a very unhealthy environment. Our profits suffered, but the crisis was over in six weeks.

FRANCIS W. "BUTCH" CASH
FORMER CHAIRMAN, PRESIDENT, AND CEO
LAQUINTA CORPORATION

> *"This is a learning organization, where we can always do things better."*

Butch Cash headed LaQuinta from 2000 until the company was acquired by The Blackstone Group and taken private in 2006. LaQuinta operated 350 limited-service hotels in the United States. Cash previously worked at Marriott Corporation and was president and CEO of Red Roof Inns.

High-performing hospitality companies focus on their customers. I spend a lot of time listening and talking to our people. I prefer informality and have no patience for highly politicized environments. I like to hold people accountable and let them run their business on a daily basis, but I do not like surprises and insist on honesty and trust.

There were three important parts of the culture at LaQuinta. First, we were never satisfied—you can always learn and do things better. We put a focus on helping each person improve through our training programs, performance evaluations, and manpower review process. Second, we put our families first. While we insist on a strong work ethic, everyone understands that families are important for balance and ultimately life success. Third, we focused on integrity in everything we did. We assumed that every decision would be on the front page of the local newspaper.

You can't have success without a strong management team. I look for people who have produced tangible results, who treat others with dignity, and who believe doing the right thing is critically important.

In running this business, I have always tried to minimize layers of management between me and the customer. I like to delegate authority and empower people to make decisions. People want the freedom and resources to do what they think is right.

JACK M. COHEN
CEO
COHEN FINANCIAL

"My hope is that people view the firm as a place to dock and gain nourishment."

Following in the footsteps of his father, Buddy Cohen, Jack Cohen has built Cohen Financial into one of the leading commercial real estate capital markets organizations. The firm, founded in 1960, now has offices in major markets across the United States. Cohen Financial funds commercial real estate loans, both directly and indirectly, through multiple capital sources. In 2006 the firm sold a significant interest in the limited partnership to First Services Inc., a public holding company headquartered in Toronto.

I divide my time between customers (borrowers), capital sources, and my sales force. I try to be inclusive, focusing on building a team and serving as a change agent, and I set the tone and vision for the organization. My hope is that people view the firm as a place to dock and gain nourishment. We provide a package of rewards which includes compensation, benefits, education, and career development. I don't intend to be above market in any component, but I want the package to be compelling.

While creating a safe haven for people is important, I want them to take measured risks. I think about 2001 and 2002, when San Francisco and other markets headed into the real estate doldrums. Against the tide and at the cost of $2 million, I hired 18 new producers nationwide, including eight in San Francisco. Three years later that class of producers produced $7 million a year (and has continued to do so since). The investment in other people ultimately paid off. It was a measured risk worth taking.

PETER F. DONOVAN
SENIOR MANAGING DIRECTOR, MULTI-HOUSING
    CAPITAL MARKETS
CB RICHARD ELLIS

> *"This is a leadership-starved industry. The only way for me to be*
> *successful in growing and managing a larger business was to focus*
> *on developing leadership skills from within and delegating more."*

Peter Donovan was CEO of Deutsche Bank Berkshire Mortgage, one of the nation's largest commercial mortgage lenders, with a $20 billion portfolio. He had been instrumental in the company's startup in 1987 as Berkshire Mortgage Finance, becoming president in 1991. He significantly expanded the origination network and investor base, and was named CEO in 1998. Deutsche Bank acquired the company in 2005. After leaving Deutsche Bank, Donovan assumed a leadership role at CB Richard Ellis, overseeing its multifamily capital markets business.

I spent much of my time on cultural and leadership issues, as well as setting business strategy. It became increasingly clear that this is a leadership-starved industry. The only way for me to be successful in growing and managing a larger business was to focus on developing leadership skills from within and delegating more. I promoted an individual to president and embarked on a leadership development program where common principles and values were established. I created an executive committee of 20 executives, who met formally two times a year, to review values and the company's mission and vision and to conduct leadership and management skills training. We wanted everyone to use a common language, values, and skills, in order to respond appropriately to any issues that might arise. As part of this leadership development program, I had every person focus on "one big thing," a pattern of behavior each exhibited that was both a strength and a weakness. Although some of their personal behavior may be counterproductive, people are often unwilling to change or unable to change—because of their assumptions, preconceived notions, fears, and long-term patterns of behavior and because it creates uncertainty for them. This process helped raise self-awareness, leading to self-improvement and a better sense of one's impact on other individuals and the organization.

The lack of leadership in the industry is only accentuated by ongoing consolidation, because larger, merged, and more complex organizations require a higher level of leadership. The only solution for us was to develop people internally. Effective delegation and accountability became the fulcrum by which we would leverage our talent. I firmly believe that people are the most important asset of any company, and our guiding principles must help shape their behavior. As a company, we were focused on being the best at what we do, concentrating on quality, not volume. My style was to be passionate, committed, and core value–driven. I wanted to show confidence and yet be approachable.

When we had an underwriting crisis in California, the sequential legacy system could not efficiently handle the volume going through our system. I acknowledged a crisis internally and informed both Fannie Mae and Freddie Mac of the problems. While that was a risky move, it helped focus our resources so as to direct all energies to solving the problem rather than minimizing it.

Many leaders struggle with gauging the impact of an issue on their business appropriately, out of concern about how it will reflect on them. However, the way a company responds to an issue is predominantly influenced by how the issue is presented internally. Simply put, declaring a crisis will elicit a more comprehensive response than downplaying an issue. Crisis identification and mobilization are the hallmarks of an effective leader.

JOHN S. GATES, JR.
CHAIRMAN AND CEO
PORTAECO LLC

"We always had fun at the job and built a tremendous amount of flexibility into the company. We never overpaid our people but went out of our way to fund their academic dreams, provide excellent insurance benefits, and build them a world-class exercise facility. This all combined to create a very special culture."

John S. Gates, Jr., headed CenterPoint Properties Trust since its formation in 1993. CenterPoint is the largest owner of industrial properties in the Chicago market. He retired in 2006 and formed a family office investment business, Portaeco, after the REIT was taken private in an acquisition by Cal East Global Logistics.

We were successful at CenterPoint because of a laser-like focus on our business strategy. We put the right team in place to execute, then added value where others couldn't.

I learned from Martin Barber, my partner in the business, the importance of integrity and reputation. You're only going to build a successful franchise if your customers and investors trust you. Then you have to recruit and motivate the right team. We always had fun at the job and built a tremendous amount of flexibility into the company. We never overpaid our people but went out of our way to fund their academic dreams, provide excellent insurance benefits, and build them a world-class exercise facility. This all combined to create a very special culture.

We always hired experienced, entrepreneurial people into the company, typically out of the brokerage or construction business. We recognized that we didn't have the resources to train people, so we attracted people who we knew through the industry and whose capabilities we trusted. Our compensation plan had objective measurements—people knew how much they were going to get paid if they performed. We assessed company, business unit, and individual performance. Everybody felt they were treated fairly.

As a leader, my style was to explain where we were going and why we were going there. Some argued that I encouraged too much debate, but I believe in an open and inclusive culture. Once we made decisions, we executed well. I felt it was important to have a fun place to work, and I spent a tremendous amount of time with our employees. They recognized that integrity and reputation needed to be at the forefront of whatever we did. They understood that accountability and process were also very important to me.

Leadership is always about testing one's limits. I remember when we were merging Four Columns, which was Bobby Stovall's company, into Capital & Regional, which was the company that Martin Barber and I controlled. It was 1993. We brought systems and processes to the merged entity, while Four Columns contributed the entrepreneurial deal makers. Simultaneously, we were taking the combined company public as the first sizable industrial REIT. We knew each other well, and the openness and trust allowed us to consummate the merger and ultimately go public. It taught our people the lesson of coming together as a team for the overall good of the enterprise.

Once when we were switching audit partners within the same firm— long before Sarbanes-Oxley—our new partner disagreed with the way in which our former audit partner had accounted for 1031 exchanges. Due to their disagreement, CenterPoint would need to restate earnings. We faced the decision of whether to do nothing and hope the problem went away or to take it public. Acknowledging that we needed to treat our investors as partners, we decided to disclose and see where the chips would fall. Well, the stock went down only marginally. It took us a month to restate earnings, but it turned out to be a positive restatement (that is, earnings increased because of it). The stock price more than recovered. This is but one example of a consistent effort to be 100 percent candid. As a result, we earned a trust in the public markets that we never lost. If you have the trust of your tenants and your investors, your enterprise value will continue to prosper.

THOMAS F. GILBANE, JR.
CHAIRMAN AND CEO
GILBANE BUILDING COMPANY

> *"Employee engagement yields outstanding customer satisfaction*
> *and service, which is all about running a great services platform."*

Founded in 1873, Gilbane Building is one of the nation's oldest and largest construction firms. With annual revenues in recent years exceeding $2.5 billion and more than 25 offices across the United States, the firm is now led by fourth-generation family members. Core values of integrity, teamwork, dedication to excellence, loyalty, and discipline have been the foundation of the business for more than 130 years.

The great firms in the construction and architectural/engineering space bring a discipline to the business—it's all about blocking and tackling. We're a people business, and the firm needs to attract and retain the right people who can fit into our culture, which is an extraordinarily important part of running a great business. They have to be comfortable that you'll back them when they're making decisions. Employee engagement yields outstanding customer satisfaction and service, which is all about running a great services platform.

Besides being a capable operator, high-performing firms have a clear vision. They set strategic plans and communicate their objectives clearly throughout the company, so that there's buy-in. And if necessary, they reinvent themselves. In our business, it's important to understand the risks and exposures. With any of our projects, there are continuously a lot of changes. So our people are invested with the authority to respond accordingly.

I'm the fourth generation of family members to be running this business. We've been in business for over 130 years, and I'm proud of the fact that we are a private, family-owned concern. My father and uncle, who ran the business before my generation took over, were extraordinary leadership examples. They showed everyone in the company how important it was to work as a team. They also reflected other important values, including integrity, hard work, commitment to the community, and a balanced life with family as an important component. In fact, we really treat our employees as family and create a culture where they appreciate how much we value them. Our core values are so fundamental to who we are. We clearly try to be the best, but profitability is not our number one objective. We invest in our people and we work hard, but we also try to have fun. After all, we spend a lot of hours in this business.

My leadership style is engaged and hands-on. I like to create and share a vision, and provide leadership for the organization. Nothing gets built in my office. It's the people in our regional offices who find and do the work. And I strongly encourage our people to speak what's on their minds. I like to think of the firm as an inverted pyramid, where I am here to support our people, and our people are here to take care of our customers.

HENRY "GREG" D. GREGORY
FORMER PRESIDENT AND CEO
INDUSTRIAL DEVELOPMENTS INTERNATIONAL

> *"I try to spend as much time with my people as I can. We have developed a strong culture centered on teamwork, ethics, family orientation, and inclusiveness."*

Owned by a Japanese parent, Kajima Corporation, Industrial Developments International (IDI) develops, owns, and leases industrial properties in the United

States and Mexico. Greg Gregory founded the company in 1989 and retired as CEO in 2007.

My top priority was developing the firm's mission statement, keeping it dynamic and up to date, and communicating it to our people. Mission is all about defining market opportunity. We spent a lot of time on strategic planning and leadership. Our strategic planning committee met five to six times a year. At our leadership symposium, we invited the next generation of leaders in the company twice a year to discuss an agenda formulated by them. It gave me an opportunity to get to know them and gave them an opportunity to speak what was on their minds.

I was a journalism major, so much of my business success has been instinctive. I tried to spend as much time with my people as I could. We developed a strong culture—one of teamwork, ethics, family orientation, and inclusiveness. We also understood the importance of paying people well to reinforce the mission and culture of the company.

GREGORY C. HAUSER
FOUNDER
CRANE ISLAND ADVISORS, LLC

> *"While compensation is not unimportant, I found that interpersonal compatibility makes a huge difference. People must feel bonded in running and building a business. And a business that constantly grows offers the best career opportunities."*

Greg Hauser started his career at Principal Real Estate Investors in 1982 as an investment analyst. He worked in a variety of roles including mortgage lending, acquisitions, development, and portfolio management. He became CEO in 1998, managing a staff of 400 people and building the company into one of the largest real estate funds manager in the United States, with $30 billion under management. He retired in 2004, forming a private investment firm, Crane Island Advisors.

Performance all gets back to a firm's people and how they perform for clients. Successful companies in our industry deliver consistently on growth and earnings. They attract and retain people not only with fair compensation but also by developing strong cultures and attractive work environments.

Leadership priorities change depending on where a business is in its own evolution. In investment management a leader has to focus first on raising capital, then concentrate on running the business, including product development and pricing. While compensation is not unimportant in attracting and retaining people, I found interpersonal compatibility makes a huge difference. People must feel bonded in running and building a business. And the business that constantly grows offers the best career opportunities. As companies get bigger, you can't let your people get lost in the shuffle—they need to be appreciated and be given the opportunity to grow.

LAWRENCE P. HEARD
PRESIDENT AND CEO
TRANSWESTERN

> *"We are intentional about recruiting the best and brightest,*
> *fully supporting them in their day-to-day activities, and then*
> *empowering them to succeed."*

Transwestern is a leading commercial real estate services firm with offices throughout the United States. Larry Heard has been president and CEO since 2002; he joined the private company in 1983.

Our executive team has adopted a servant leadership approach when working with our team members in each region throughout the country. We first attempt to equip our people with the tools required for success and then empower them to represent the firm in the best manner possible. The key to our success has been in recruiting and retention. We are intentional about recruiting the best and brightest, fully supporting them in their day-to-day

activities and then empowering them to succeed. We look for folks with
the brains, energy, and values that our firm is known for in the industry. We
value entrepreneurs and an entrepreneurial approach to the business but
must have people that can also work in a team environment. The most successful people at Transwestern are team players.

All of us on the leadership team spend time with our clients. We listen
closely to their needs and then develop strategies to stay on top of constant
changes in our economic environment. If we need to make course corrections, we do so quickly and without a lot of fanfare.

Lastly, an area of people management that I believe in strongly but our
busy and fast-paced industry sometimes undervalues is the art of encouragement. I begin with the fundamental premise that people come to work every
day and try to do their best on the job. However, market forces, a miscalcula-
tion that leads to a mistake, or the loss of a piece of business can wear people
down. We try to set a course, stay in tune with the market and our plan, and
then encourage folks to persevere. Proper levels of encouragement can actually help people elevate their performance to new heights.

LAURENCE E. HIRSCH
CHAIRMAN
EAGLE MATERIALS

> *"The best-performing companies in homebuilding are*
> *homegrown. They spend a tremendous amount of time and money*
> *investing in infrastructure from systems to developing people.*
> *This is the only way to sustain long-term growth."*

Eagle Materials is a NYSE-traded construction products company that manu-
factures and distributes gypsum wallboard, cement, ready-mix concrete, recycled
board, and paperboard. It is a spin-off of Centex Corporation, a leading home-
builder, where Hirsch was CEO from 1988 to 2004. He is also the chairman of
Highlander Partners, a private equity firm.

I am a lawyer by training and had the extraordinary fortune to run a public, diversified company when I was only 29 years old. I spent the majority of my career, 19 years, with Centex and take pride in having transformed the culture from an opportunistic land acquisition business to a production-oriented, process-driven environment. The best-performing companies in homebuilding are homegrown. They spend a tremendous amount of time and money investing in infrastructure, from systems to developing people. This is the only way to sustain long-term growth.

Within any company, a strong work ethic is extremely important to success. At Centex I created a tough-minded culture where nonperformers were warned and if they didn't turn around, weren't protected. Maintaining an organization with the highest-quality people is extraordinarily important and has a positive trickle-down effect. At the end of the day, the B players simply don't make it.

I was always concerned about our culture becoming too insulated. I intentionally hired people from outside the company and always focused on ways in which the company could improve, regardless of how well my people thought the organization was performing. I always tested best practices and pushed people to recognize that they're not as good as they think they are.

My style was open, analytical, and energized. I tried to set an example. We were fortunate to have minimal turnover in the business. The culture was collaborative, not intimidating. But accountability was always a hallmark.

Employees are different today. Any CEO needs to recognize his or her people want information and are uncomfortable with a top-down, directive-oriented environment. But a culture of accountability can be blended with this participative approach. Whenever I was recruiting people, I looked for track records of success and long-term commitments to employers. The best fits in our organization were high-energy people who were accomplishment driven but not ego intensive.

RICHARD D. KINCAID
FORMER PRESIDENT AND CEO
EQUITY OFFICE PROPERTIES TRUST

> *"I traveled extensively, visiting every region and MSA once a*
> *year. I am a strong believer in creating a culture where people*
> *come to work for a reason rather than just collecting a paycheck.*
> *When I visited a region, I would have dinner with our regional*
> *leadership and then visit with small groups of employees*
> *throughout the day."*

Headed by Sam Zell, Equity Office Properties (EOP) was a REIT and the largest
property owner of office buildings in the United States after the federal govern-
ment. It was taken private by the Blackstone Group in early 2007. Richard Kin-
caid became president of EOP in 2002 and CEO from 2003 to 2007. Previously,
he served as EOP's executive vice president and chief operating officer, during
which time he initiated a major operational restructuring of the business.

One of my top priorities was having the right management team and organization structure in place to execute our strategy. Historically, the human
resources discipline never added much value at EOP, nor was much time
and attention paid to people development, simply because the company
was run early on as an entrepreneurial entity dominated by its founder, Sam
Zell. This is not unusual in the real estate industry, which has been dominated by private market players who view their companies more as trading
vehicles than long-term organizations that need to be fostered and cared
for. I paid a lot of attention to cultural fit.

    I also challenged my senior management team to think much more
strategically. I wanted to run the firm on a portfolio management basis,
where we matched investment trends to economic cycles. Historically, we
overemphasized the revenue side, attempting to maximize the value of
leasing transactions. Achieving cost advantages was never a high priority.

I was focused on process optimization, in either achieving scale or exiting markets. We needed to recycle capital out of mature markets and reinvest where the upside was strong.

In order to implement our strategic vision, I needed to stay in touch with the company as well as the markets. So I traveled extensively, visiting every region and MSA (metropolitan statistical area) once a year. I am a strong believer in creating a culture where people come to work for a reason other than just collecting a paycheck. When I visited a region, I would have dinner with our regional leaders and then visit with small groups of employees throughout the day. To effectively run a national platform, I pushed functional expertise into each region rather than relying on too many generalists. I also visited with brokers in each market. I instituted service-level standards in the company, making our people understand the value of having positive relationships with the brokerage community.

My vision only worked if there was a structure and clarity to the organization. All of our activities reported to one person, a chief operating officer, who ensured that the appropriate national standards and programs were put in place across the regions. If we had the right organizational structure in place to carry out our strategy and the right people "in the right boxes," we stood a reasonable chance of success.

EDWARD E. MACE

FORMER PRESIDENT

VAIL RESORTS LODGING COMPANY

> *"Balance in one's life is critical to success. This business is a marathon, not a sprint. No one has all the answers, and nothing changes overnight. Success is a blend of urgency and patience, and this comes with maturity. You have to play the whole game to win and many games to have a winning season."*

Ed Mace has led some of America's most prominent resort companies. He was president of RockResorts and president of Vail Resorts Lodging Company. Mace also has been president and CEO of Fairmont Hotels and CEO of Lincoln Hotels. He has also been a partner at Lincoln Property Company and managing partner of Lincoln Property Company of Europe.

Great CEOs share their vision and ensure that everyone is motivated, aligned, and empowered to implement it. Communication is critical in aligning senior management with the vision. Articulation of values is important too, because everyone needs to understand the types of behaviors to be reinforced in the organization. Debate is good, but ultimately decisions have to be made and everyone needs to move on. CEOs need to encourage an entrepreneurial environment; otherwise, bureaucracy reigns supreme.

Patience and focus have been critical to my success. When Canadian Pacific acquired and merged into Fairmont Hotels, Canadian Pacific was a public company headquartered in Canada and the subsidiary of a railroad. Fairmont Hotels, meanwhile, was an American company, entrepreneurial, and privately held. Fairmont ran its corporate office with 35 people, while Canadian Pacific had 240. In short, focus needed to be achieved quickly and a rapid integration had to occur. I put aside many minor political issues that could have derailed the merger. I went out of my way to bond together the senior people across the two companies, even though some of the Fairmont team would not have long-term prospects in the new entity. We rewarded them fairly and did everything possible to keep focus on the integration. Later, we worked hard to find new opportunities for those who were let go as a result of the merger. I recognized that Canadian Pacific was buying Fairmont, they owned it, and they would do what they wanted. To their credit, they worked hard to learn the Fairmont brand and to understand where Fairmont added value.

Balance in one's life is critical to success. This business is a marathon, not a sprint. No one has all of the answers, and nothing changes overnight. Success is a blend of urgency and patience, and this comes with maturity. You have to play the whole game to win, and many games to have a winning season.

JAY MANTZ
MANAGING DIRECTOR AND CO-HEAD, MERCHANT
    BANKING DIVISION
MORGAN STANLEY

> *"A partnership and ownership culture has the entire team aligned to work together to achieve the best results—top-tier investment performance and first-class client service."*

Morgan Stanley has had a dedicated real estate business since 1969, the longest uninterrupted presence in the real estate industry of any Wall Street firm. Today, Morgan Stanley Real Estate provides a complete range of products and services in the real estate sector, including mergers and acquisitions, restructuring and re-capitalization advice, public and private debt and equity underwriting, mortgage financing, and investment management. Jay Mantz is responsible for the Morgan Stanley Real Estate Investing business, the Morgan Stanley Infrastructure Fund, and other private equity funds.

There are a number of reasons why certain organizations are superior performers. First of all, their leaders need to be electable, so they are not in their roles by appointment or because they are the most senior people in an organization. Simply put, they add value, and the team comes to them for leadership and direction. They typically run a flat organization and are out there every day interfacing with clients. In short, they make a difference.

Another hallmark of an outstanding organization—and we do this here at Morgan Stanley—is that we're not afraid to promote young people and challenge them with responsibility. An organization has to be built on meritocracy. For example, Sonny Kalsi, who now co-heads the real estate investing business globally, ran the Asia operation when he was 32 years old.

Another hallmark of an outstanding organization is that they "invest-ment spend." We were early investors in many parts of Asia, including China and Japan. We persevered through some extraordinarily slow times and purposely sent an "A Team" to each new market. Too many organizations compromise on the quality of people they send into new markets, and then they wonder why they are unsuccessful. Today, the majority of our revenues are from outside the United States. We believe in gaining that geographical footprint and hiring teams that are reflective of the local cultures.

And there are two other cultural attributes important to us at Morgan Stanley, as well as all other high-performing firms. First of all, we put the client first. You need to remember that "the world is round." I learned this when I was working in Europe, and the markets were exceedingly tough. Because we had capital we could drive hard bargains, but we knew that one day capital would return and we wouldn't have that competitive advantage. And our clients were facing tough issues, whether it was selling corporate real estate to liquefy their balance sheets or struggling through under-performing businesses, etc. In short, we've tried to treat our clients fairly throughout the cycles, and it stood us in good stead.

PETER A. MARCHETTO
FORMER CEO
BOVIS LEND LEASE HOLDINGS, INC.

> "I view the United States as a giant chessboard—and you can't keep all your good players in one corner. You need to promote people throughout your network of offices and across the country. These growth prospects excite and retain them."

A subsidiary of Australian real estate firm Lend Lease, Bovis Lend Lease provides project management and construction services throughout 40 countries. High-profile jobs include Kuala Lumpur's Petronas Towers, New York's Trump World Tower, and Paris's EuroDisney. Peter Marchetto had served as president of Lehrer

McGovern Bovis before its acquisition by Lend Lease; he was then appointed
CEO of Bovis Lend Lease–Americas, which he left in 2008.

I was the third employee to work at Lehrer McGovern, the predecessor company to Bovis Lend Lease. I learned from Peter Lehrer that we're
here to serve clients and their interests come first. From Gene McGovern
I learned that there aren't any shortcuts to doing the job right. Successful
companies are all about successful people. The right people will serve clients
in an outstanding fashion. And if you don't have the right people on your
management team, you need to make the difficult decisions and put the
right players on the field. I believe you can develop a lot of skills in a person,
because no one has 100 percent of everything. But I always hire for motivation. If someone isn't motivated, it's virtually impossible to stoke that fire.

We now employ 2,800 people and have offices all over the country. I
view the United States as a giant chessboard—and you can't keep all your
good players in one corner. You need to promote people throughout your
network of offices and across the country. These growth prospects excite
and retain them.

I spend the majority of my time managing my team. It's impossible for
one person to run an organization. If they're successful, we'll be successful
as a company. I go out of my way to be open and communicate with them. If
they understand my expectations, we'll be a much more successful business.
My door is always open, and I invite questions and solicit opinions. I run the
company as a democracy, but everyone understands that if you want to succeed, you need to perform. We recently took the leadership team to Gettys-
burg. We studied why the battle was won and what leadership lessons could
be learned. One was that armies win battles, not generals.

I also spend a fair amount of my time selling new work, as well as
interfacing with existing clients. After all, that's the business we're in. Our
clients want to see that I have an interest and that we are committed.

My role was epitomized about five years ago when I got a call from
Steve Ross at The Related Companies about building the AOL Time Warner

Center. There were seven partners in the deal, and they wanted us to guarantee the cost as well as the time to construct. This was going to be the largest project built in New York City, short of the reconstruction of the World Trade Center. It involved 3 million square feet of residential, office, retail, and hotel. I met with the principals and told them I would have an answer in 24 hours. At 5 p.m. that same day, I assembled 35 of our senior people. Thirty-two were too busy to commit to the project, but three wanted to be involved and assume a leadership role. Keep in mind that this project would ultimately require 100 people. The four of us stayed up all night drafting a contract, and I got approval from our parent company in Sydney, Australia. I brought the leadership team over to meet with Steve the next day, and we won the business. This leadership moment exemplifies the role I liked to play at Bovis Lend Lease.

LAURALEE E. MARTIN
GLOBAL CHIEF OPERATING AND FINANCIAL OFFICER
    AND DIRECTOR
JONES LANG LASALLE, INC.

> *"We're not all about compensation but focus on the development of our people for the benefit of our clients."*

Since 2005, Lauralee Martin has been responsible for enhancing the productivity and improving the financial performance of Jones Lang LaSalle, Inc., a leader in real estate services and investment management with a rich history of client service. In her current position, Martin has aggressively upgraded the finance function and is an integral member of the management team that is improving the firm's global businesses.

Our business at Jones Lang LaSalle is all about people. Unlike many other businesses, you can't export what we do to India. Clearly, a strategy needs to be put in place, but then it's all about motivating and retaining the best people to execute. We tend to be a very inclusive culture, and I am simply one member of the team. We push everyone on the team to innovate, because spotting value while simultaneously assessing risk is the key to our business—especially on behalf of our clients. Unquestionably, we put our clients first; the firm is the next priority. We sincerely have a mutual respect for one another, which creates a very strong culture.

In the real estate industry, egos are all too common, given that almost everyone grows up in a deal-making culture. Some of the greatest names in the business have left huge legacies. However, as the industry becomes more global and institutional, a team—not simply one individual—provides the answer. In fact, at Jones Lang LaSalle, we do not have a star culture. We go out of our way to hire, mentor, and develop team players. We also put a premium on communications. We're not all about compensation but focus on the development of our people for the benefit of our clients. As an example, our client relationship managers are individuals who have rotated through multiple functional responsibilities.

In the end, the real estate business is a long-term game. This is a cyclical industry; however, as an industry, we are developing more of an institutional memory, and reputation is increasingly critical. Hence, building a culture that focuses on serving clients and developing a reputation are critical to any firm's long-term success.

PAUL H. MCDOWELL
CEO
CAPITAL LEASE FUNDING INC.

> *"The firm's culture is familial and inclusive. There is a genuine caring for everyone and loyalty, probably to a fault."*

Paul McDowell was a founder with Lewis Ranieri of Capital Lease Funding (CapLease), a diversified public REIT that owns and finances primarily net-leased, single-tenant commercial real estate assets. Before joining CapLease, McDowell was corporate counsel at Sumitomo Corporation of America.

I stay very close to the day-to-day management of the business and specifically to investment decision making. We want to build scale and diversify,
which is why a strategic thought process is so critical. Since our founding,
CapLease has gone from a small, private, first-mortgage lender with a
gain-on-sale business and $13 million of capital to a NYSE-traded, diversi-
fied, public REIT that invests at all levels of the net-lease capital structure,
including first-mortgage loans, mezzanine loans, and direct equity investments, with billions of dollars in assets.

I have an easygoing style and spend a lot of time with our staff. The
firm's culture is familial and inclusive. There is a genuine caring for everyone—and loyalty, probably to a fault. The company has probably retained
some people longer than it should have, but because we are loyal to our
employees they have been tremendously loyal to our company. This deliberate strategy has allowed us to build the strongest and most cohesive team in
the net lease business. We refuse to hire "stars," who look to be individual
contributors at the expense of others. Instead, we look for intelligent, highly
energized people who have leadership potential and are team oriented. I
am a consensus builder and strive to be a good communicator, both with
our team here at CapLease and with the multitude of outside constituencies like investors, customers, and vendors. I try to constantly monitor what
our ever-changing range of opportunities is and what the hurdles to getting
there are, so we can successfully adjust our strategy as an organization in
getting it done.

In any firm, especially in a smaller one, the test is getting through a
crisis. Ours was in 1998, when the financial markets basically melted down.
At the time, we had very little equity capital but had a very large, and highly
leveraged, loan portfolio. As the financial world seemed to be crashing
down around us, our lenders told us the game was over unless we were
able to meet margin calls and protect them. We were able to survive because
we were honest, had integrity, and were willing to deliver the bad news to
our lenders and equity investors on a real-time basis. As partners, the senior
management team at CapLease subsumed their personal ambitions for

the benefit of both investors and employees, and we stood by the company during its darkest hour. In the end, the investors received their returns, the banks were made whole, and the employees received bonuses. No one gave up, and there was tremendous loyalty to the firm. We survived a very difficult learning experience because we did the right thing under enormous pressure, when it would have been so easy to just go home.

ARTHUR J. MIRANTE II
PRESIDENT, GLOBAL CLIENT DEVELOPMENT
CUSHMAN & WAKEFIELD

> *"I spent a tremendous amount of time interviewing executives for employment by Cushman & Wakefield. I found that if they had character, ambition, and empathy, they had a reasonable chance of success at the firm."*

Cushman & Wakefield has 198 offices in 55 countries and is majority controlled by IFIL, the investment group of the Agnelli family. Arthur Mirante retired as CEO in 2005. He joined the firm in 1971 and served as general counsel, national director of Management Services, and New York Area regional director. He was the first CEO at Cushman & Wakefield not to have risen through the ranks as a broker.

When I was CEO of Cushman & Wakefield, my most important priority was to walk the talk. I felt it was extraordinarily important to set an example by respecting other people, having a strong work ethic, and being of the highest character. At Cushman & Wakefield, we believe strongly in giving back to the community and in diversity. It was always important for me and other members of our senior management to practice a strong value system, making sure the system was incorporated into our vision of the firm. The critical factor was repeating, again and again, what these values are and what the firm stands for. The dots need to be connected through real examples of strong values demonstrated by senior management. When this positive behavior is rewarded, the values are correlated with people's success and growth within the firm.

A large part of my success has been surrounding myself with smart people and then listening to them. They do much of the day-to-day management of the firm, and I've encouraged them to learn by making mistakes, even though it may be painful. I spent a tremendous amount of my time interviewing executives for employment by Cushman & Wakefield. I found that if they had character, ambition, and empathy, they had a reasonable chance of success at the firm.

Leadership is about taking risks and underwriting those risks through instinct and judgment. In 1992, I pushed to move into Europe. Coldwell Banker and Grubb & Ellis were already there, and I felt it was an opportunity to export Cushman & Wakefield's services while protecting our franchise. If our competitors started working with one of our clients in Europe, then our business in the United States was potentially at risk. So, in essence, a good offense would provide a sound defense. I was meticulous in executing the strategy. I found the right people and integrated them successfully into the firm without compromising our values. In many countries, a service provider is often asked to do inappropriate things that might ultimately allow them to win the business. No piece of business was ever that important to us.

I also led Cushman & Wakefield into the corporate services business. I felt it was important to hire salaried people who were designated as client relationship professionals and I did this, although it was not popular with our brokers. We ultimately became a leader in the industry. There was a real opportunity to provide corporate America with high-quality real estate services. Despite significant resistance to the corporate services concept and having salaried professionals managing our corporate accounts with the brokers, this move ultimately proved to be in the best interests of the firm.

LARRY A. MIZEL
CHAIRMAN AND CEO
M.D.C. HOLDINGS, INC.

> *"We want customers to be proud of buying a Richmond American*
> *home. We try to convey that homebuilding is one of the noblest*
> *professions, because we are building the largest and most*
> *important asset that any family will ever own."*

Now listed on the NYSE, M.D.C. Holdings, Inc., was founded by Larry Mizel
in 1972. Operating nationally, M.D.C.'s Richmond American subsidiaries build
and sell single-family detached homes and townhomes. Its subsidiaries also offer
mortgage loans, title services, and insurance.

I focus on providing strategic leadership to the business, constantly researching
global economics and demographics, working to understand how trends may
impact our homebuilding business. Every land purchase at M.D.C. is approved
by an investment committee, irrespective of whether it is one lot or a major
parcel. My belief is that a homebuilder should be like a bank, with separate
production and credit/underwriting units. Well-managed homebuilders acquire
real estate only after careful review of the risks associated with the asset.

In 1972, M.D.C. started as a homebuilder with a net worth of $50,000.
More recently, we commanded a market capitalization of approximately $2.5
billion. We were the fourth of eight publicly traded homebuilders to receive investment grade ratings from the three major rating agencies—a confirmation of
our strategy and the market's confidence in our ability to execute. Much of our
success derives from the culture we have created. We focus on communication,
loyalty, and balance. We take our profession very seriously. We want customers to be proud of buying a Richmond American home. We try to convey that
homebuilding is one of the noblest professions because we are building the
largest and most important asset that any family will ever own.

In 1993, M.D.C. was an aggregation of various operating businesses
and had neither a common marketing message nor a common culture.

Employee satisfaction was low, and employees felt the company was run without opportunities for personal or professional growth. In September 2000, 20 of our company's leaders signed our first "Declaration of Change and Common Principles." They accepted responsibility for transforming the company's culture. On September 11, 2001, we planned to celebrate the first year of this cultural transformation. Seven hundred employees were gathered in a theatre in Denver, and the theme, interestingly enough, was "Red, White, and Blue," where all employees could show their pride for being affiliated with the company as well as for being Americans. Fifteen minutes before the event was to begin, the planes hit the towers. Amid obvious uncertainty, I decided to move forward with the event and appeared in front of our people, telling them to remain strong and stay unified so we could persevere through adversity. It turned out to be a very compelling event and achieved more than we expected. Today, M.D.C./Richmond American Homes Foundation is a significant contributor to the Homeland Defense Foundation, which donates money to individuals and their families who have served in the wars in Iraq and Afghanistan. We believe very strongly in making sure that our employees have balanced lives and are committed to their families, as well as to important outside causes.

ANTONIO B. MON
EXECUTIVE VICE CHAIRMAN, PRESIDENT, AND CEO
TECHNICAL OLYMPIC USA, INC.

> *"I preach that our business is an inverted pyramid. Our customers are at the top of the pyramid, our employees are in the middle, and I'm supporting everyone. In short, I work for our people, and our people work for our customers."*

A publicly traded homebuilder, Technical Olympic operates nearly 250 communities in 16 metropolitan markets in Florida, Texas, the West, and the Mid-Atlantic states. The company has grown by acquiring other homebuilders. Technical Olym-

pic specializes in selling homes to first-time and move-up buyers, as well as people relocating. It also operates home mortgage and land title subsidiaries. Tony Mon has been president and CEO since 2002. Earlier, he cofounded Pacific Greystone Corporation, a West Coast homebuilder that merged with Lennar Corporation, and previously worked in various positions for the Ryland Group, a publicly traded homebuilder headquartered in California.

In a business as cyclical as homebuilding, I take great pride in managing through crisis. I'm very patient and always encourage our people to focus on the longer term and avoid concentrating on the bleak times. From my perspective, what separates the high-performing homebuilders is their ability to execute. In many ways, this is still a "mom and pop" industry. Eighty percent of our product is unremarkable, so the tactics that we utilize to execute the business are the clear differentiators. You'll see more people coming into homebuilding from other industries where they've been taught how to execute.

I run a very decentralized company with strong financial controls, a direct reflection of my financial background. I try to bring a strategic orientation to the business, establish goals, and then point my people in the right direction to accomplish those goals. I don't get too involved in how they accomplish their objectives. One of my challenges from a leadership perspective is that I don't always cut and run soon enough. But I'm a big believer that too much change is not good for an organization.

I refer to Technical Olympic as a "soup in the making." The company has been together for four years, after a series of mergers. I think we've instilled some important core values such as integrity, team orientation, and a customer focus. In fact, I preach that our business is an inverted pyramid. Our customers are at the top of the pyramid, our employees are in the middle, and I'm supporting everyone. In short, I work for our people, and our people work for our customers.

I don't panic but prefer to communicate the facts and then say, "This is what we're planning to do to manage through the crisis." I try to inspire our people and focus on the bigger picture. It's helped me enormously in persevering through the inevitable downturns.

BRUCE E. MOSLER
PRESIDENT AND CHIEF EXECUTIVE OFFICER
CUSHMAN & WAKEFIELD, INC.

"At the end of the day, culture counts."

Bruce Mosler leads the world's largest independent real estate services firm and serves on its board of directors. Cushman & Wakefield employs more than 15,000 professionals operating from 221 offices in 58 countries; in 2007 its revenues were in excess of $2.1 billion.

In order to run a successful business, I believe you need three things:
- The quality of your people needs to be extraordinary.
- People need to understand and believe in the vision of your business.
- Your business needs to be diverse, from both a product and a geographic perspective. Today, our business at Cushman & Wakefield is split virtually evenly between U.S. and international activities. That wasn't the case five years ago.

Of equal importance is the consistency of service delivery. The quality of service you receive from our firm in India has to parallel what you receive in Tokyo. And I strongly believe that growth needs to be balanced. Too much growth, too quickly—typically in the form of big acquisitions—carries the potential to undermine a culture. A rush to market in this way can compromise the processes and procedures one needs to have in place in order to manage a business successfully. After all, at the end of the day, culture counts—particularly in a service industry like ours. Our culture is what differentiates Cushman & Wakefield.

Culture does not exist in the abstract—it must be experienced. As a result, my leadership style has always been hands-on. The CEO has to set the vision and strategy, and in my view, it's the CEO who should deliver the message. I like to meet with as many of our people as I can, typically in town hall–style, face-to-face sessions. I also like to stay close to our clients, to make sure we're performing consistently for them and also get their assessment of the competition. If I do right by our people, I will do right by our clients.

People often ask what makes a good CEO. I came up in this business as a broker, and a personal record in the business can give one credibility as a CEO. But other elements need to be learned, and there is no better way to learn them than from a strong mentor who has sat in that chair and been successful. My predecessor and one of my greatest mentors, Arthur Mirante, taught me the value of patience, how valuable it is to simply listen to people.

One also needs to know the difference between being liked and earning respect. Earlier in my career, I wanted everybody to like me. But a leader must show the ability to do things and make decisions that are difficult or unpopular. In the final analysis, as the leader of this organization, I need to do what I think is right, even though that might be contrarian to what else is going on the industry.

Finally, no leader can go it alone. That's equally true of a CEO or the head of a small team. I go out of my way to surround myself with individuals whose skills complement my skill set. Knowing your own limitations and then engaging and inspiring those who have the skills and talent you need are central to leadership at all levels.

THOMAS J. O'NEILL
FORMER CHAIRMAN AND CEO
PB INC.

"I've been fortunate to surround myself with complementary people. I have a very diverse senior management team, both

male and female, who harken from all over the world including
the United States, England, and Australia. They bring some
of the visionary and marketing skills which complement my
background."

Founded in 1885, PB is a private, employee-owned, global planning, engineer-
ing, project management, and construction management firm that consults on
infrastructure—buildings, environment, power, highways, transit, and telecom-
munications. With 150 offices and more than 10,000 employees, it operates in 80
countries. Tom O'Neill was elected president and CEO of PB in 1996 and chair-
man of the board in 2004. He retired in 2008.

Integrity and honesty are inviolate in everything a leader does, setting the
tone for the entire organization. Employees are the only asset we have.
It's important to treat them the way that we want to be treated. While our
culture at PB values its heritage and its employees, we try to be a modern
company in a modern era. We stress the longevity of the firm and how
clients are paramount. We don't try to maximize profitability but balance
profit with reinvesting in the firm and our people. We try to make PB a nice
place to work and value all people equally. While our goal has always been
to grow from within, we also believe in bringing in outsiders—typically
people from the engineering and construction industry—so the firm never
becomes too insular. Business simply changes too frequently.

Since I'm an operations person by background, I tended to take a
fairly hands-on approach, erring on the side of speaking up if I get uncomfortable about something. I've always tried to recognize my limitations. I've
been fortunate enough to surround myself with complementary people. I
had a very diverse senior management team, both male and female, who
hailed from all over the world, including the United States, England, and
Australia. They brought vision and marketing skills that complemented my
background. I see myself as quite patient, although the people who worked

for me may not see me that same way. While achieving our numbers was important, it is not the sole driving force in this business.

Leadership is all about overcoming adversity. We bought a U.K. company with a pension plan that we had a net asset position in, but quickly went into a large net deficit position. The liabilities were simply not matched with the pension fund's ability to pay out capital. Our book-value shares dropped by 40 percent, but in a few short months we successfully addressed the problem. We took steps to protect shareholder value, while also taking steps to fund the deficit over time. We did not try to fix blame; we fixed the problem. While it could have led to a sharp decline of the business, cooler heads prevailed.

MATTHEW OUIMET
FORMER PRESIDENT, HOTEL GROUP
STARWOOD HOTELS & RESORTS WORLDWIDE, INC.

> *"Sincerely investing in the people around you ensures both professional success and personal satisfaction."*

Starwood is one of the world's largest hotel and leisure companies, conducting hotel and leisure business both directly and through its subsidiaries. Before joining Starwood in 2006, Matt Ouimet spent 17 years at the Walt Disney Company including assignments as the president of the Disney Cruise Line and the president of the Disneyland Resort. In his role as president of Starwood, Ouimet oversaw hotel operations worldwide for Starwood Hotels & Resorts Worldwide, Inc., which includes the company's nine hotel brands consisting of more than 900 hotels in 95 countries. He left Starwood in 2008.

I do believe strongly in servant leadership; I try to make the lives of those I work with better. This is especially important in the hospitality industry, where a caring attitude cascades down to customers. Sincerely

investing in the people around you ensures both professional success
and personal satisfaction.

Secondly, I think that creativity and innovation in business are driven
by a diversity of experiences and points of view. I saw the importance of
respecting alternative perspectives when I was running Disney's cruise line
business. The Disney culture was fairly well defined, and initially we worked
very hard to embed this culture within the ship. However, what we failed to
recognize was that the maritime culture—which many of the officers and
crew were familiar with—had some wonderful attributes that, although different from what Disney had traditionally done, resulted in a better experience for the crew and the guests—and better business results.

There were also more than 50 nationalities represented in the ship's
crew, including a significant number of young women who would leave
their children for six to nine months to work on our cruise ships. As a young
father at the time, I had a hard time understanding why someone would
choose to be away from their family like this. However, as I came to know
the crew, they explained to me how there were not many good jobs available in their home countries and serving on our ship allowed them to earn
enough money to take care of their families. Ultimately I learned that they
were great family people, that their world was just different than mine.
Learning how to manage and motivate this culturally diverse crew and have
them perform at maximum productivity was a wonderful learning experience for me and my management team.

There is another critical element driving organizational productivity,
and that is trust among the leadership of a business. A leader has to create
effective dialogue and debate with his or her senior management team.
But this can only happen if there is a high level of mutual trust between
all of the team members. When this level of trust exists, you hear all of the
issues and alternative perspectives in a common forum. You can then make
a decision and carry that decision forward to the broader organization with
everyone feeling like they had a hand in the decision that was made. I've
told several people whom I've worked for over the years that I would work

for them as long as they listened to me, not as long as they agreed with me. Someone always has to get the extra vote, but talented people greatly value being a legitimate part of the decision process. To be a successful leader you have to remember that it isn't about you, it's about them—the people who work with you and the guests you serve.

MARK R. PATTERSON
FORMER HEAD OF GLOBAL PRINCIPAL INVESTMENTS
MERRILL LYNCH & COMPANY

"People like working for an agile organization at the forefront of many strategic opportunities in the industry."

Merrill Lynch is one of the world's leading investment banks, providing institutional sales and trading, investment banking advisory and capital-raising services to corporations, governments, and institutions worldwide. It was acquired by Bank of America at the end of 2008. Mark Patterson joined Merrill Lynch in April 2005 as the global head of Real Estate Investment Banking and became the head of Global Principal Investments. Before joining Merrill Lynch, he headed real estate investment banking at Citigroup.

Even though most of us in real estate are in the "hard asset business," any organization revolves around hiring, developing, and motivating people. Unlike a lot of investment bankers, I focused on fostering a team-oriented culture, constantly reminding our people that the competition is in the marketplace—not in our ranks. We made decisions collectively, and there was transparency in our decision-making process. We were also very strategic about how we managed and built the business. For example, we had people in Japan ahead of the REIT boom and followed a similar strategy in Europe. People like working for an agile organization at the forefront of many strategic opportunities in the industry.

Leadership is about taking calculated risks. When my team and I moved to Merrill Lynch, we became part of an integrated platform, which I felt was critical to success in our business. It was best for our clients and allowed us to be competitively positioned globally. And fortunately, we had a great team who shared the vision and belief that a globally integrated investment platform was the future for our business. We succeeded, working together as a team, focused on satisfying our clients' requirements.

WILLIAM D. PETTIT, JR.
PRESIDENT AND CHIEF OPERATING OFFICER
MERRILL GARDENS, LLC

"Interestingly, if people fail, I feel it's the company's fault versus the individual's."

Merrill Gardens is the second-largest privately held assisted living company in the country. Bill Pettit joined the firm in 1992, after 18 years in the commercial banking industry. He was instrumental in the formation of the company, which started with one community in 1993.

Even though our company is financially driven, I feel it's almost too forgiving at times. If people fail, I often feel it's the company's fault, not the individual's. I tend to give people the benefit of the doubt and am slow to make personnel changes. But this patience and nurturing has worked well for Merrill Gardens. The general manager's role is the toughest in the industry and one of the toughest of any industry. The most successful general managers are people who have run their own business and have the passion for taking care of seniors. They must be hands-on in their orientation and be willing to think outside of the box. Of the 66 properties in Merrill Garden's portfolio, 45 have been acquired, and I am proud that 40 percent of the inherited people have stuck with Merrill Gardens on a longer-term basis. I visit every facility once a year, so that my general managers know that I care about them and that I'm there to offer advice and counsel.

Having been in the banking business, I have seen a lot of industries and understand the pitfalls of rapid growth. There are benefits to structure, internal controls, and thoughtful marketing. While it is extraordinarily important to track performance, especially as a company builds scale, you must hire and develop the right people; otherwise our business simply doesn't work.

ELYSIA HOLT RAGUSA
MANAGING DIRECTOR
JONES LANG LASALLE

> *"We go out of our way to protect our culture. We build an enormous amount of trust within the company, and then we transfer that trust to our clients. If everyone in the company works as a team, the client will benefit."*

Headquartered in Addison, Texas, The Staubach Company was founded in 1977 by former Dallas Cowboy quarterback Roger Staubach. The firm was acquired by Jones Lang LaSalle in 2008. Staubach provided property tenant representation and relocation services to businesses around the world. Clients include Time Warner, O'Melveny & Myers, and Exxon Mobil. Elysia Holt Ragusa served as Staubach's president and chief operating officer from July 2001 to June 2007.

One of the keys in creating a successful company in any services business, including real estate, is establishing brand awareness. You have to be known for something, and your identity is all about the people with whom you're associated. In our case, Roger Staubach represented our brand. We decided to do something reasonably unique and focus on serving tenants only. Many people thought we were crazy to focus so narrowly, but we thought no Chinese wall would be tall enough if we entered the landlord business.

We were a competitive firm that enjoyed winning. But winning could not compromise our overarching belief in values. Values and meeting our clients' needs came first. Financial performance and our own compensation were not priorities. We recognized early on that we're in a competitive industry, made up of highly motivated salespeople. Given Roger's training at Annapolis, we recognized how important leadership and academics are to success. So, we hired many people from the service academies, virtually all of whom have added tremendous value. Roger has also perpetuated the concept of diversity. He had a strong mother, as well as four daughters, and always recognized the importance of intuition and empathy to business success.

Some of the best leaders are entrepreneurial, and they want to accept responsibility and act responsibly. An organization is best built on a decentralized basis, where people serving clients are "close to the customer." They drive the business, and that's where we distributed our wealth. We let regional leaders make decisions. Our culture was all about resilience, persistence, and persuasion.

Roger has been a great mentor to me. He believes in doing the right thing for the customer and pursuing everything with a passion. As a result, dollars will follow. He taught me to let the market dictate what will happen to a client and not to reach any negative conclusions prematurely. One never knows what a landlord will yield in concessions.

I tried to coach and bring the best out in people. Even though we had a company of brokers, we worked hard to play as a team. I'm clearly tenacious about setting and realizing goals. I stay focused on what needs to be accomplished. Roger and I always put the welfare and success of the company above any individual.

We went out of our way to protect our culture. We built an enormous amount of trust within the company, and then we transferred that trust to our clients. If everyone in the company worked as a team, the client would benefit.

About half of our people were recruited from the outside as experienced veterans. We didn't want to become myopic. Our biggest challenge was firing a proven performer who wasn't a team player. If you don't take action, the machine grinds to a halt due to the lack of trust generated when we don't walk our talk.

COLIN V. REED
CHAIRMAN, PRESIDENT, AND CEO
GAYLORD ENTERTAINMENT COMPANY

> *"At Gaylord, we believe in a culture where our 'stars come first.'*
> *The stars are our people, who in essence take care of our guests.*
> *We go out of our way to celebrate each other."*

Publicly traded on the NYSE, Gaylord Entertainment is in the hospitality and attractions business, catering to large meeting and event planners, with Nashville properties including the Grand Ole Opry, as well as resorts in Hawaii, Texas, and Florida. Colin Reed was elected president, CEO, and director in 2001 and chairman of the board in 2005. Before that, he was a member of the Office of the President of Harrah's Entertainment and earlier, chief financial officer.

Especially in the hospitality industry, the best firms have strong internal cultures, in which people take pride in the company and treat the business as if they owned it. Their caring for the customer helps build a long-term sustainable business. In contrast, shareholder-driven companies place making money as the highest priority. But companies with strong cultures will always outperform from a financial perspective.

Over my career, I had the opportunity and privilege to work with and learn from many inspirational leaders, including Phil Satre, who was chairman and CEO of Harrah's, but the person who has had the most impact on my career is Mike Rose. His all-around business acumen and customer-driven focus resulted in the creation of many world-class hospitality brands. He always said, "Our business is not about the product, it's about the people. If your people take pride in taking care of their customers, the business will work."

We own one of the largest convention hotels in the world, with about 3,000 rooms. Located in Nashville, it enjoyed a terrific reputation and was doing well financially. And then from 1998 through 2001, it went into a freefall. Large bookings declined dramatically, and I'm talking about groups of 600 people at a time. Our front-line people were just not executing and were treating guests rudely. And it happened because the staff believed management had checked out, had become arrogant, and was sitting in an ivory tower. They believed management was much more interested in cutting costs than treating the customers well and having fun in the process. Guess what? If management feels that way, employees will adopt the same behavior.

At Gaylord, we believe in a culture where our "stars come first." The stars are our people, who in essence take care of our guests. We go out of our way to celebrate each other with numerous recognition and reward systems now in place. In fact, our front-desk line staff and our hotel concierges can earn a quarterly bonus based upon customer satisfaction. I spend about one-third of my time on the front line, interacting with people. I host town hall meetings, where everyone gets to talk about what's on his or her mind. I literally spend a couple of hours with every new supervisor and manager hired by the company, imparting our beliefs in culture and customer service. I instituted a "1-800-Call-Me" telephone line, so anyone in the company can call me with recommendations or complaints. And I'm very active in leading group training sessions. Our people need to know that I care for them, and I want them to care for our customers.

We have a group of 12 people who run this business. I call it our partner group because I view each of them to be partners of mine. We cover all aspects of the business, which is a great learning experience for each of them, and the perspectives that I receive as a CEO are quite remarkable. In retrospect, when I took over the helm of this company in 2001, it could have cratered. Our team has done a remarkable job. In essence, our formula sounds quite simple but it takes extraordinary discipline to execute throughout the company. I think that's the reason you don't see it replicated across the industry—and that's good for us.

DAVID A. RIDLEY
CEO
INVESCO REAL ESTATE

"Our success is built on cultural values."

INVESCO Real Estate manages approximately $20 billion in direct real estate assets and publicly traded real estate securities. David Ridley has directed INVESCO Real Estate since its inception in 1983. He has overall responsibility for the management of the firm, its real estate investment and management strategies, and its financial planning, and has managed the steady growth of INVESCO's real estate investment business. Ridley has also overseen INVESCO's recent expansion into Europe.

My partners and I believe our long-term success can be attributed directly to our culture. From the beginning, we've embraced two primary values: people are our most important asset, and our focus on clients must never waver.

We firmly believe that to be successful in the real estate funds management business, you need to use a team-based approach. A "star" system will not work because of the complexity and management intensity of the real estate investment process. We call it IQ compounding. By working as a team, we compound the intellectual capital of our firm, which helps us make better decisions for our clients. By involving people in decisions, they become a lot more engaged and have a direct stake in making the business successful. That helps create greater stability (which our clients appreciate) and a natural path for succession (which our employees appreciate).

Our kind of environment is less "low ego" and more "shared ego." By working together, we all feel better about our business and take greater pride in the shared accomplishments of our firm. Our ability to exceed clients' expectations drives our continued well-being, so every decision we make in our firm is based on their long-term best interests. We started out as a small business with a few clients, so we were able to focus on their needs one client at a time. As we've grown, we've maintained that one-client-at-a-time approach, because we realize how critical they are to our success.

Because we value the relationship we have with each of our clients, we firmly believe they should be treated with the highest degree of respect, dignity, and humility. You can't do that day in and day out unless that is ingrained in the culture of your company. Because we use a team approach, which engenders strong depth and stability of our employee base, I'm able to spend most of my time on strategic planning, communicating with our clients, overseeing our risk management systems, and ensuring that we have the right processes in place to deliver on our promises.

As a result of our dedication to our cultural values, we've been able to create a captivating work environment that enables us to attract and retain some of the best people in the business. My partners and I have been together for over 20 years, and many of our employees have been with us a decade or longer. Just as important, I believe our clients appreciate our cultural values, and that is reflected in the stability of those relationships and the long-term success of our business.

MICHAEL D. ROSE
CHAIRMAN OF THE BOARD'S EXECUTIVE COMMITTEE
GAYLORD ENTERTAINMENT INC.

> *"I'm one of the few people in the hospitality industry who didn't grow up in it. I was a partner in a law firm, where I learned some valuable management leadership practices. Law firms are run by partners, who rely on each other, and trust each other. Each partner has accountability to and for the whole firm."*

Mike Rose started his career as an attorney, before shifting gears to head Holiday Inns and Promus Hotel Corporation. He has served on numerous corporate boards and in 2000, was named one of "corporate America's ten outstanding directors."

I'm one of the few people in the hospitality industry who didn't grow up in it. I was a partner in a law firm, where I learned some valuable management leadership practices. Law firms are run by partners, who rely on each other and trust each other. Each partner has accountability to and for the whole firm. In the companies I ran, I instituted a Partner Group, which served as an executive management team for strategy, policy, and major operational decisions. The Partner Group consisted of about 12 people and included both operating business heads and senior staff like the chief financial officer and head of human resources. This participative management approach, where each person had a say in major decisions that affected the whole company, was critical to our success.

I always ran companies with a culture that was values driven. The businesses were based on principles that were communicated to every employee, verbally and in written form. All of our speeches and presentations reiterated these principles, as did our written materials.

I take great pride in identifying and developing potential talent. I created an assistant to the CEO role, in which a high-potential person would shadow me for a year. Two of the hospitality industry's outstanding CEOs, Chuck Ledsinger and Colin Reed, occupied this chair. I delegated extensively to them, and they learned senior executive skills early in their careers.

It's important not to deviate from quality standards, whether in product design or in customer service. Marriott International probably has the most disciplined program. When I took over Holiday Inns, customer service was simply inconsistent. We put in place a customer quality guarantee program in Hampton Inns, Embassy Suites, and Homewood Suites, which made employees much more accountable and made our franchising business much more quality and service sensitive.

Oftentimes, leadership is about taking large but calculated risks. In 1986, in the midst of a hostile takeover wave, Donald Trump took a run at our firm, Holiday Inns. Real estate values had appreciated greatly but were not reflected in our stock price. We wanted to stay independent so we embarked on a huge and risky recapitalization, borrowing $3 billion and paying shareholders a $2.6 billion dividend. If we failed, we risked losing all our equity in the company. With the company highly leveraged, heaven forbid the economy should sour at the same time. I had to convince everyone that this recapitalization made sense. Eventually, we sold the real estate, paid off our debt, and transitioned into a franchising company. Prior to the recapitalization, we traded at $50 per share. In the recapitalization, we paid our shareholders a one-time dividend of $65 per share. After the dividend, the stock dropped to a low of $15, but we drove the share price to $100 after selling our Holiday Inn division in 1990.

DANIEL J. SMITH
FORMER MANAGING DIRECTOR, REAL ESTATE
   MORTGAGE CAPITAL
RBC CAPITAL MARKETS

> *"Our people viewed themselves as coworkers and collaborators, not competitors. They understood their businesses needed to perform up to expectation, but the culture did not pit them against one another."*

Part of GE Commercial Finance, GE Real Estate is one of the largest global players in the industry and active throughout North America, Europe, Asia, and Australia. Dan Smith was responsible for GE Real Estate's Debt Group, overseeing commercial real estate lending in the United States and Canada. He joined GE Real Estate in 1996. He ran the Real Estate Mortgage Capital Group for RBC Capital Markets from 2006 to 2009.

I was in constant communication with my direct reports and spent a tremendous amount of time in the field. We had succession plans in place for every position. In fact, every person in the business was ranked from strongest to weakest—20 percent are listed as top performers, 70 percent as valued performers, and 10 percent as weak performers. I was constantly focused on how to retain my good people and improve their capabilities from management skills to technical strengths.

GE Capital was tremendously supportive in helping manage human capital issues. Virtually all of my reviews were paperless meetings. Everything was computerized, ranging from performance reviews to organization charts (including pictures of every person), an assessment of the strengths of each person and the areas where he or she needed to develop, with each person's comments on where they would like to grow. People were then matched with opportunities in the business on a global basis.

On strategic growth, I met with each of my direct reports, in either the late summer or the early fall. We generated ideas for new businesses, many coming from people who were in the field, dealing directly with customers.

My style is open and approachable. I try to foster collegiality. People viewed themselves as coworkers and collaborators, not competitors. They understood their businesses needed to perform up to expectation, but the culture did not pit them against one another. The company offered tremendous professional and personnel growth opportunities and promoted a work–family life balance, where technology allowed people to spend more time at home. GE Capital and RBC recognized not only their high-performing producers but also others who made contributions, such as administrative assistants, through a variety of programs, including trips. Everyone was recognized for his or her contribution.

DAVID P. STOCKERT
PRESIDENT AND CEO
POST PROPERTIES, INC.

> *"No one person can push an organization of this size, but great things happen when a group of talented people pull toward a commonly understood set of goals and aspirations."*

Dave Stockert became the CEO of Post Properties in 2002, having served as chief operating officer. He helped turn around one of the premier apartment ownership and management companies. Previously, Stockert worked for Duke Realty. He begin his career in investment banking with Dean Witter.

I prioritize my time between guiding the company's strategic direction, helping other executives set and achieve priorities, fostering relationships, celebrating accomplishments, and communicating with the many people who contribute to our success. I also believe we owe something back to the community, so I and others at Post invest time in various civic and charitable activities.

One of the things that make Post a great company is that our people believe they're the best. We have a 35-year tradition of quality and customer service. Our people take pride in being part of that, which creates a strong and unique culture. My job is to encourage creativity, initiative, and an entrepreneurial spirit, while also setting out the plan and the benchmarks to which we are all accountable.

We spend a lot of time hiring terrific people and then communicate frequently and openly about our plans and goals. I know I am doing my job well when there is alignment among our board, our management team, our investors, and our associates as to where we are headed and how we plan to get there. No one person can push an organization of this size, but great things happen when a group of talented people pull toward a commonly understood set of goals and aspirations.

We also spend time listening to our customers and studying our competitors. Our residents can reach me personally, if need be, and often do. In the real estate business, the focus is often on location and design, but companies like ours understand that service is a huge differentiator.

A leader must believe in him- or herself, especially in difficult times. Throughout a public proxy fight several years ago, our team tried always to take the high road. This was very important in keeping the company together. As a new and untested CEO, the way I handled that adversity impacted my relationships with the board, our associates, and our investors positively.

In many ways, I feel fortunate to have had that experience. Persevering through trying (and humbling) times is a key ingredient in good leadership.

J. RONALD TERWILLIGER
CHAIRMAN AND CEO
TRAMMELL CROW RESIDENTIAL

> *"I have high expectations for myself and my people, and I try to manage by exception. I delegate, but not to the point of putting someone at risk. I espouse servant leadership where I try to help my people be successful."*

Trammell Crow Residential is one of the largest multifamily developers and owners in the country. It operates with national and regional partners, who have developed more than 200,000 units. The company split off from Trammell Crow in 1977 but remains associated with the Crow family. Ron Terwilliger became chairman and CEO in 1986.

We run the company on a decentralized basis—business unit leaders are empowered to run their businesses. I try to provide a strategic overview and monitor quality. I honestly believe our people are proud of the company, and we try to support them through down cycles. We have had a lot of success in hiring people who are well liked and self motivated, and show strong financial acumen. Our people stay close to the real estate, where they make most decisions. They share a focus on quality, and all of our interests are fundamentally aligned.

I have high expectations of myself and our associates, and I try to manage by exception. I delegate, but not to the point of putting someone at risk. I espouse the concept of servant leadership, where I try to help our people be successful. But I watch the details and serve as a check and balance on the company's financial performance.

The true test of leadership is surviving in difficult times. When the apartment business was in serious trouble back in 1991, I wondered whether it made sense to continue. No capital was available and the economy was weak. People were deeding properties to lenders. Even though we had limited financial support, I decided to stay in the rental apartment business. We closed seven businesses unrelated to our multifamily operations and shut two field offices. We right-sized and rationalized the organization. As times got somewhat better, we spun off two REITs to liquefy the business. I recognized that if we survived, we would have a great opportunity when the economy improved because many competitors had gone out of business. Few apartments were built in 1992, 1993, and 1994, but business was terrific from 1994 to 2000, and we were one of the few players left standing.

LAWRENCE P. WASHINGTON
CHAIRMAN AND CEO
MERRILL LYNCH CREDIT CORPORATION

"I spend time supporting my people and enjoy being in the field on the front line."

Merrill Lynch Credit Corporation is the home financing arm of Merrill Lynch Bank & Trust, Co., FSB, offering residential mortgages, home equity loans, and other financing to homebuyers and homeowners. Its correspondent group purchases prime mortgages on the secondary market, concentrating on jumbo mortgages. Larry Washington has been the group's chairman and CEO since 2003 and has been the president and chief operating officer of Merrill Lynch Bank & Trust Co., FSB since 2006.

I interface with the various Merrill Lynch constituencies, especially my peers in the private client advisory business. Over 90 percent of our production comes through Merrill Lynch's network of more than 15,000 financial advisers. Since mortgages are not their specialty, it's important for me to keep our product on the top of their mind and provide greater support than a tradi-tional mortgage company. I'm always thinking about new products, channels, and distribution opportunities, as well as supporting my people. I prefer to give them a lot of rope, and I enjoy being in the field on the front line. That way, I can gather direct intelligence from clients on what is going on in the market and gauge how our salespeople are feeling. I can also get constructive feedback on process improvements and gaps in our product line.

Despite my accountant background, I tend to spend more time creating and cheerleading. But I'm also a pragmatist and try to look at everything objectively, so that we do the right thing for our people, clients, and the firm. I don't believe that just paying a lot of money to your people creates satisfaction or makes for a successful business. People want to be treated fairly, be part of a vibrant business, and have fun. I participate in our employee events and support our local charities. You need to be visible and add a personal element to your role—like washing cars for the United Way, when many of my peers wouldn't think of doing something like this. It's all about being a part of a team and working alongside everyone.

Leadership success often turns on personal resolve. Prior to Merrill Lynch, I served as the senior executive vice president of First Nationwide Mortgage. I had a wide range of responsibilities over the years and was often asked to take responsibility for areas that were experiencing difficulty. In each case, I felt it was essential to take the time to listen carefully, fully understand all sides to the issues, and be compassionate and objective. In the end, I would reach out to others in the organization, especially those with different perspectives than mine, to get their views on my conclusions and then make the changes that were necessary.

My most valuable lesson—learned early in my career—was to listen carefully and always be aware of what you do not know. Telling others more knowledgeable what to do has never worked for me. Rather, I seek to understand and then be understood. Teddy Roosevelt said it best: "The best executive is the one who has sense enough to pick good men to do what he wants done and self-restraint enough to keep from meddling with them while they do it." He was a wise man.

BERNARD WINOGRAD
EXECUTIVE VICE PRESIDENT AND CHIEF OPERATING OFFICER
PRUDENTIAL FINANCIAL AND PRUDENTIAL INSURANCE

"While there has to be pay for performance, other intangibles are extraordinarily important, ranging from collegiality to intellectual learning environments."

With about $400 billion in assets under management, Prudential Investment Management provides expertise in equity, fixed-income, real estate, and commercial mortgage investment management. Bernard Winograd had been CEO of Prudential Real Estate Investors and, before that, chief financial officer of the Taubman Company, a retail REIT. In January 2008, Winograd was promoted to executive vice president of Prudential Financial and Prudential Insurance. Earlier, he was president and CEO of Prudential Investment Management, a subsidiary of Prudential Financial.

Even though I'm not active in the day-to-day real estate investment management business anymore, I grew up in the industry and have some perspective. I firmly believe successful real estate companies have a deep knowledge of a specific aspect of the business. For equity players, it has to be some market or property expertise. For intermediaries, it has to be some piece of the capital markets chain. Developing a performance-oriented culture is not solely about compensation. While there has to be pay for performance, other intangibles are extraordinarily important, ranging from collegiality to intellectual learning environments.

Increasingly, real estate companies will be large organizations so the people who run these businesses must be able managers. They need to have both emotional maturity and interpersonal skills. It is extraordinarily important that these businesses attract and retain talented people, and their leaders must have the patience and skills to hire and motivate effectively. Obviously, these leaders must know real estate and have strong investment skills, but they must be comfortable in a large-scale operating environment, too.

ROBERT H. ZERBST
CHAIRMAN
CB RICHARD ELLIS INVESTORS, LLC

> *"Fifty percent of our assets, people, and investors are now outside*
> *of the United States. Internationally we like to hire locals with*
> *strong academic backgrounds . . . and prior experience working*
> *for American companies. We've had success in branding our*
> *investment programs, where many investors are now committed*
> *to multiple funds. We have an organization marked by a*
> *cohesiveness of culture and yet our people are entrepreneurs."*

With an M.A. in economics, an M.B.A., and a Ph.D. in finance and real estate economics from Ohio State University, Robert Zerbst began his career in education and real estate research in 1974. He founded and served as CEO of Piedmont Realty Advisors starting in 1982. The firm was acquired by the RREEF Funds in 1991. He joined CB Richard Ellis Investors as president in 1997, and he has built the business from slightly more than $3 billion low-risk, domestic core assets into a multistrategy, global investment organization now managing more than $30 billion.

In the investment management business, best-in-class firms generate superior performance and provide outstanding client service. You must also provide investors with increasing transparency and communication, especially when performance may be lagging. The firm's interests and employee compensation need to be aligned with client objectives. Fifty percent of our assets, people, and investors are now located outside the United States. Internationally, we like to hire locals, with strong academic backgrounds and good local connections, and prior experience working for American companies. We've had success in branding our investment programs, where many investors are now committed to multiple funds. We have an organization marked by a cohesive culture yet we encourage our people to be entrepreneurs. The head of our European fund never lets us forget that the word "entrepreneur" is French.

I have a somewhat unusual background for a real estate investment manager CEO. In graduate school, I emphasized finance and quantitative subjects and never was terribly interested in organizational behavior. After leaving academia, I quickly learned that leadership, communication, and creating the correct alignment of interests were every bit as important as investment decisions in building a successful organization. I'm also very entrepreneurial. Even though I was a tenured professor at SMU, I went to California on a sabbatical and enjoyed the West Coast so much that I started a pension consulting firm in San Francisco, building on my academic research on real estate as an asset class. A year later one of our pension accounts, the Chicago Transit Authority, asked us to invest $120 million, and that launched my career in investment management.

My leadership style is to articulate where we're going and how we're going to get there. I then try to hire the best people and give them room to experiment—including making mistakes. Aligning their rewards with performance is extraordinarily important. Today, all of our investment professionals are compensated on a formulaic basis as a percentage of either carried interests or firm profitability. Based on this philosophy, we've grown assets under management from $3 billion to more than $30 billion by the end of 2006.

When I assumed the leadership of CB Richard Ellis's investment management business, which was then called Westmark Realty Advisors, we had numerous personnel, financial, and client issues. In addition, many investors and consultants viewed the ownership of an investment manager by a brokerage firm as an inherent conflict of interest. I believed that we could reverse this impression if we could harness the resources of the world's largest real estate services organization for the benefit of our investors. By creating an independently managed business structure and utilizing the parent company's resources on an arm's length basis, we were able to reverse the market impression and CBRE has become our strongest suit. During my tenure, we have evolved from a domestic pension adviser to a global, multistrategy investment management organization sponsoring funds across the risk-return spectrum, to different classes of investors, on three continents.

CHAPTER FOUR

PRAY FOR FORGIVENESS, NOT PERMISSION

L eaders come to understand they have no security at the top and need to run their businesses cloaked in the possibility of failure. But entrepreneurial personalities carry an innate dissatisfaction with the status quo and crave new initiatives that can lead to growth and performance gains. They realize fear of disappointment can compromise chances for success and risk-taking creates opportunity. Truly, the easiest way to fail at any business is not to take risk. Standout leaders have an inner compass—the ability to set the right course instinctively based on intelligence, experience, and innate good judgment. They also create environments where people can learn and grow from successes as well as mistakes, ultimately benefiting their business. "Doing what you feel is right is the responsibility of a leader," says Chris Nassetta of Hilton Hotels. Says Tom Hefner, retired CEO of Duke Realty, a REIT: "You just need to know when to stand up and do what you believe, even when it is unpleasant or controversial."

Leaders rise to the top and stay there because they consistently make the right decisions in weighing risk. And when they occasionally misfire, the enduring CEOs shrug it off, staying motivated and challenged. "They simply reset," says Sam Zell of The Equity Group. "They have extraordinary self-confidence and the courage of their convictions."

Facilitating an entrepreneurial "go from the gut" culture requires an environment in which leaders tolerate mistakes so people can learn from them. "[I]t is important for our people to recognize that taking risk is critical, and failing is okay," says Michael Cryan of Windsor Capital Group, a private, hotel investment firm. "People can celebrate failure, if they learn from their missteps." That sort of culture can really only stem from strong leaders who understand that mistakes are the inevitable byproduct of taking risks and trying new things—both integral to the entrepreneurial mission. Bob Larson of Lazard Freres Real Estate Investors believes healthy organizations allow "people to pray for forgiveness, not for permission" as long as their actions are well considered, ethical, and carried out with integrity.

Successful leaders of any organization set examples. And the beauty of the real estate industry is that most individuals grow up in the business as entrepreneurs, where they are accountable for their own success. Success is all about taking calculated risks and winning a lot more than one loses. By modeling this type of behavior, leaders are sending a clear message to their people. While companies don't have to reinvent the wheel to be successful, everyone in the organization needs to take risks in order for a company to grow and remain competitive. Inevitably, people will fail—and in well-managed organizations, this is expected.

And, as many say—from Mike Fascitelli at Vornado to Sam Zell—the great leaders do fail, and they simply dust themselves off and start again. Unsuccessful leaders personalize failure. And inherent in this message is an unwillingness to accept nothing short of greatness, as Martin Fenton of the Senior Resource Group acknowledges. Standards have to be high, and then they have to be pursued with zealousness. Furthermore, as Peter Lowy of The Westfield Group emphasizes, senior people in any organization must have a fire in their belly. That then must be emulated by others in the organization. Otherwise, any company will ultimately lose its edge.

In short, taking risks is part of the recipe for success. As Chris Nassetta of Hilton Hotels emphasizes, any CEO's success is driven by a great
strategy and the discipline to stick with it. However, there is no automatic
pilot. It involves a lot of hard work, mistakes, and sleepless nights. CEOs
who make sacrifices teach their people to do the same thing. David Simon
articulates this quite well.

KENNETH J. BACON
EXECUTIVE VICE PRESIDENT, HOUSING AND
   COMMUNITY DEVELOPMENT
FANNIE MAE

> *"I pride myself on pushing controversial initiatives, as long as*
> *they are right for Fannie Mae. Leadership is about the courage of*
> *your convictions."*

Ken Bacon is responsible for Fannie Mae's efforts to increase the nation's supply of
affordable housing, including multifamily lending, equity investments, invest-
ments in low-income housing tax credits, lending for community development and
acquisition, and development and construction financing. He managed a $127
billion book of business (as of December 2006), including the DUSTM program
and low-income housing tax credit (LIHTC) Program investments.

I view myself as a conductor of the orchestra, controlling the tempo and tweak-
ing the sound. My job is to ensure people work well together. And I assume
personal responsibility for the next generation of business opportunities.

   I believe strongly in pursuing the right culture for our business. We
don't want rogue credit cowboys; integrity and ethics are critically important. The mission of my Housing and Community Development (HCD)
business is to increase the supply of affordable housing, develop communities, serve demographic segments in need of affordable housing, help
rebuild the Gulf Coast, and maximize shareholder value. To accomplish this

mission, HCD brings reliability and a focus on service to our partners and provides value to all of our stakeholders. And we never deviate from this position. Everyone works together to be part of a progressive, supportive environment where people feel good about their contribution.

A month after I became head of HCD, Hurricane Katrina struck and I was asked to lead the company's hurricane relief response. In the early days after the storm, everyone wanted to do the right thing, but nobody wanted to take on unquantifiable risk or take a loss. But I believe that leadership is about doing the right thing, even when it's not all that comfortable for you. You have to quickly adapt to rapidly changing needs in order to be effective. And the situation in the Gulf demanded that Fannie Mae do right by the people and the partners that were depending on us.

I remember one of the lenders we worked with had a loan on a multifamily property that was supposed to close the day after the storm hit. The property was heavily damaged, but our partners kept calling us and saying "We've got to get the money to do this deal." While the risk environment in the Gulf Coast was great, we realized it was important to invest prudently in the affected regions. After a lot of serious consideration and debate, we provided $80 million in financing for the development. We also provided 1,500 real estate–owned properties with rent-free leasing for up to 18 months.

This happened time and again. When our partners told us they needed investment capital to rebuild, we created a $110 million LIHTC fund solely dedicated to the Gulf Coast. When our partners told us that home-owners needed cash to repair their homes, we tailored our existing cash-out refinancing product and a renovation loan product to get them the cash they needed. And when our partners said they needed to get more apartments online faster, we told one of our best underwriters: "If somebody wants to do a deal and it's hard to underwrite, take a long hard look to see if there is any way to make it happen." And, many times we found a way.

TERRY CONSIDINE
CHAIRMAN, CEO, AND PRESIDENT
APARTMENT INVESTMENT AND MANAGEMENT COMPANY

"In our culture, I'd like to think that nothing's off limits, and
we're willing to debate openly and get the issues on the table."

Headquartered in Denver, Colorado, Apartment Investment and Management
Company (AIMCO) is the nation's largest owner and operator of apartment com-
munities, with nearly 1,163 communities that include 202,337 units. Operat-
ing as a REIT, AIMCO engages in the acquisition, ownership, management, and
redevelopment of apartment communities in 46 states, the District of Columbia,
and Puerto Rico. Terry Considine has been chairman of the board and CEO since
July 1994.

Over my career, I've learned that leaders in the real estate business can be
unique and yet successful. By nature, they are optimistic people and move
ahead undeterred. There are some who have great dreams and can picture
the real estate long before it's built. I think of Gerry Blakely, with whom
I worked early in my career at Cabot, Cabot and Forbes, or Jim Rouse or
Arthur Cohen. Conversely, there are terrific leaders in our industry who are
finance people, first and foremost. They understand what the numbers need
to generate. However, whatever your profile, ours is an industry where the
smart leaders understand the requirement to avoid excess leverage.

My passion is in doing deals. The more complicated the structure,
the better I like it. I very much enjoy figuring out how it all fits together.
However, the deal business in real estate is getting more efficient, with the
advent of the REITs, CMBS, and private equity. I have tried to transform our
business into an efficient operating model.

Everyone recognizes that I can be hard on people; that is often uninten-
tional. However, I'm constantly after the right answer, and I expect our people
to know what the answer is, after doing their homework to figure it out. In

our culture, I'd like to think that nothing's off limits and that we're willing to debate openly and get the issues on the table. However, at the same time, I do see us as a family business. I get paid after everyone else does. There also have been numerous situations where our people have become sick or they've gone off to war in Iraq, and we continue to pay them what they were earning previously. While ours is a demanding culture, we've lost very few people that we didn't want to lose, and I'm proud of that.

THOMAS J. CORCORAN, JR.
CHAIRMAN
FELCOR LODGING TRUST INC.

> *"Successful people ultimately do what they think is right and don't worry about the risks involved."*

Tom Corcoran cofounded FelCor, Inc., in 1991 with Hervey Feldman and has served as president and CEO. In early 2006 he became chairman of the board. In 1994, FelCor went public as a hotel REIT with a market capitalization of approximately $120 million. During Corcoran's tenure as CEO, FelCor grew from six to 117 hotels, with a market capitalization of $3.2 billion.

I'm a patient but "can do" person. I led by example and didn't sit in an ivory tower. I had an open door policy and spent a lot of time walking around the office. I believed strongly in communicating with my people: Employees were invited to our board of directors' dinners, and I circulated my monthly board report to everyone in the company.

I am extremely proud of our culture. It's family oriented, entrepreneurial, fun, and hard working. One of our unique events is the monthly chairman's luncheon, where a group of FelCor employees can get better acquainted with fellow team members. I started this tradition of cooking and fun when my partner Hervey Feldman and I founded the company. The chairman's luncheon is a great team-building exercise. On alternating months, I passed the spatula and chef's hat to fellow team members, regardless of their cooking experience. A handful of employees were selected at random, told the culinary theme, then given the menu at 7 a.m. on the day of the lunch. After shopping for ingredients, the chosen few spent the morning slaving over a hot stove to create a five- to seven-course meal from scratch.

A CEO must be an optimist and be willing to take risks. People want to be led. Successful people ultimately do what they think is right and don't worry about the risks involved.

MICHAEL D. CRYAN
PRESIDENT AND CHIEF OPERATING OFFICER
WINDSOR CAPITAL GROUP

"I encourage our people to celebrate their failures."

Privately held Windsor Capital Group invests in the hospitality business. Michael Cryan, its president and chief operating officer, has more than 30 years of experience in the lodging industry. He previously worked for Sheraton Hotels and Homestead Village.

I establish goals, achieve buy-in, and make sure that these goals are understood throughout the system. I am very open to hearing people's thoughts on alternative strategies and feel that it is important that everyone has a voice in strategic decision making, as well as in implementation. We go out of our way to utilize all the skills and resources of our people. The whole is always greater than the sum of its parts. So, the company's strength is a reflection of our aggregate human capital. Our people need to recognize that taking risks is critical and it is okay to fail. In fact, I encourage our people to celebrate their failures, sharing these lessons equally with the successes. They need to learn from their mistakes.

We are starting to hire young people right out of school and allow them to run a department in a hotel, like the restaurant. We want them to be entrepreneurial, and we go out of our way to educate them and provide them with outstanding career development. We also promote from within, where pedigrees are not nearly as important as performance. We have executive chefs who once were dishwashers and controllers and general managers who started out as accounts payable clerks. You have to create an environment where people can continuously learn and grow.

We also attempt to keep the management team as close to the hotels as possible. We have very few staff positions at corporate. In fact, our regional vice presidents live at the hotels. They remain close to their customers and the younger people who run the operations. They also don't generate many reports or policies, so the business avoids becoming too bureaucratic.

A leader must willingly take risks, while focusing on the long term. In 1991, at Sheraton I was asked to become director of strategic projects. The new president and I made a decision to recommend moving into the all-suite business, and I focused on buying six all-suites hotels from Marriott International. At the time, Marriott had never sold an asset to a competitor, and I had to be dogged to conclude a transaction. Simultaneously, it took the new president and me 18 months to convince the cautious ITT Sheraton Board that this all-suite initiative made sense. At one point, I delayed the start of vacation and sent my family to Hawaii, because of an important presentation to the board. After the presentation, I was absolutely convinced that I had destroyed my career. But the chairman of ITT Sheraton sent a bottle of champagne to my hotel room in Hawaii, saying that it had been well received. In the end, it took another six months to gain board approval for the Marriott purchase, but perseverance paid off and it was a very successful acquisition.

GARY A. DELAPP

PRESIDENT AND CEO

HVM LLC (EXTENDED STAY HOTELS)

> *"The best people in our organization are self-starters, who are willing to make decisions and take risks. They take initiative for the betterment of the organization."*

Homestead Studio Suites was acquired by The Blackstone Group in 2001. Extended Stay America was acquired in 2004. With the last acquisition, the company became Extended Stay Hotels, operating 680 hotels in 44 states. HVM LLC (Homestead Village Management, Limited Liability Company) is the operator of Extended Stay Hotels.

What makes a company successful in our business is hiring and retaining the right people. I believe strongly in giving people the tools and autonomy to do their jobs well and rewarding them accordingly. If the company does well, then they should participate in the upside. I find the best people in our organization are self-starters who are willing to make decisions and take risks. They take initiative for the betterment of the organization.

My mentors in the hospitality business taught me one fundamental aspect of leadership. A leader needs to be tenacious in learning all aspects of the business and understanding the whole picture. It is not necessary to be an expert in any one discipline, but a leader in the hospitality industry needs to understand each—and most importantly, how they integrate the different parts of the business toward the success of an overall enterprise.

Our culture engenders a high sense of urgency. We run fast, but we also have a lot of fun. We communicate efficiently. Everybody rolls up their sleeves and gets things done. We are an inclusive organization with virtually no hierarchy or levels of importance. I have an open door policy, and people e-mail me regularly about a variety of issues. While I travel a lot and attend many meetings, I try to be as accessible as possible and always respond personally to all my e-mail messages.

I ask and expect a lot from my team, and in turn, I set the example by expecting a lot from myself. I set an example of commitment, and our people appreciate that. In fact, we have one of the lowest turnover rates in the entire industry. There's mutual respect here.

My greatest leadership moments occurred during the first year of the merger between Homestead Studio Suites (132 hotels) and Extended Stay America (475 hotels) and the acquisition of 37 Wellesley Inn and Suites hotels. We experienced phenomenal growth, increasing our portfolio from 132 properties to 644 within seven months. The company faced a multitude of significant changes, and I challenged our management team and associates to think like an owner—to create excellence every day in every way possible. During that first year, we successfully integrated technology platforms, operating procedures, and benefit plans; realigned our sales force; launched new Web sites; rolled out high-speed Internet access chainwide; and began upgrading our product—all while operating the business. We introduced excellent cost controls, minimized discounted rates, expanded our online reach, realized strong EBITDA growth, and achieved outstanding guest satisfaction scores. It was a tremendous challenge to our organization and any successful leader.

MICHAEL D. FASCITELLI
PRESIDENT
VORNADO REALTY TRUST

> "[In our culture] there is a certain toughness in consummating transactions. . . . Leadership is about regrouping and making the best of strategic opportunities."

Vornado Realty, a NYSE-listed real estate company, is one of the largest equity real estate investment trusts in the United States. Since joining the firm in 1996, Mike

Fascitelli has been a driving force in developing Vornado's position in the industry. The firm is one of the largest commercial landlords in New York City and Washington, D.C. Before joining Vornado, he ran the real estate investment banking business at Goldman Sachs.

Successful firms in our industry have smart people who can strategically decide what asset sectors make the most sense. Capital-intensive businesses need only a small number of people to make a big impact. Even though there is not a lot of differentiation among various asset classes, consolidation will inevitably lead to differentiation, which will benefit firms that demonstrate strong performance.

I spend the majority of my time working on transactions that will lead to corporate growth and financing those transactions. Along with Steve Roth, I have tried to create a culture of teamwork, risk taking, mentorship, delegation, and autonomy. We look for value-oriented players, who show a certain toughness and drive in consummating transactions. People like working here because our deals are interesting and complicated, and they can learn and contribute a lot. We tend to compensate our top people quite aggressively.

Leadership is about regrouping and making the best of strategic opportunities. In the late 1980s and early 1990s, I was asked to restructure the real estate investment banking group at Goldman Sachs. We reduced the group from 130 to 40 people. I was honest and compassionate, and went out of my way to find new opportunities inside and outside Goldman Sachs for the people we displaced. Unfortunately, I was slow to react in hiring new people when there was an upswing in the real estate capital markets. In fact, Goldman's real estate private equity business was born out of the difficulties of the real estate recession. There was no liquidity in the market, and we couldn't sell assets. Since we couldn't sell assets, we determined that we might as well be buyers. And we had an excess of talented people who we could deploy into the real estate private equity business. This was an enormously successful strategic move.

MARTIN FENTON
CHAIRMAN
SENIOR RESOURCE GROUP

"When excellence is possible, good is not enough."

Martin Fenton started Senior Resource Group in 1988 with his partner, Michael Grust. It is a company that has always opted for quality, not quantity, and now is a co-owner with pension fund investors of a portfolio of 11 communities in Oregon, California, and Arizona. Senior Resource Group manages these communities and three others, one in California and two in Florida. The company typically develops larger "campus" communities that offer a broad range of residential alternatives to the expanding seniors market it serves. The largest campus offers fully independent apartments, full-service independent living, assisted living, and dementia care.

When excellence is achievable, good is not enough. That mantra applies to design, execution, and service to our residents. People need to be unwilling to settle for less and should seek to challenge themselves and to grow in the process. We view ourselves, and our fellows in the seniors' housing industry, as pioneers. We are inventing a business, and while each of us may have a sepa-rate template, we tend to share a commitment to the welfare of our residents.

Our particular focus is to do everything that we can to augment their quality of life. We must listen and we must learn and we must be flexible. My style is to be a cheerleader and to set goals that are a stretch for us all. A mistake is simply a lesson learned for the next time. Ours is a practice of managing by walking around. The most important people in the company are those who have a daily interaction with our residents; our task is to sup-port them in that effort.

We concentrate on markets that we know and view the notion of exporting a management culture to far-flung regions to be one of the greatest challenges, simply because travel imposes limitations on anyone's management style. A company needs to attract and to retain the right people: individuals with a positive attitude, passion, and a sense of humor. And successful companies are but catalysts, recognizing trends and opportunities in the marketplace and then synthesizing responses to satisfy those market needs.

I remember walking back from a dinner in Florida many years ago, 1979, when we were in the community development business. I walked 79 blocks passing many retired senior citizens sitting outside their small homes in aluminum chairs with nylon webbing for seats, looking onto the street. I realized then and there that there was opportunity in the seniors' housing business.

MARK FINERMAN
FORMER MANAGING DIRECTOR AND HEAD OF
    REAL ESTATE FINANCE
RBS GREENWICH CAPITAL

> *"I've learned to lead by having the best people on the ground.
> A leader needs to trust the instincts of his or her people who
> are with clients every day and doing the business since the best
> decisions are not always made at the top of an organization."*

A subsidiary of the Royal Bank of Scotland, Greenwich Capital Markets, known as RBS Greenwich Capital, has been one of the leading originators and securitizers of commercial mortgage debt. Mark Finerman previously served as managing director and head of the Real Estate Finance and Securitization Group for CS First Boston and was a founder of Nomura's Commercial Mortgage Group. He recently left the firm to start a new fund, LoanCore Capital.

High-performing firms in our business know how to strategize and execute. The key is to form relationships, because our industry is built on relationships. It's much harder to build a business than to simply manage one, because you have to take clients away from your competitors. Our success at Greenwich was driven by our focus on customers. When we were starting the CMBS business in the early 1990s, Nordstrom was the role model for retailers, and we treated our borrowers in a fashion similar to the way Nordstrom treated its customers—that is, better than the competition.

I previously worked for SunAmerica, Nomura, and First Boston, where I learned some important life lessons, including what was good and what was bad. Allan Nussenblatt at SunAmerica taught me the importance of credit, and Ethan Penner taught me the importance of marketing and serving one's clients. Andy Stone at First Boston was a great trader and taught me there was a correlation, albeit imperfect, between real value and relative value, which enables a practical person in the capital markets to take advantage of the arbitrage.

Our culture at Greenwich was grown-up, but we weren't overly mature. We did come up together in the industry and learned some of life's lessons the hard way. We worked as a team, we were apolitical, and it was a relaxed, open, and honest environment. We prided ourselves on retaining our employees and lived by the concept that performance merits recognition.

I've learned to lead by having the best people on the ground. A leader needs to trust the instincts of his or her people who are with clients every day and doing the business, since the best decisions are not always made at the top of an organization. In the CMBS business you can't underwrite from afar, because mistakes are made from a distance. The better firms know how to delegate. There's also a motivational factor to this leadership approach. If a leader pushes down responsibility to people who are self-motivated, they honestly feel like they're making a difference. When motivated people think they're making a difference, this is a recipe for business success.

Successful leadership is all about taking risk, and doing what you think is right. When we restarted the Greenwich CMBS business in 2002, the market was overbanked, with about 40 competitors already in the business. To be successful in a mature market, one needs to differentiate products to add value. I knew we had to be aggressive, in order to differentiate ourselves. We needed to create our own brand and securitize our own product to retain control. We couldn't originate loans and then participate in someone else's securitization, thus letting someone else control our destiny.

Our mantra was "better leverage for better properties." We were forced to do larger transactions. Not only did we need to originate larger loans, which were tough to find given the competitive environment, but we also had to do more of them, because any successful securitization requires diversification. The success of the securitization, and ultimately our business, depended upon the respect that we earned from both investors and lenders. Having been in businesses that failed before, our team understood what would be successful; but in order to be taken seriously, we had a very limited window to work in. The fear of failure is a wonderful motivator, and often that fear creates the motivation that determines who will be ultimately successful.

LAURENCE GELLER
PRESIDENT AND CEO
STRATEGIC HOTELS AND RESORTS INC.

> *"My people have been loyal to me, and I have always tried to be honest and transparent, sharing as much information as possible."*

Strategic Hotels and Resorts, Inc., a publicly traded, self-managed hotel investment company—a REIT—acquires and manages full-service, upscale, and luxury hotels, including the Hotel del Coronado in San Diego. The company has ownership interests in more than 200 properties totaling 8,500 rooms. Laurence Geller founded the company.

Our success is driven by my interest in measuring performance. While I give my people a lot of rope in order to be successful, I do hold them accountable. And I try to spend a lot of time listening, whether it is to our guests, our shareholders, our advisers, or my own organization. I am very goal oriented and preach that facts are friendly. I am also willing to admit when I am wrong, and people can change my opinion.

At Strategic Hotels and Resorts, we have been in a cathartic state of catalytic change. My people have been loyal to me, and I have always tried to be honest and transparent, sharing as much information as possible. I am constantly focused on hiring risk takers and putting people into challenges that are over their head. The good ones will figure it out. I have no problem paying the superstars much more aggressively than the rest of the organization. Given the dynamics of the hotel business, flexibility and nimbleness are critical features to winning the race. This all gets back to the people you hire, develop, and motivate.

THOMAS L. HEFNER
CEO
HEFNER INVESTMENTS

> *"Great leaders understand when to step up and to do the right thing, even though it might be unpleasant. Having the instinct to do the right thing is what it's all about."*

Duke Realty Investments, a REIT headquartered in Indianapolis, is a fully integrated real estate company that owns interests in a diversified portfolio of industrial, office, and retail properties totaling more than 105 million square feet. Tom Hefner was CEO from 1993 to 2004, prior to retiring and forming Hefner Investments.

Great companies have a clear mission and strategy, which need to be understood by everyone and the company needs to stick to them. You can't change based upon market whims. Conversely, you can't be shy about replacing people who haven't measured up. Without the right people to implement the strategy, you can't run an operating business.

I spent a lot of time on recruitment and compensation. I interviewed virtually all senior people, and I always liked to meet their spouses. I wanted to make sure that any candidate was well grounded and looked for honesty, intelligence, and a strong work ethic. I always try to exhibit these character-istics in leading by example. On the compensation front, I tried to teach our people to be patient. Serious net worth is built up over time.

While we tried to promote from within, bringing in new blood was important to keep the organization from drinking from the same pitcher. New ideas and new perspectives are constantly needed to deal with a world in flux. While we would always listen for Wall Street's perspective, we did what we felt was right for the company. I tried to be loyal to my people, and in return, they were loyal to me. I stressed that the company is more important than any individual. We also worked hard to maintain an entre-preneurial spirit, where people could make a lot of money if the company performed. Everyone knows the game plan—we even developed a depth chart mapping how people would grow through the top 100 positions.

Great leaders must put themselves in other people's shoes and have the sensitivity to do what is right. It's all about learning from their own ex-periences. They understand when to step up and to do the right thing, even though it might be unpleasant. Having the instinct to do the right thing is what it's all about.

THOMAS J. HUTCHISON III
FORMER CEO
CNL HOTELS & RESORTS, INC.

> *"When I speak to our employees or prospective hires, I constantly reiterate the word 'trust.' Our people need to understand that sharing bad news is not a negative, because mistakes happen. The issue is to own up at an early stage."*

CNL Hotels & Resorts, Inc., was one of the nation's largest REITs in the lodging industry before being acquired by Morgan Stanley. Before joining CNL, from 1978 to 1986, Tom Hutchison was the president and CEO of Murdock Development Corporation and Murdock Investment Corporation.

When I spoke to our employees or prospective hires, I constantly reiterated the word "trust." Our people needed to understand that sharing bad news is not a negative, because mistakes happen. The issue is to own up at an early stage.

I adopted a nurturing approach in running our organization. Strategy and people are closely aligned. Part of my job was complementing and supporting our people and encouraging mutual respect. Frankly, I'm most concerned about the generation of people behind the baby boomers, who have a different view of business standards. They need to have a long-term perspective and appreciate the importance of relationships, which are both personal and professional.

I have tried to provide many of our young people with positions of significant responsibility at an early age. That's how I developed early in my own career. I spent ten years with David Murdock, who offered me enormous accountability and responsibility. At 35, I was running nine companies. I took companies private and even orchestrated the merger between Occidental Petroleum and City Service. I learned to work with strong personalities and make important decisions. Murdock taught me to be comfortable in communicating bad news, as well as to lead by example.

ROBERT C. LARSON
CHAIRMAN
LAZARD REAL ESTATE PARTNERS, LLC

> *"Collaborative leadership yields the best results. Characteristics that I look for in people include integrity, self-confidence, and diversity of thought, ideas, and experience."*

Bob Larson is managing director of Lazard Alternative Investments and chairman of Lazard Real Estate Partners. He serves as a director of InterContinental Hotels Group, a global hospitality operator based in London, and is chairman of United Dominion Realty Trust (UDR), one of the largest multifamily REITs. In addition, he represents Lazard as a director of Atria Senior Living Group, Destinations

Limited, Commonwealth Atlantic Properties, and ARV Assisted Living. Before joining Lazard, Larson spent most of his real estate career with regional mall developer Taubman Company, retiring as vice chairman.

I've always focused on two issues when running a business. The first is the "care and feeding" of people, and the second is setting a clear vision and strategy for the business. You need the right organizational structure to implement the business plan and the right people to make it all work. Retention and motivation of people is critical. Collaborative leadership yields the best results. Characteristics that I look for in people include integrity, self-confidence, and diversity of thought, ideas, and experience. I like a culture where people feel free to take initiative and, if necessary, "pray for forgiveness, not permission."

Being strategic requires a CEO to step back from day-to-day operations. It can't be easily delegated. I try to spend time with leaders from a variety of industries in an attempt to understand their perspective and the lessons they've learned. Making leadership decisions can be tough and often lonely. Leadership in the real estate industry will be increasingly challenging due to increased consolidation and globalization, but there always will be opportunities for innovative entrepreneurs who operate under the radar screen and outperform the big boys.

To be effective, I believe boards of directors must be both collegial and challenging. At UDR, a national multifamily REIT in which Lazard had a major investment, the board demonstrated these qualities in leading fundamental change in a company that had lost its strategic direction and was dramatically underperforming its peers. We asked the longstanding CEO to step down, relocated the executive headquarters from Richmond to Denver, recruited a dynamic new chief executive, and repositioned the business without major incident, loss of key personnel, or loss of investor support. During that process, I spent a lot of time with each board member, listening to their concerns, insights, and ideas. As a sage once observed, "There's a reason why God gave us two ears and only one mouth." I try to do a lot of listening before making any decision, but ultimately follow my instincts. The decisions we made during the leadership transition and repositioning of UDR had high risks but proved to be successful due, in large part, to the board's effective working relationship with the newly recruited CEO.

EDWARD H. LINDE
CEO
BOSTON PROPERTIES, INC.

> *"People like working for a winner. Making mistakes is not a*
> *negative—in fact, it points to people making decisions and*
> *doing things."*

Boston Properties owns high-profile, well-leased office buildings in leading markets, including Manhattan, Washington, D.C., Boston, and San Francisco. Ed Linde cofounded Boston Properties in 1970. With his partner, Mort Zuckerman, Linde has built the company into one of the most highly regarded office REITs in the industry.

In this business, leaders can never get too far from the real estate. You need to stay highly involved in the substance of the business in addition to managing the enterprise. High-performing companies give the management team a significant ownership stake in the business. We also allow our regional offices a tremendous amount of autonomy, so they develop their own style and approach suitable to their market. But corporate always maintains certain controls. People like working for a winner. Making mistakes is not a negative—in fact, it points to people making decisions and doing things. Of course, if the ratio of mistakes to wins gets too high, we've made the mistake of picking the wrong person.

I spend a lot of time mentoring and coaching our senior people. I much prefer face-to-face meetings over voice mail or e-mail. I try to treat people with the same genuineness with which I want to be treated. I emphasize the need to do the right thing and take pride in doing something well.

PETER S. LOWY
CO-GROUP MANAGING DIRECTOR
WESTFIELD GROUP

> *"I'm always concerned that the fire is not in the belly of our*
> *senior people, which is how a company ultimately loses its edge."*

The Westfield Group, an Australian public company, is one of the world's largest
real estate companies and owner of regional shopping centers. Westfield operates
39 centers in Australia and 61 centers and six airport plazas in the United States,
11 malls in New Zealand, and seven in the United Kingdom.

At Westfield, we split the operating side of the business from finance. I focus more on acquisitions, financing, and interfacing with investors and Wall
Street. While it is not black and white, my brother Steven mainly handles
the global operating side of the business. It is quite efficient to split operations and finance. For example, when we were in the process of acquiring
Rodamco, I was spending two weeks a month in Amsterdam, and there was
no way that the operating side of the business could have received virtually
any of my attention. During the acquisition though, due to this structure,
our operations did not miss a beat.

From a finance point of view, we literally reproject our five-year global
business plan every eight weeks, and our top executives meet to analyze
those numbers and understand what they need in the near term, over the
next 24 months, and over the next five years. Our redevelopment pipeline is
critical to the company's financial success, and it has to be reanalyzed on a
regular basis. Occasionally, immediate course corrections need to be made,
and many strategic decisions emanate from this ongoing financial analysis.
In short, we run the company by the numbers, and the numbers have a
large influence on our strategy.

We have had an investor focus, creating shareholder value and driving
income since we went public 45 years ago. Ours is a demanding culture,

where people either deliver or move on. But our senior management team
has been with the company on average ten-plus years. We encourage open
discussion and debate at meetings and, as the company grows larger, do
everything to fight bureaucracy and indecisiveness. If we can't achieve
consensus, senior managers are quite comfortable making decisions and
carrying them out. I am concerned that the fire is not always in the belly
of our senior people, which is how a company ultimately loses its edge. I
think that high-performing companies have a great attention to detail and
one core philosophy, where every employee knows the direction in which
the company is heading. I also believe that the great companies are conser-
vatively managed from a financial perspective, retain cash on their balance
sheet, and don't become too aggressive with leverage. When the cycle turns
down, we want to have cash to buy underperforming assets.

Leadership is about making often-difficult decisions without full
information. At the end of the day, a leader must pursue his or her instincts. We controlled the retail space at the World Trade Center when the
planes hit on September 11. I was on a conference call about 4:30 a.m. at
my home in California. When the first plane hit, I knew that something
had happened but didn't understand the magnitude of it. I went into the
office in my sweats and with more information understood that this was a
terrorist event, but it was hard to know the implications for my family and
the company. I proceeded to shut the office down, and 12 executives plus
four lawyers reconvened at my home. Ten of our people in New York were
missing, and I had a team focus on finding them. Our lawyers immediately
accessed the insurance documents and quickly understood what the insurance implications were. At about 11 a.m. we closed all of our domestic malls
and started drafting a statement outlining our position for the opening of
the Australian stock market, which was needed by 2 p.m.

PHILIP "FLIP" MARITZ
MANAGING DIRECTOR
MARITZ, WOLFF & COMPANY

"Our success has been driven by the principles of passion,
ambition, and a willingness to make tough decisions."

Founded in 1992 by Flip Maritz and Lew Wolff, Maritz Wolff is a private invest-
ment fund which owns luxury resorts, hotels, and office properties. Its hotel hold-
ings include the Mansion on Turtle Creek in Dallas and The Carlyle in New York.
Maritz earlier worked for Morgan Stanley and Spieker Properties.

The best operating companies develop outstanding teams and strong bench
strength to deliver service. These operators have enduring cultures, like Four
Seasons, and are not media-driven or public relations–driven hotel chains,
which market a great experience but often don't deliver. On the ownership side, the high-performing companies have leaders who are financially
oriented and sophisticated investors. They also have an appreciation for
operations, knowing how to drive growth and success.

Our success has been driven by passion, ambition, and a willingness
to make tough decisions. For example, we own the Four Seasons Resort in
Nevis, West Indies, in the Caribbean. In 1999, it was virtually destroyed by
a hurricane—up to nine feet of sand covered lower-level guest rooms and
facilities near the ocean. My first responsibility was to shareholders. I had
some inclination to simply walk away from the asset. It would have been
easier than negotiating with the insurer, the lender, Four Seasons, and the
local government.

Believe it or not, there were bigger issues. The hotel employed 900
people on an island of 9,000 people. It was a company town, and the
hotel was the company. The resort represented something on the order of
30 percent of the country's gross domestic product. We had to recognize
our responsibilities and how walking away might impact our reputation.

The government had no resources to help us, and we had to go through a lengthy suit with our insurers to try to get as much as we deserved. Nonetheless, given the potential of the investment, as well as our responsibility to the community, we reinvested the time and money to open the asset again. Ultimately, the insurance settlement was $84 million, and we invested another $20 million of new equity on top of that. We closed the hotel for one year in order to renovate it and literally stripped it to the studs. The end result was a substantially improved asset with significantly stronger financial results. We have subsequently refinanced and returned equity—in the end, a major win for all constituents.

CHRISTOPHER J. NASSETTA
PRESIDENT AND CEO
HILTON HOTELS CORPORATION

> *"Transforming a company from 'Bad Co.' to a world-class business requires a great strategy (and the discipline to stick with it), great people, a lot of hard work, and some sleepless nights."*

Chris Nassetta was appointed president and CEO of Hilton Hotels after Blackstone took the company private in 2008. Earlier he had served as executive vice president, then was elected chief operating officer, and in 2000 became CEO at Host Hotels and Resorts, the largest hospitality REIT. He also chairs the commercial real estate industry's most influential lobbying organization, the Real Estate Roundtable.

When Host Hotels & Resorts split from Marriott International, 200 people separated from 200,000. Marriott International was a large organization, with all of the good and bad that comes with that size of company. We had to develop a strategy to transform the company and develop a culture more appropriate for our business. We needed to make sure we had a disciplined approach to our business but also cultivated an entrepreneurial spirit. We set a new course by delegating and empowering people with responsibility and autonomy, providing the management team with leadership development and with review and performance management (compensation) systems that encouraged independent thinking and accountability.

The tone of any organization comes from the top, and the CEO can never underestimate the importance of internal and external communications. I spend considerable time with employees at all levels of the company as well as our board, Wall Street, and the investment community—for their benefit, as well as mine.

Probably our greatest success was the transformation of Host following the split from Marriott International. Host Marriott had been a limited-service business, with a hodgepodge of assets, a weak balance sheet, limited geography, and brand diversification. Our management team has transformed the company into the largest owner of luxury and upscale hotels with one of the strongest balance sheets in the business, with hotels in 50 markets and eight countries around the world and 18 distinct brands.

Transforming the company took many years and involved significant change and risk. It is never easy or quick to execute a transformational strategy, but good leadership is about setting the right course, creating the right culture, and tackling adversity to move the enterprise to the next level.

DAVID J. NEITHERCUT
PRESIDENT, CEO, AND TRUSTEE
EQUITY RESIDENTIAL

> *"To be successful, your senior management team must be focused on the success of the company, not themselves or their business unit."*

Equity Residential is an S&P 500 company recently named one of America's most admired companies by Fortune *magazine. It is the largest publicly traded owner and operator of multifamily housing in the United States, with nearly 150,000 apartment units in 23 states and the District of Columbia.*

The CEO of a public company, as they say, is stretched a mile wide and an inch deep. In addition to being responsible for all aspects of your business, you have numerous external responsibilities, such as dealing with investors and other stakeholders, representing the company within its industry, and interfacing with your board. Therefore, it is critically important for a CEO to have the right people in senior management roles. Their goals and objectives need to be clearly understood and aligned with the corporate strategy. And then you must have sufficient confidence and trust in them to give them the freedom to do their job. If you have to micromanage them, they are either the wrong people or in the wrong role. If you have built your team correctly, their roles will be a showcase for their talents, to the great benefit of the entire organization.

To be successful, your senior management team must be focused on the success of the company, not themselves or their business unit. They must understand the mission of the organization and how they can contribute to the success of that mission. Each year our senior team collaborates to set five to six important corporate goals, and the executives, in turn, establish goals for their business units that align with and support the company's goals. And our compensation program is based on both business unit and company success.

At Equity Residential, collaboration is essential because so much of our success is dependent on business units working together. When our senior management team meets to review progress, we spend little time on our successes, so we can focus on the areas in need of improvement. And no matter how successful an organization is, there is always room for improvement. For this process to work, people must be open, honest, and willing to acknowledge lack of success. Your team must be willing and able to challenge one another and engage in serious debate. And the only way to make this happen is to create a culture of trust that allows people to be candid with themselves and with others.

Our culture is extremely important to us, and we have worked hard to preserve it over the years. It has evolved from what our chairman Sam

Zell and his late partner Bob Lurie created many years ago at Equity Group Investments. Since our beginnings in the early 1970s, through our IPO in 1993, through rapid growth into an S&P 500 company, through good times and bad, our culture has guided us well. "Ten Ways to be a Winner" is the foundation of how we do business at Equity Residential:

- ↬ *Question authority:* "We've always done it that way" is a poor way to justify your actions in the workplace. When something appears inefficient, ineffective, or just plain wrong, question the direction, offer new ideas, and help us make the right decision.

- ↬ *Take educated risks:* Question traditional ways of doing things, estimate the upside—and consider the downside—of trying something new. If the good outweighs the bad, go for it.

- ↬ *Test your limits:* Winners don't settle. They continually push themselves past their present comfort zone, trying more-challenging things and reaching new levels of success. We can't grow unless you grow.

- ↬ *Listen, not just hear:* Listening is a skill few people have mastered. It means giving someone your full attention, taking in—and acknowledging—what they're saying. Words are wasted on people who only hear and don't listen.

- ↬ *Share knowledge:* If we're not sharing knowledge with our coworkers, we're not doing our jobs. Some believe if they hold all the "knowledge cards," they have job security. These people have put their self-interests above those of others and wind up compromising themselves, their coworkers, and the company. Be a student and a teacher every day.

- ↬ *Walk the talk:* Do what you say. Practice what you preach.

- ↬ *See the glass half full:* You can choose to see the glass half full each day or see it half empty. Be optimistic, maintain a positive attitude, and "whistle while you work." Even the most mundane or difficult tasks won't seem so bad, and people will like being around you more.

- ↬ *Do the right thing:* Get all the facts, weigh all the alternatives, and listen to all opinions, then make the right decision. Let your conscience and your good sense be your guide. It's better to do the right thing, than to do things right.

☞ *Share the spotlight:* Our own success always involves the efforts of others. Recognize those people who have contributed to your success. They'll feel appreciated and you will have gained their respect.

☞ *Enjoy the ride:* When you consider the time we spend in the workplace, it's important that you like what you're doing and that you're having a good time. If you're not having fun in your job, change it.

MICHAEL PRENTISS
FORMER CHAIRMAN
PRENTISS PROPERTIES TRUST

> *"I believe in putting issues on the table, including when I'm at fault, and then moving on without any grudges. This tough love is important in running any real estate business well."*

Michael Prentiss founded Prentiss Properties Trust, an office and industrial REIT, in 1987. It was acquired in 2005 by Brandywine Realty Trust in a deal valued at some $3.3 billion.

My success has been due to luck, hard work, and taking advantage of op-portunities. While I pride myself in being flexible and taking some risk, I would not gamble on losing everything. I never signed a guarantee. I bought a portfolio of assets from Cadillac Fairview in 1988 to form Prentiss Properties, shortly after the industry went into its tailspin. Tom August and I set up a third-party asset management business and counted the Federal Deposit Insurance Corporation (FDIC) and the Resolution Trust Corpora-tion (RTC) as important clients of the firm. And then, as the world got bet-ter, we developed a relationship with IBM, where we did nine joint ventures and became the preferred provider for their office space requirements across the country. We earned their respect because we developed to a budget and never had cost overruns. The credibility of IBM helped us in pursuing new business with other equity partners.

I learned that a leader needs to complement himself with a strong group of people who can manage a business successfully. Unlike many entrepreneurs, I've been able to delegate both responsibility and authority. I've been fortunate to have Tom August as a partner, who ultimately became the CEO of our company. I think our people recognized I had good real estate judgment. While I'm a strong personality, I believe in putting the issues on the table—including when I'm at fault—and then moving on without any grudges. This tough love is important to running any real estate business well.

ALBERT B. RATNER
CO-CHAIRMAN
FOREST CITY ENTERPRISES, INC.

> *"We've made a lot of mistakes over time, but work hard to correct them. We believe strongly in relationships and forgive people when they make honest mistakes."*

Founded in 1921 as a lumber dealer, Forest City Enterprises now focuses on real estate development across the United States. Headquartered in Cleveland, Al Ratner has been in the commercial and residential real estate industry since the late 1940s and is acknowledged as a long-time community booster of Cleveland.

We pride ourselves as a values-driven organization at Forest City. We treat people with integrity and honesty, and don't focus on making money as our top priority. We've made a lot of mistakes over time but work hard to correct them. We believe strongly in relationships and forgive people when they make honest mistakes. People are attracted to our culture because they want to be entrepreneurial and run businesses. We tend to be very protective of our people and try to do the right thing by them.

In the early 1990s, when the real estate industry basically became illiquid, we didn't leverage our challenges to cause problems for our lenders. We did not give properties back to the lenders, making the excuse that we couldn't pay off the mortgage debt. At the end of the day, we did the right thing.

DAVID E. SIMON

CEO

SIMON PROPERTY GROUP

> *"I try to lead this company by example. I am tough and aggressive but I have the same standards for myself. I sacrifice in the same fashion that I ask my people to sacrifice."*

Simon Property Group is the nation's largest shopping mall owner and one of the biggest REITs. It owns malls, community shopping centers, and outlet centers in 40 states as well as in France, Italy, Poland, Japan, and Mexico. David Simon joined the Simon organization as chief financial officer in 1990 and was promoted to CEO in 1995. Earlier, he worked on mergers and acquisitions and leveraged buyouts for Wasserstein Perella and Company.

I am tough and aggressive and ask my people to sacrifice like I do. We try to run this company as a family with as little bureaucracy as possible, even though it's a big business. We have an open-door policy where communication and interaction are encouraged. But people really come to work at Simon because of our highly energized culture—they know exciting things go on here. We constantly pursue new business initiatives and look at most transactions.

A CEO often must make decisions in the face of considerable uncertainty and market skepticism. Successful companies balance the entrepreneurial ability to grow with a professionally and efficiently managed business. When we acquired Corporate Property Investors, I faced the prospect of considerable market skepticism. In the middle of the negotiation, I found myself at 3 a.m. sitting in my office with our chief financial officer, communicating with our New York team, including our lawyers. Corporate Property Investors was owned by some savvy, institutional investors who were tough negotiators. Despite my best efforts and an aggressive offer, I felt the deal could go either way. If we won, I expected negative feedback from the market because everyone would accuse me of overpaying. I was only about three years into my tenure as CEO, and Corporate Property Investors represented a $6 billion transaction—when our existing market cap was only $7 billion. I enlisted input from a variety of people, stuck to my convictions, and turned out to be right.

DAVID A. TWARDOCK
PRESIDENT
PRUDENTIAL MORTGAGE CAPITAL COMPANY

> *"I'm not a cheerleader but someone who has to make the tough*
> *decisions, including having the right people in the business.*
> *I push for a sense of urgency, which is necessary in any*
> *performance-driven organization."*

Dave Twardock is responsible for managing all of Prudential's commercial real estate finance activities. He joined Prudential in 1982 and worked in both the acquisitions and the property management areas before joining the company's mortgage organization in 1984. He directed the company's efforts to reduce direct ownership and increased positions in public and private real estate operating companies.

I prioritize my time by thinking through the business's strategic objectives and how we will ultimately meet them. I want my direct reports to focus on the right issues in running the business, and I go out of my way to communicate our performance, on a face-to-face basis, whenever possible. I try to delegate, collaborate, and empower people. I'm not a cheerleader but someone who has to make the tough decisions, including having the right people in the business. I push for a sense of urgency, which is necessary in any performance-driven organization.

Managing through difficult times is one of the best reflections of effective leadership. In 1996, I was asked to dramatically transform and shrink Prudential's real estate equity portfolio so the company could focus on its asset management business. We were charged with selling or swapping $6 billion of assets in a difficult environment where there were few buyers. It was a daunting prospect. Staff knew they were working themselves out of jobs and faced tough career decisions. I offered everyone the chance to leave, with a severance package of one times salary, which gave them a cushion. Next, I put a compensation plan into effect, primarily for the deal people, where if the group sold the assets at a particular premium, they could earn a one-time bonus, which could be multiple times their salaries. Ultimately, about 25 percent of the people left immediately, and the balance worked together in an enormously rewarding effort for Prudential.

The project provided a learning experience for a number of people, and they were excited about the prospect of doing new things, like swapping assets for REIT shares. People's skill sets were enhanced for their next opportunity. We were ultimately successful in making the effort fun and profitable, and provided the right type of culture in which individuals had the authority and accountability to do the business in creative and opportunistic ways.

RAYMOND E. WIRTA
FORMER CEO
CB RICHARD ELLIS GROUP, INC.

> *"We focus on training our people and empowering them to*
> *be leaders in local markets. It's important for us to keep the*
> *organization flat and delegate as much as possible."*

Publicly traded on the NYSE, CB Richard Ellis is the largest commercial property manager in the world, with operations in 35 countries. The company undertakes brokerage, market research, mortgage banking, asset management, and advisory

services. Now retired, Ray Wirta was the firm's CEO from 1999 until 2005, a
period when the firm bought Insignia Financial, privatized, and subsequently
went public again.

Because of our long history, we built on a tradition of ethics and mentorship. We focused on training our people, empowering them to be leaders in
local markets. It was important for us to keep the organization flat and delegate as much as possible. We focused on constantly improving quality and
encourage risk taking. I delegated, hired good people, and let them exercise
their judgment. I tended to hold people to a high level of accountability and
tried to keep my messages to the organization simple and clear. I wanted
an entrepreneurial company culture that was highly ethical and competitive
but friendly.

My greatest leadership challenge was taking over from Jim Didion. We
needed to transition from Jim's command-and-control style to a decentralized leadership structure. Jim had been with CB Richard Ellis for 37 years and
was CEO for 12 years. He had built the business into a U.S.-based sales and
leasing organization. His management style was appropriate for its time, but
then changes occurred, largely at his initiation. The company went public and
acquired other firms, including Melody, Koll, and TCW Investment Advisors,
and moved into overseas markets. With these changes Jim, to his credit, recognized that new leadership was required to lead the company going forward
and picked me as his successor.

When I inherited the company, the production people viewed the back-
office people skeptically since the back-office people were paid to police the
producers. The organization was also populated by people who could execute
but were not focused on the broader issues. That had been largely Jim's role.
For starters, I tried to eliminate the dysfunction between the back office and
the producers. I hired leadership in the back office who had much better
people skills and understood their role to service the producers, not constrain
them. And I evaluated all of the line managers and replaced those who had
become complacent, typically promoting from within.

DONALD C. WOOD

PRESIDENT AND CEO

FEDERAL REALTY INVESTMENT TRUST

> *"Leadership is all about taking risk and standing by your*
> *convictions."*

Federal Realty is a REIT that owns more than 100 community and neighborhood
shopping centers in the northeast United States. Don Wood joined Federal in 1998
as chief financial officer. He had been chief financial officer of Caesar's World, a
wholly owned subsidiary of ITT Corporation.

Leadership is about taking educated risks and standing by your convictions.
As one of the oldest public REITs in the country, Federal had been at the
shopping center game for nearly 40 years by 2001. After having developed a
solid reputation as a leader and innovator in the 1970s and 1980s, Federal had
lost its way in the 1990s by allocating the majority of its financial and human
capital to the development of large-scale, mixed-use projects to the detriment
of its well-located, time-tested, necessity-based shopping centers.

As chief operating officer of the company and then president (but not
the CEO), what do you do when you don't believe in the growth strategy
and risk profile that the company is following but you're expected to add
shareholder value by virtue of your title and position? That was the situation
I was in, and both the internal and the external struggles that were necessary to convince the critical players that a complete change in direction
was necessary were huge. The answer lay in the way we communicated the
proposed changes, the veracity of the arguments, and the clarity and consistency with which we presented them.

By late 2002, the board agreed to make a change at the top of Federal and to embrace a new business plan focused on internal growth (i.e.,
re-leasing, remerchandising, and redeveloping those assets that we already
owned or controlled) with acquisitions meant only to supplement that re-

development pipeline. In my view, the board agreed to the change because the arguments we made for this plan were based on solid facts, clearly laid out and substantiated, with all the potential pitfalls also openly discussed and debated. Emotions were downplayed and all members of the Federal management team were made part of, and ultimately embraced, the new plan. Those that were unable to get behind it had to leave.

It's now five years later, and it appears as though those decisions must have been easy to make. I can assure you they were not, as changes such as this aren't made with the benefit of hindsight. At the time, the stakes were high, but the analytical review of the facts coupled with clear, level-headed communication and a good helping of plain old luck helped make the case.

SAMUEL ZELL
CHAIRMAN AND CEO
EQUITY GROUP INC.

> *"Good leaders always want to be challenged and are motivated when they don't achieve their goals. They simply reset. They have high energy, extraordinary self-confidence, the courage of their convictions, and an instinct for doing the right thing."*

A real estate industry luminary, Zell and his partner, Bob Lurie, founded Equity Group Investments in 1968. Today, the REIT portfolio of this multibillion-dollar investment company includes Equity Lifestyle Properties and Equity Residential Properties. Equity Office Properties was sold to The Blackstone Group in 2007. A visionary in the business, Zell has long been a proponent of the securitization of the commercial real estate industry.

Leadership is about setting an example. I constantly ask myself: Where can I have the biggest impact? But you can't take yourself too seriously, and I constantly poke fun at myself in public. Good leaders always want to be challenged and are motivated when they don't achieve their goals. They simply reset. They have high energy, extraordinary self-confidence, the courage of their convictions, and an instinct for doing the right thing.

Leadership is also about creating an open and sharing culture. At Equity Office Properties in the late 1990s, I had to convince the management team that our enemy was without and that we needed to trade information and communicate more effectively within the organization. I used the analogy of circling the wagon train and defending against outside aggression. Information is currency, and people in a bureaucracy control the flow of information to secure power. When people within an organization don't share information, the business becomes dysfunctional. Ultimately, not having a transparent internal organization dramatically increases the risks of making investments.

Our industry is long on transactionalists and short on conceptualizers. We need people who are entrepreneurs but can manage as well. I try to blend both. When my partner, Bob Lurie, died in 1990, the real estate industry was in the depths of a depression. We employed 1,200 people, and I had to set a vision and execute it. I needed to turn down the emotion, get focused, and get it done. The experiences of the early 1990s reminded me again that being responsible was often a lonely adventure. The problem in the early 1990s was a dearth of capital available to real estate, and yet the opportunities appeared extraordinary. We thus began the first real estate opportunity fund, which gave us the capital to exercise our vision.

CHAPTER FIVE

HIRE HARD,
MANAGE EASY

Team building necessarily consumes significant CEO time and attention. Hiring right allows CEOs to delegate comfortably, and providing autonomy gives subordinate executives the desired opportunity to grow and flourish. Today, the company management team and employee lineup is the key differentiator in the marketplace. Attracting and developing high-quality people is the only thing a competitor cannot duplicate. In real estate businesses, "high-performing companies recognize they must run people-centered organizations where employee loyalty is valued and people are rewarded if the business performs," says Regina Lowrie, retired CEO of Gateway Funding, a residential mortgage lender. "Recruiting can be arduous but must be discerning. You keep good people by giving them room to operate, but making sure they are held accountable."

Recruiting Standards

No single set of criteria serves every company in evaluating new hires. A generic profile includes the familiar catch words—values, integrity, character, empathy, smarts, driven, and passionate. Many CEOs look for people smarter than themselves. Nelson Rising, CEO of Maguire Properties, finds "a direct correlation" between an executive's willingness to accept accountability and highly sought after "human qualities—judgment, work ethic, and intelligence." "Our people need to be self-motivated and interested in learning as well as sharing information," says Jay Sugarman of iStar Financial.

Avoid Prima Donnas

Winning management teams discourage "rock star" hires—executives who use company platforms to launch personal success rather than fostering company achievement through working with others to build platforms. Rock stars typically require coddling and ego stroking, at the expense of common team culture. They often set demands and expect special treatment that can create resentment among other executives as well as the rank and file.

Let Smart People Alone

Once high-octane performers are attracted to a company, they need to be managed, motivated, and retained. CEOs should set expectations and performance thresholds but then give their people ample flexibility to run their departments or businesses. Testing their mettle requires giving them enough room to learn from their successes and mistakes. "My inclination is to throw responsibility at people and see how much they can handle," says Tom Toomey of United Dominion Trust, a multifamily REIT.

The lesson learned in this chapter is that the great CEOs spend the time and make the effort to hire quality people. There is nothing that can supplant the time invested in this effort. And what do the great leaders look for in people? They look for people who are smart, both intellectually and instinctually, as well as individuals who are competitive yet team oriented, who accept accountability and want to make decisions. Interestingly enough, if a company is successful in hiring these types of people, there has to be a commitment from the organization to allow them to take on responsibility and make their fair share of mistakes. That's why organizations where people can assume responsibility for a business early in their career are more attractive places in which to work. Simply put, great people don't want a bit in their mouths; they want to drive down the road, have the ability to move into the passing lane, and yet have the guardrails on either side of the road to make sure they don't drive off the cliff.

Art Coppola of Macerich emphasizes that he has created a culture where people are delegated to but are encouraged to visit with him regarding any concerns or questions. "People have to accept that they don't have all of the answers and should come for help before making silly mistakes. Setting goals for people and then holding them accountable is key to creating a performance-oriented culture." As Doug Crocker articulates, "Your people need to have the same passion as their leader, and their leader needs to support his people or the equation simply breaks down." People like to work in organizations where they can trust their own instincts and do what is right. Following the pack is not the answer. And there is acknowledgment that an organization run on a decentralized basis, where autonomy is prized, and that supports different styles integrated into a successful platform is the right recipe.

DANIEL A. ARRIGONI
PRESIDENT AND CEO
U.S. BANK HOME MORTGAGE

"My leadership style embodies harmony, empathy, responsibility, consistency, and people development."

As head of U.S. Bank Home Mortgage since 1996, Dan Arrigoni leads an organization of more than 2,400 employees nationwide. In 2005, he was named to the board of directors of the National Mortgage Bankers Association.

I spend a lot of my time interfacing with our major shareholder, U.S. Bank, and try to shield the company from many corporate challenges as they keep tabs on our performance. They are very numbers oriented, and I am constantly reforecasting while I let my direct reports run the business day to day.

My leadership style embodies harmony, empathy, responsibility, consistency, and people development. I require harmony and teamwork among my direct reports. I try to practice empathy by putting myself in their positions. I recognize the importance of consistency in all decision making, and I delegate, acknowledging that it is important for my team members to have autonomy in running their disciplines.

Our management team has been together a long time, and that's because we work well together. Responsibility is delegated and achievement is acknowledged. I communicate goals and performance well throughout the company. I push everyone to be empathetic. While our people are fairly compensated, they aren't compensated at the top end of the market—a demonstration of how culture can drive high performance in a business. I'm especially proud of how our organization has shaved peaks and filled in valleys. Our ability to provide stability to the business keeps morale high.

GERALD "JERRY" L. BAKER
PRESIDENT AND CEO
FIRST HORIZON NATIONAL CORPORATION

> *"Decision making needs to remain as close to the customer as possible, and greater local autonomy is critically important to attract qualified, experienced management talent."*

First Tennessee National Corporation changed its name to First Horizon National in 2004 to reflect its growth beyond Tennessee. Jerry Baker earlier served as president of Mortgage Banking, president and CEO at First Horizon Home Loan Corporation, and chief operating officer of First Horizon National Corporation.

My priorities are strategy development and looking forward. It's critical to know what is working and what's not working, in all areas. Meetings and interactions with staff and management provide valuable insights—what I call discovery. With appropriate systems and a disciplined process, continuous performance reviews can be accomplished.

High-performing companies have a clearly defined strategy, and all business units have a common and singular focus. Instilling discipline can avoid distractions and wasting resources. Execution must be solid and consistent.

I try to set a clear strategic vision with well-understood goals. Our people need to understand those goals, and the action steps required to accomplish the desired results must be frequently reviewed. People must have room to perform. I try to lead by example, expect what has been promised, and show confidence but not arrogance.

Many organizations in the residential mortgage business, as well as other financial services companies, increasingly move toward greater centralization of support services, including processing, underwriting, and document preparation. This is a dangerous trend. Decision making needs to remain as close to the customer as possible, and greater local autonomy and decision making is critically important to attract qualified, experienced management talent.

RICHARD CAMPO
CHAIRMAN AND CEO
CAMDEN PROPERTY TRUST

> *"We look for people who are adaptable and thrive on solving problems. They are team players, who add value."*

Camden is one of the largest multifamily REITs in the nation and specializes in several disciplines within the residential real estate industry. It provides expertise in the ownership, development, and management of apartment communities; in the acquisition, disposition, and redevelopment of properties; and in consulting, building, and construction services for third-party clients. As the chairman and

CEO since May 1993, Richard Campo holds strategic roles within the real estate industry. He serves on the Executive Board as the chairman for the National Multi-Housing Council, is an executive committee member for the Urban Land Institute (ULI–Houston Regional), and sits on the board of directors for the National Association of Real Estate Investment Trusts (NAREIT).

Within Camden, I'm known as a "hallway manager." I'm not big on long meetings, except where they are necessary, such as board meetings. I much more enjoy interacting with our people and encourage them to adopt the same styles. Interestingly enough, I've only had one job out of school. Keith Oden and I ended up buying this company from its founders and transformed it from a "pirate ship culture." In other words, too much time was spent politicking with the captain, and Keith and I learned from that experience what we didn't want to be.

We have tried hard to create a special culture at Camden. We are very careful about hiring the right kind of people, and once those people are in the company, we provide a supportive environment that is both collegial and fun. Our values are enormously important to us. Even in the toughest of times, we try to put a smile on our face. We're not looking for the smartest people or the most technical, but those individuals to whom ethics are important and who have a high energy level and work ethic. We look for people who are adaptable and thrive on solving problems. They are team players, who add value.

Communications are extraordinarily important to me. I spend a lot of time on the road. In fact, during the first quarter, Keith Oden and I visit each one of our 16 operating regions and also bring people back to the corporate office. And we go into the field not as some high-ranking executive, but as one of the troops. In fact, when we consummated our acquisition of Summit, I traveled to Charlotte in blue jeans, a maintenance shirt, and sneakers. A number of the Summit employees were surprised that Camden would send a "maintenance man" to integrate the businesses.

Last year, Camden was honored as one of Fortune's Top 100 Companies. We were the first REIT ever to be included in this group, as well as the first multifamily company. From our perspective, it proves the theory that there is a strong correlation between culture and performance. And at the end of the day, it's all about substance. I knew the Enron executive team well. And they were a classic example of painting the right corporate picture but not having the value system to support it. At Camden, we have worked hard at walking the talk, and I think we've been pretty successful at accomplishing that mission.

ARTHUR M. COPPOLA
PRESIDENT AND CEO
THE MACERICH COMPANY

> *"You have to be hands off, but head in. People want the*
> *autonomy, and you need to delegate it to them. But I want them to*
> *come to me with any concerns or questions."*

Headquartered outside Los Angeles, Macerich is a REIT and one of the largest owners of regional shopping centers and community shopping centers. A lawyer and accountant by training, Art Coppola has been in the shopping center industry for 30 years. Coppola is the chair of the NAREIT.

Companies differentiate themselves in the retail real estate industry with a tight concept, a strong culture, and ability to raise capital. We started buying regional malls and redeveloping them, and now we do ground-up development as well as mixed-use projects. But our concept has always been well defined in particular markets we know well.

We are entrepreneurial and yet cohesive. We know what we stand for, and our behavior is ethical beyond a doubt. I learned a lot about culture from my father, as well as my partner, Mace Siegel. My father taught me that a strong work ethic and honesty are core values that can never be compromised. You need to be the best that you can be. One of the great travesties is if you have talent and don't have the work ethic to take advantage of it. Conversely, people with strong work ethics and limited talent can do quite well. Mace Siegel's guiding principle was that you need to treat employees, customers, and vendors the same way that you want to be treated. What I've learned is that you have to be hands off, but head in. People want autonomy, and you need to delegate it to them. But I want them to come to me with any concerns or questions. I like to prioritize my time in pursuing new business opportunities and don't like too many meetings.

As we grow the company, we only hire people that we know extremely well. Otherwise we promote from within. As my father used to say, "Spend your time on hiring and not firing." When David Contis recently left our firm as chief operating officer, we took a lot of time considering the right person for his replacement. We decided upon Tony Grossi, then the chief operating officer of Cadillac Fairview, because we had known Tony for over ten years and had been partners with Cadillac Fairview for over ten years. With this approach, I think we maintain a very healthy culture. We work hard and play hard. We are liberal with flextime. And our people all have different interests. In fact, we encourage diversity. My father used to tell me that one of the keys to success is to surround yourself with people that are smarter at what they do than you could ever be. As a naïve young man, I found that hard to imagine, but now I am very comfortable that we have achieved that at Macerich—and it is the key to the great company that we have here.

When we bought Westcor, a private mall developer based in Phoenix, everyone felt that we were overpaying, which is not a good situation when you're a public company. They brought a development expertise which we did not have internally, and they were a group of talented people who fit well into our culture. In fact, we asked our people to list their friends in the industry, and virtually every one of them named at least one person at Westcor. Westcor also brought a terrific development pipeline to us. We clearly stretched to do the deal, taking on $1 billion in unsecured debt. However, we bought ten malls, got a great team, and got a wonderful pipeline. I took the risk, and it worked.

ROB COUCH
GENERAL COUNSEL
U.S. DEPARTMENT OF HOUSING AND URBAN DEVELOPMENT

> *"People want to have goals set for them; it's best to let
> them perform."*

*A former chairman of the Mortgage Bankers Association, Rob Couch was ap-
pointed president of the Government National Mortgage Association (Ginnie
Mae) in 2006. In June 2007, he was confirmed by the U.S. Senate as general
counsel of the U.S. Department of Housing and Urban Development. Earlier,
Couch headed New South Federal Savings and was managing director of Collateral Mortgage, Ltd. The bank has some 40 residential mortgage origination offices
in more than a dozen states, mainly in the South.*

My people would describe my management style as results oriented and
demanding. I want to see the numbers. I would characterize any business
that I have managed as efficient, cost-conscious, opportunistic, and nimble.
In the early 1990s, we bought a lot of assets from the RTC and made a significant amount of money from those purchases.

I push people to reach their full potential. I strongly believe in training and investing in people and acknowledging their performance. Every
month, at New South, before our manager's meeting, we acknowledged
"our core values hero" in the company. This is someone who has accomplished something which is reflective of our four key values—integrity,
service, community, and profitability.

People want to have goals set for them; it's best to let them perform.
I can remember when our organization was number four in residential
mortgage production in Birmingham. I wanted us to be number one in the
market, especially given that our headquarters is here. I told my production
people that, if they were to achieve the number one ranking, I would kiss
the rear end of Vulcan, who is the god of iron steel, planted firmly on top of

a mountain outside of Birmingham. We had to dislodge SouthTrust from the top position. Interestingly enough, Vulcan's elbow fell off, and the city cut the entire statue into ten-foot sections. It was brought down from the mountain and disassembled in a parking lot, and Vulcan's rear end was about six feet off the ground. When my Birmingham production team achieved their number one spot, I followed up on my end of the bargain and "barely" was able to kiss Vulcan's rear end. It was clearly a motivator for many of our people.

DOUGLAS CROCKER II
PARTNER
DC PARTNERS, LLC

> *"I turned over a fair amount of people, because I believe in hiring and firing for attitude. Everyone needed passion and to pull hard like I did."*

Doug Crocker is former vice chairman of the board of trustees and the CEO of Equity Residential (NYSE:EQR) before he founded his own firm, DC Partners. He serves on the board of directors of Ventas, Wellsford Real Properties, National Water and Power, Inc., Acadia Realty Trust, and Post Properties. Crocker previously served as chairman of the board of directors of the National Multi Housing Council and as a trustee of the Urban Land Institute. Top industry honors awarded to Crocker by leading industry publications include five-time Multifamily Executive of the Year, three-time REIT Executive of the Year, three-time Outstanding CEO, and two-time CEO of the Year.

My focus was to walk the talk and create a team-oriented environment where people believed in the company. Because of our multiple corporate acquisitions, it was important to knock down fiefdoms. We communicated corporate messages clearly throughout the business, and I required my senior management team to listen to what was being said throughout the organization. I didn't want people's titles to establish some type of rank order and wanted everyone viewed as a partner in running the business. I turned over a fair amount of people, because I believe in hiring and firing for attitude. Everyone needed passion and to pull hard like I did. I also had to transition the culture from a deal-oriented shop into an operating business.

In an effort to empower people throughout the organization, I created committees to address various topics important in formulating our culture. It was quite an honor to be selected and participants included vice presidents, assistant vice presidents, property managers, and even cleaning people. These committees made recommendations on issues ranging from operations to legal and human resources, and presented to the senior management team. My challenge was to keep people stimulated after rapid growth had passed, and as we transitioned into an operating mode. We instituted 360-degree feedback reviews across the company to allow people to better understand their strengths and weaknesses. We also introduced a policy enabling everyone to take their children to their first day of school, which didn't cost anything but yielded tremendous benefits.

I always try to be passionate about leadership. My people knew that I would do anything I ever asked of them. And I also felt it was important for all of us to commit to our communities and support national industry organizations.

JOHN C. GOFF

CO-FOUNDER, FORMER VICE CHAIRMAN, AND CEO
CRESCENT REAL ESTATE EQUITIES LTD.

> *"Leaders are effective delegators, who recruit good people who can make the right decisions. They let their people grow. This 'land of opportunity' mindset creates a competitive advantage."*

Crescent Real Estate Equities, a REIT invested in office and hotel properties as well as ownership positions in upscale residential developments, was founded by John Goff and Richard Rainwater. Goff served as CEO from the company's inception in 1994 through 1996 and returned in 1999, leading the successful turnaround of the business. It was sold to Morgan Stanley in 2007.

My responsibility was to make our organization aware of macro trends, anticipate change, and take action whether corrective or opportunistic. We needed a flexible balance sheet, a healthy skepticism in decision making, and a lean organization, where noncritical functions are outsourced. Running a business today can be complex, and having the right mix of skill and talent is the art of management.

High-performance companies are known for their creative leadership and high energy level. They combine expertise in staying focused on the big picture with skillful addressing of day-to-day operations. Their leaders are effective delegators, who recruit people who can make the right decisions. They let their people grow. This "land of opportunity" mindset creates a competitive advantage.

We tried to embrace these best practices. I wanted to be kept well informed and involved, but my greatest added value was as a strategist. I tried to stay focused on the horizon and not the trees. I often defined myself as a cheerleader—I'm good at identifying and recruiting strong people into the organization and then cheering them on. We tried to maintain a reasonably flat organization so we could make decisions quickly.

LEO E. KNIGHT, JR.
RETIRED CHAIRMAN
NATIONAL CITY MORTGAGE

> *"I've tried to hire the smartest people and let them do their jobs. I set expectations and performance thresholds, and then give people the flexibility to run their own businesses."*

Leo Knight retired as chairman and chief executive officer of National City Mortgage in 2005. Owned by National City Corporation, the Cleveland-based residen-

*tial mortgage bank ranks among the top ten home lenders in the United States,
with 200 lending offices in 28 states. National City Corporation was merged into
PNC financial Services Group, Inc., in 2008. Knight served on the National Mortgage Bankers Association Residential Board of Directors.*

I concentrate on strategic issues. While I try to stay close to the operating
business, I've always had a chief operating officer to focus on the day-to-
day operations. The chief operating officer also spends a fair amount of time
focused on continuity and culture. I've tried to hire the smartest people and
let them do their jobs. I set expectations and performance thresholds, then
give people the flexibility to run their own businesses. In National City we
had a strong work ethic, but trust was also a key factor. Whenever there was
a problem in the business, everyone rallied around to solve it.

In perpetuating a common culture and philosophy, I've always tried
to maintain the entrepreneurial spirit of our sales force and let our branches
run their own businesses, rewarding profitability. They were accountable
for volume and expenses. The support staff and the rest of the organization
recognized they must respond to the origination machine. I did everything
in my power to avoid letting bureaucratization from the parent company
impact our entrepreneurial business.

As a leader, I always stayed very visible with both customers and employees. Employees took heart in my taking the time and making the effort
to interface with customers, and it reinforced our customer-centric culture.
Internally, I've always encouraged an open communication system. Since
1981 five different banks owned our business. Amazingly, I lost only one senior person throughout all that change. My success in retaining people has
resulted from overcommunicating. I can remember at one meeting where I
honestly said I had "nothing to report." That may appear inconsequential to
many, but conveying to them that their interest was paramount to me made
a huge difference. It all gets back to trust and people feeling that they are
valued and respected.

REGINA M. LOWRIE
FORMER CEO
GATEWAY FUNDING DIVERSIFIED MORTGAGE COMPANY

"We hire hard and manage easy."

Gateway Funding Diversified Mortgage Company ranked as the greater Philadelphia area's largest independent mortgage company. Regina Lowrie, who founded Gateway in 1994, built the company from seven employees and $1.5 million in startup capital to 800 employees in 58 offices, who have originated more than $3 billion in loans annually in recent years. Lowrie was the 2006 chairman of the Mortgage Bankers Association.

Every year, we refreshed our strategic plan, and every three years, we wiped the slate clean. I had two partners in the business, and the three of us decided on expectations relative to return on equity. I then articulated a vision that would generate the anticipated return. I discussed my vision at an off-site meeting with the management team, and then we all agreed on the vision and decided how to best implement it. If the management team does not buy in, there is simply no way a strategic plan will be successfully executed.

In order to be successful in this business, a leader needs to take risks, and never back away from a challenge, no matter how big or difficult. Our turning point came in 1996, two years after Gateway was founded. We were doing about $100 million in production. Provident Bank put up for sale a $300 million mortgage company with five branches that complemented Gateway perfectly. Unlike many other bidders, I offered a deal for the top two people of the mortgage company, which gave them an earn-out over two years and allowed them to participate in the overall profitability of their business. I also let the business stand alone and retain its name. The other bidders would have gotten rid of the two people and assimilated the business into their larger entities. While we were somewhat of a fish swallowing a whale, we consummated the transaction by being sensitive to what the principals wanted to achieve and recognizing that they had a voice at the table. This deal looked impossible but put us on the map.

Leaders in the residential mortgage banking industry understand that the best companies are sensitized to human resources issues. If a company doesn't get the people thing right, it's impossible to acquire and retain talent. Once in the company, people need to be trained and developed, and knowledge needs to be transferred. You need to make an investment here.

DENNIS "DENNY" D. OKLAK
CHAIRMAN AND CEO
DUKE REALTY CORPORATION

> *"My preference is to allow our people to run their businesses . . .*
> *I want to create a culture which generates free thought and where*
> *good ideas can be implemented. Nonetheless, I am acutely aware*
> *of the importance of a disciplined process."*

Duke Realty Corp., an NYSE-traded REIT, owns and develops suburban office, industrial, retail, and medical office properties throughout the United States. The company's service operations include construction and development, asset and property management, and leasing. Denny Oklak has headed Duke since 2004.

My management style is laid back—I delegate decision making to my people. But I'm not afraid to express my opinion or make decisions when necessary. I try to be a visible leader, visiting all of our 18 offices each year, and I believe strongly in communications. Each quarter, I host an associates' conference call, typically after our board meeting and a subsequent analyst call. All of our people are invited to hear what is going on in the company. My preference is to allow our people to run their businesses, and I want to create a culture which generates free thought and where good ideas can be implemented. Nonetheless, I am acutely aware of the importance of a disciplined process.

Duke has become an employer of choice because of our entrepreneurial culture, where many people make important decisions. Our compensation plans have a very attractive, long-term component, and our strategic planning teams allow a wide range of people to have input on the company's strategy. We also constantly assess the top 120 people in the company, monitoring and developing their career paths.

Much of leadership is about persevering. I can remember when we took the company public in 1993. It was a transforming moment. We were unique among REITs since we owned about 10 million square feet, managed another 10 million square feet of properties for third parties, and had a construction company. We also specialized in both office and industrial assets. Not only was 1993 a difficult time to take a REIT public, because of all the troubles in the real estate industry, but investors also had trouble "quantifying" us, given the breadth of our businesses. The IPO process was challenging and lengthy, but we persevered, and it's worked out well.

EDWARD PADILLA
CEO
NORTHMARQ CAPITAL, INC.

> *"I delegate to create a true sense of autonomy. If you truly hold people accountable for the bottom line, you need to let them make decisions and run their businesses in a way they feel comfortable. They're responsible for drawing their own road map. The ones who need specific direction won't fit into our organization."*

NorthMarq is one of the nation's largest commercial mortgage banks, providing around $13 billion in financing for commercial real estate transactions annually in recent years. The company is owned by the Pohlad family. Ed Padilla joined NorthMarq in 1991.

Successful companies, especially service firms, depend upon highly motivated, ethical people to distinguish themselves from the competition. Performance is driven by financial rewards and peer competition. The competitive self-motivator is quite often the type of person we seek out; people need to achieve in their own style within the basic guidelines of the overall organization, but act as entrepreneurs.

We have 28 offices, which are all ultimately judged by the profitability of their businesses. The cultures of our offices depend upon the markets in which they operate and their customer base. So the successful offices hire the right people, motivate them well, but give them flexibility in how they execute. If the people are not right, it simply won't work. We have acquired seven firms over the course of our history, and the first criterion is fit. If it's not there, there's no reason to look at the numbers. Fundamentally, I don't believe that you can be successful converting people throughout a national system.

Our culture has always been driven by doing the right thing for our clients and customers first. In an organization of 400 people, we have minimized the number of people in senior management. The rest of our senior leadership are producing and managing directors who run regional offices. Ours is not a sales-managed, rah-rah culture. We require plans and budgets from each office, and we're there to support them. We believe in a locally based relationship, and the home office role is to provide the resources and platform to execute the business plan. Running a business in this fashion can put limitations on growth. Because of this style, we may never be the biggest in regard to production or servicing volume, but we'll be profitable and hopefully have happy clients. Also, in large part because of this style, our employee retention rate is one of the highest in the industry.

My style is reflective of the business we've built. I am low key by nature and always try to be accessible. I spend a lot of time visiting our offices, as well as with our capital sources and clients. I delegate to create a true sense of autonomy. If you truly hold people accountable for the bottom line, you need to let them make decisions and run their businesses in a way that they feel is comfortable. They're responsible for drawing their own road map. The ones who need specific direction won't fit into our organization. You can't make people act like entrepreneurs by talking about it. You need to create a system that empowers and rewards them.

The year 1998 was a watershed year for our firm, and specifically our leadership team. Our owners at the time, the Hamm family, decided to retain Goldman Sachs to sell the business. I told our owners and many of our suitors that the management team would not be comfortable with some of the acquisition scenarios. I ultimately decided to approach the Pohlad family. I, along with the rest of management, was obviously taking a risk, as I openly stated a preference for a specific buyer. Toward the end of the process, we were actually closely aligned with the Pohlad family. Fortunately, the Pohlads were our ultimate acquirer and have been a great partner as we've built the business. Ninety-five percent of the key leaders who were with our company then are still with us today. As a leader, a time will come when you need to take a risk. You have to live with the consequences; if you believe your position is right, you need to stay true to your convictions. Every time we see an acquisition opportunity, someone in our organization takes that position of being an advocate. Those who are good at it make a call and are prepared to be accountable.

DOUGLAS M. PASQUALE
CEO
NATIONWIDE HEALTH PROPERTIES, INC.

> *"I focus on people who are driven, who believe that they can always achieve extraordinary results, and don't take no for an answer. The best senior housing firms are ones that are people driven and are passionate about doing the best job they can."*

Nationwide Health Properties, one of the nation's largest health care REITs, specializes in seniors' housing, long-term care facilities, and medical office buildings. It owns more than 500 assets in 42 states. Doug Pasquale is a veteran of the hospitality industry.

In transitioning the culture of Nationwide, the key leadership ingredients have been integrity, reliability, and doing whatever it takes to get the job done. I view running the business as a partnership, and people are an extraordinarily important part of the equation. I focus on people who are driven, who believe that they can always achieve extraordinary results, and who don't take no for an answer. The best firms in seniors' housing are ones that are people driven and are passionate about doing the best job they can.

Successful companies will never be content—that is a recipe for disaster. The high performers will continue to reinvent themselves, even in good times.

STEPHEN R. QUAZZO
CEO
TRANSWESTERN INVESTMENT COMPANY, LLC

> *"The real estate investment business requires a healthy paranoia,*
> *or in other words, a strong sense of urgency. Too many people*
> *want to play in the space, and it's been that way for generations.*
> *In fact, real estate has offered one of the best vehicles for the*
> *preservation and transfer of generational wealth."*

Transwestern Investment Company, LLC, is a real estate principal investment firm with around $4 billion under management, cofounded in 1996 by Stephen Quazzo. Previously he was president of Equity Institutional Investors, Inc., a subsidiary of Equity Group Investments, Inc., a holding company controlled by Sam Zell.

The real estate business differs from many other investment businesses in corporate America in two ways: it's labor intensive and highly inefficient. You need to have local knowledge and representation in order to acquire assets well and manage them efficiently.

Successful leaders are entrepreneurial, but they require the right infrastructure to manage the business. They need to hire good people, provide them a meaningful financial stake, and then delegate. Alignment is key.

Also, you have to manage by consensus, so your people buy into your strategies. "My way or the highway" doesn't work. The concept of mutual accountability is also important—everybody must be accountable for performance. In this business, you are only as good as your people.

The real estate investment business requires a healthy paranoia or, in other words, a strong sense of urgency. Too many people want to play in the space, and it's been that way for generations. In fact, real estate has offered one of the best vehicles for the preservation and transfer of generational wealth. It's the second oldest profession.

I've had great mentors in my life. I think of John Weinberg, who was the chairman of Goldman Sachs, as well as one of Goldman's clients, Tom Murphy at ABC. They were humble, self-deprecating, and related well to people around them. They weren't autocratic. I also think about Sam Zell. One of Sam's greatest attributes is that he is open minded; he never makes snap decisions. His door is always open, and he wants to hear other perspectives. Now, he isn't always right, but he has the good instinct to listen before he makes decisions.

At Transwestern, I try to be very consensus oriented and encourage mutual respect. We engage the management team on a regular basis, and I try to explain what I'm thinking and get their reaction. They all have a financial stake in the business and a voice. I also implemented 360-degree reviews. We pay people for being team players—there are no silos in acquisitions, finance, due diligence, or elsewhere.

When we hire people, I tend to favor those who are willing to pick up the phone and make something happen. I assume everyone has the fundamental analytical skills, but the successful people take the bull by the horns, even if they might make mistakes. I also look for good communicators and team players, critical attributes in our culture. I try to interview virtually everyone we hire, including executive assistants. Culture is important.

Our clients invest with us because they rely on our integrity. We try to be totally transparent. They know we won't take excess risk and embarrass them. And they also know that our turnover has been minimal, a big differentiator with our clients. As John Weinberg at Goldman Sachs said, "If the firm takes care of its clients, that's the best investment that an organization can make." It's better to be long-term, rather than short-term, greedy.

My greatest leadership moment occurred when the firm was put in the position of having to suddenly buy out one of the founding partners. His leaving created a number of problematic issues and the firm could have imploded, but that didn't happen. I convinced my other cofounder to broaden ownership stakes in the company, so that other partners could participate more directly in the firm's success. We also decided to share the firm's full financials with all partners. And we created an Executive Committee and Management Committee, so that others could have key roles in helping run the organization. This participative approach allowed us to retain the team through this difficult time, and committed them for the long term to the organization.

NELSON C. RISING
PRESIDENT AND CEO
MAGUIRE PROPERTIES, INC.

> "There is a direct correlation between one's willingness to accept
> accountability and strong human fundamentals—integrity,
> judgment, work ethic, and intelligence. We are comfortable with
> giving authority to our senior management and accept the fact
> they may make mistakes, so long as they acknowledge them and
> ultimately learn from them."

Maguire Properties is an office REIT based in Los Angeles. A veteran of more than 33 years in the real estate industry, Nelson Rising previously served as chairman and CEO of Catellus, an industrial REIT which was acquired by ProLogis. Over an 11-year period, Rising oversaw Catellus' successful evolution from a railroad land company to a diversified development company and ultimately its conversion to a REIT in 2004. He also is the chairman emeritus of the Real Estate

Roundtable, the most powerful public policy advocacy organization for the real es-
tate industry, and former chairman of the Federal Reserve Bank of San Francisco.

My priorities focused on two fundamental issues: the company's strategic
direction and attracting, retaining, and motivating our people to implement
it. Executing the strategy largely falls in the hands of our management team.
And I preferred to manage our people through a management by objective
process where we mutually set objectives, and then I provided autonomy to
them for making decisions. We found a direct correlation between one's willingness to accept accountability and strong human fundamentals—integrity,
judgment, work ethic, and intelligence. We are comfortable with giving
authority to our senior management and accept the fact they may make mistakes, so long as they acknowledge them and ultimately learn from them.

It is also an important part of the CEO's role to be an effective
spokesperson. The strategic, organizational, and spokesperson responsibilities are always prioritized depending upon the challenges facing any
particular organization. And no CEO incorporates all three of these as equal
strengths. Each leader needs to focus on what they do well and then hire
people who complement their weaknesses.

When I joined Catellus, it was a dysfunctional organization with a
badly broken model. The culture was paralyzed, not entrepreneurial—real
estate assets were utilized to serve the railroad. I had no idea of the challenge in front of me. I needed to understand the facts, have some sense of
how to move the business forward, and then identify the right talent to help
me achieve my objectives. I then had to attract these people and form them
into a management team. One key factor in my success is that I have never
been threatened by people and eagerly anticipated their contributions.

WARREN "NED" E. SPIEKER, JR.
PARTNER
SPIEKER PARTNERS

> *"I had the courage to let younger people run with their*
> *responsibilities, trying to support them. I told them it was okay*
> *to make mistakes. I would have killed the organization by*
> *micromanaging and second-guessing other's decisions."*

Ned Spieker left Trammell Crow in 1992 and built one of the most highly regarded
office and industrial development firms in the western United States. In 1998, he
took Spieker Properties public as a REIT, operating more than 250 properties with
40 million square feet. Equity Office Properties bought the firm in 2001.

My most important responsibility was reinforcing the firm's culture. As the
company grew, we needed strong people committed to achieving outstanding results. In essence, I tried to create a cult. It required considerable
face time, but I provided an historical perspective to new employees and
assumed hands-on responsibility for cultural orientation. I didn't want to
convey a bunch of platitudes, but people needed to understand that success
was about having a balanced life. I think workaholics are boring and unpro-
ductive people. The only way to communicate my message was to get out
into the regions and meet with people.

I also spent time tracking macroeconomic cycles. We were invested in
12 different markets, and we needed to understand their cyclical positions.
Was it time to buy, sell, or develop? As CEO, I examined the big picture and
ensured each region was functioning to the corporate plan. I stayed close
to the senior management team—obtaining everyone's input and getting
them to execute on the same page.

I learned a lot from Trammell Crow. Most importantly, he taught that
it's vital to share everything with your partners including money, responsibility, and credit. When Spieker went public, we shared stock options across

the company. Trammell also taught me what not to do. He always knew where the accelerator was but too often had trouble finding the brake. I happen to think the best offense is a good defense.

My greatest accomplishment was guiding and building a terrific organization, which truly worked as a team. We all believed in this concept of sharing. In managing the business, I had the courage to let younger people run with their responsibilities, trying to support them. I told them it was okay to make mistakes. I would have killed the organization by micromanaging and second-guessing others' decisions.

MARTIN "HAP" E. STEIN, JR.
CHAIRMAN AND CEO
REGENCY CENTERS CORPORATION

"I have had the good sense to provide the team with the responsibility and authority to realize our vision and build a great company."

Hap Stein has led Regency Centers, a leading owner and developer of grocery-anchored shopping centers, for more than two decades. Stein joined Regency Group, Inc., in 1976. He became president of the real estate division in 1981 and was appointed president and CEO in 1988. In 1993 Stein took the company public, growing the business from $150 million in assets to more than $3 billion in total capitalization.

One of my top priorities is spending quality time with our team, especially Regency's high performers. I reinforce Regency's strategy, mission, and values, and I articulate expectations, reward performance, and point out areas for improvement. Just as important, I can learn from them the challenges they're encountering. Second, I try to enhance relationships with our customers, including major retailers, development partners, property owners, and brokers. These parties control new investment opportunities and are key to our growth. Third, I spend a good amount of time with Regency's financial stakeholders, including investors and joint venture partners. We endeavor to be good stewards and are committed to transparency. If our stakeholders understand our strategy and are comfortable with our team, they will be more inclined to provide capital on a cost-effective basis when needed.

Culture is extremely important at Regency. We value customers, investors, and especially employees. I believe that engaged employees will better serve customers and create value for shareholders. My senior management team and I are dedicated to instituting Regency's values in everything we do.

I am most proud of the vision we have set for Regency to be the leading national owner, operator, and developer of grocery-anchored shopping centers. The key has been to assemble and motivate a talented and engaged team that shares Regency's core values and vision. I have had the good sense to provide the team with the responsibility and authority to realize our vision and build a great company.

THOMAS W. TOOMEY
PRESIDENT AND CEO
UNITED DOMINION REALTY TRUST

> *"I throw a lot of responsibility at people and see how they do. We have to be decentralized and give people as much responsibility as they can handle."*

Tom Toomey has been CEO of United Dominion Realty Trust (UDR) since 2001. He was recruited to reposition the firm, taking over from John McCann, a legend in the apartment business. The board of UDR thought enough of Toomey to relocate the company's headquarters from Richmond, Virginia, to Denver, where Toomey was living and working. Toomey has lived up to investors' expectations, turning around the business. Earlier he worked at AIMCO, a large multifamily REIT, and at Lincoln Property Company.

As our company's leader, my job is to provide strategic direction and empower people to do the best job they can to accomplish our objectives. So, I spend the majority of my time on cultural issues and developing my key people. I make sure that we execute our strategy appropriately and put out fires where necessary. I want my direct reports to be advocates for the organization and for the organization to look to me for direction and support—not micromanagement.

I throw a lot of responsibility at people and see how they do. We have to be decentralized and give people as much responsibility as they can handle. If they have a high energy level and good communications skills, I believe they can develop into strong leaders and decision makers.

Our organization will be successful if we view ourselves as winners and focus as a team executing our strategies and serving our customers. I want people proudly focused on working for the enterprise, not their boss in the organization. We need strong systems, good capital flows, and people development programs. Ultimately, we need to compensate and recognize people. And we need to be open to change. Today's approach may not be the right answer for the future. The best recognition programs and the best motivators derive from customer feedback on performance.

One of my greatest challenges was taking over for John McCann, who was a legend in the multifamily industry, and had built UDR virtually from scratch. I didn't want to alienate anyone, but I also recognized the need for change. I took aside everyone in senior management and readily admitted that I didn't know everything. These people were quite competent, and I wanted to discuss with them and agree upon business philosophy and prioritizing objectives. For me, it was a tightrope walk, but eventually it worked quite successfully, because everyone gave each other the benefit of the doubt.

_____

WILLIAM H. WALTON III
MANAGING MEMBER
ROCKPOINT GROUP, LLC

> *"We typically hire younger, smart, self-motivated people and*
> *give them lots of latitude and responsibility once they have*
> *demonstrated maturity and judgment. Our culture is fair but*
> *tough: people know what they need to accomplish."*

Bill Walton is a managing member of Rockpoint Group, LLC, a global real estate
investment management firm he cofounded in 2003. He also is a managing
member of Westbrook Real Estate Partners, LLC, a real estate investment man-
agement company he cofounded in 1994 after spending 15 years with Morgan
Stanley Realty.

High-performing real estate private equity companies create positive cultures, underpinned by hiring and retaining the right people. Professionals should be motivated, ambitious, and commercially minded, but balanced with integrity and high standards. Great companies don't seem to be composed of people motivated by money alone. Without this balance, it just won't work over the long term.

We almost always hire only people we know. Many of our initial hires worked with us at Morgan Stanley. We never bought solely experience, and we have been unwilling to compromise anyone's fit within the organization. We typically hire younger, smart, self-motivated people and give them lots of latitude and responsibility once they have demonstrated maturity and judgment. Our culture is fair but tough: people know what they need to accomplish. They get paid well, probably better than most in the industry, from generous equity participation.

High-performing firms proactively seek out investors who can provide not only investment capital, but who can also contribute in other ways. We think of our investors as true partners. We make our business transparent to our partners and strive to provide accurate, comprehensive, and regular reporting to them. We are fortunate to have developed a solid investment track record and, in any new fund that we raise, most of our investors have invested with us in prior funds.

In managing our business, we source and evaluate transactions and try to stay in front of potential operating partners. We are always thinking about the strategic mix in our business—the risks, asset mix, and geographic diversification. Since our people are mature and self-motivated, management of the enterprise doesn't take much time.

CHAPTER SIX

LEARN WHAT NOT TO DO

Learn what not to do" is all about maintaining a corporate focus and emphasizing the firm's core competency. It's all about understanding and concentrating on what works for the company—and more important, what doesn't. A company needs to be comfortable in its own skin. Not playing to a company's strengths may mean making mistakes. Leaders should stay the course but constantly challenge assumptions.

Avoid Distractions

"The best homebuilders have simple and straightforward objectives and stay away from experimenting with non-essential issues," says Dwight Schar of NVR Homes.

As management researcher Jim Collins notes in Good to Great, great companies focus equally on what to do—and what to stop doing. Great companies, he says, especially those that have turned themselves around, are like hedgehogs. They are simple, doughty creatures that know one big thing and stick to it. Unlike foxes, which are crafty, cunning animals that know many things and yet lack consistency, hedgehogs understand what they are deeply passionate about, what they can be best at, and what drives their economic engine.

Prevent Complacency

Part of learning what not to do is to keep an eye on the bottom line and avoid complacency. Wandering too far afield may have fiscal consequences. Stuart Miller, the chairman and chief executive officer of Lennar Corporation, another leading homebuilder, says, "I run this business with one foot on the brake, and the other on the accelerator." Complacency can kill any business—you can't take anything for granted. High-performing companies can never rest on their laurels. Fear of failure "is a constant" in high-performing companies, creating "a tenaciousness in culture" that pushes people "to do the business well," says Preston Butcher, CEO of commercial developer Legacy Partners.

See the Big Picture

Insularity, marked by building organizations only through internal growth, can lead to complacency and missed opportunities. "Continuity is important, but some new outside blood can rejuvenate businesses" and provide different perspectives, says John Johnson, president and CEO of Mortgage America, a residential mortgage lender. Leaders need to be constantly generating new ideas for the long term. Short-term decision making does not lead to an enduring high-performing business enterprise.

Concentrate on the Customer

Successful companies know what their customers want and meet or exceed their expectations. "We focus on doing the right thing for the client," says Rob Brennan of CS First Boston, one of the largest global CMBS players. Chief executives need to reach out and listen to customers, who can highlight perceived company strengths and weaknesses, identify staffing issues or product weaknesses, and generate ideas for new products or services. "High-performing firms in our space are client oriented and perform with integrity," says mortgage banker John Fowler of Holliday Fenoglio Fowler. "An adviser can never risk abusing client trust. We present the facts objectively, so that everyone involved can make an informed decision."

Make Decisions

High-performing CEOs recognize their responsibility to make tough decisions, even if those decisions are unpopular, and avoid skirting issues. Hearing people out and listening to different points of view helps them to grasp issues. "My style is collaborative, but I don't run a company as a democracy," says Tim Callahan, who has led two of the nation's biggest office REITs. "After hearing other people's insights, I must formulate my own conclusions." Winnowing out weak performers can raise particularly difficult personal conflicts, but taking action sends important signals to all employees.

Don't Let Issues Fester

CEOs need to bring management and business problems to the surface, then address and resolve them quickly. "Operate a company with substantial transparency and foster communications," says Lance Shaner of Shaner Hotel Group. "Issues will inevitably arise, but don't let them fester." Otherwise, they will become more time-consuming and destructive.

Take Responsibility

By taking responsibility for mistakes, leaders underscore the importance of accountability throughout the organization and help establish a strong value system for people to support each other, as well as encouraging collaboration. "Once a strategy is decided, leaders support other people's decisions, run interference where helpful, credit them for successes, and assume responsibility for failures," says Daniel Neidich, who headed the real estate private equity business at Goldman Sachs and recently cofounded his own private equity business, Dune Capital. Interestingly enough, too many companies fail because they lack focus and don't appreciate their core competencies. While this sounds simple, the roadway of business history is littered with the carnage of companies that had the potential to be great but tried to be too many things to too many people.

This concept is an interesting blend of ideas. A company must differentiate itself from its competition, yet there are qualities that all companies should emulate in order to be successful. Focusing on the customer and delivering results are important priorities for success in any business. Mike Brennan, formerly of First Industrial, points this out. "This is all part of seeing the big picture. Avoiding distractions is of equal importance. Then the leaders of an organization need to send to the right message. They need to avoid complacency, make decisions, and take responsibility. "Preston Butcher articulates it well. "There has to be tenaciousness in the culture, starting with the CEO." A work ethic and the willingness to make tough decisions is all part of leadership, as both Debbie Cafaro and Tim Callahan emphasize. It's okay to acknowledge that the future is uncertain and the firm can be both cautious and proactive, as Stuart Miller of Lennar acknowledges.

THOMAS F. AUGUST
EXECUTIVE VICE PRESIDENT AND CHIEF OPERATING OFFICER
BEHRINGER HARVARD REAL ESTATE INVESTMENTS

"The key in this business is to remain as focused as possible and differentiate your organization from competitors in the public markets."

Prentiss Properties was a REIT with interests in office and industrial properties in metropolitan areas across the United States, including Dallas, Chicago, Houston, San Diego, Sacramento, and Washington, D.C. Tom August served as president, CEO, and trustee of Prentiss until its 2005 acquisition by Brandywine. He had

*been president and chief operating officer of Prentiss since its initial public offering
in 1996. He joined Behringer Harvard in 2008.*

I spent a tremendous amount of my time with investors. At Prentiss, ours
was a conservative organization, focused on the management and leasing of
assets. We tried to concentrate everyone on the success of the firm. My style
was to be consensus driven, and I wanted to be kept informed to limit surprises as much as possible. I pushed the team-oriented environment hard,
and I tried to stay visible and accessible. As much as possible, I visited with
all levels of our people. Communication was critical. We hosted quarterly
teleconferences in which everyone in the company could hear from me for
20 minutes, about the company's strategy and performance, and then I an-
swered questions for the next half-hour. We transformed our company from
one of the best real estate deal shops in the industry, pursuing the flavor of
the day, into a must-own stock.

Mike Prentiss and I had a good partnership. My style and financial
background better prepared me for running a public company, while Mike
is a great entrepreneur. Together we brought a more disciplined and more
focused approach to managing the business. We reduced the number of
markets in which we did business from 19 to seven. Also, we focused on
the office business and moved away from industrial markets, selling more
than 10 million square feet of assets. The key in this business is to remain
as focused as possible and to differentiate your organization among your
competitors in the public markets.

KEITH F. BARKET

MANAGING DIRECTOR–REAL ESTATE

ANGELO, GORDON & CO., LP

> *"Investors recognize our approach and appreciate it. They
> understand we know how to add value by operating assets,
> in addition to using our financial skills. We make money
> by partnering with smart, local entrepreneurs who are good
> operators and who help us to significantly improve the
> performance of an asset."*

*Keith Barket is a senior managing director of Angelo, Gordon and a member of the
firm's five-person executive committee. He joined Angelo, Gordon in 1997 and oversees
the firm's global real estate activities. He has more than 20 years of direct real estate
ownership and operating experience, involving more than $10 billion in assets. Before
joining Angelo, Gordon, he was one of the firm's first real estate operating partners.*

Downturns have taught me that you can't control the cycles, but you can try
to protect your business. We buy assets at a discount to replacement cost and
make money by adding value—i.e., significantly improving operations and
cash flow. Because of this approach, we believe that we can make money even
when the economy turns against us. However, we are not afraid to sit on the
sidelines when pricing is unreasonable or we can't find assets at discounts
to replacement cost. I am fully prepared to wait out the cycle. Investors in
Angelo, Gordon recognize and appreciate this approach. They understand
that we know how to operate assets and leverage our financial skills.

Part of my success relates to the fact that I grew up in the real estate
business. I've leased office space, renovated apartments, and worked on
single-family construction sites for my father since I was ten years old. I
know all aspects of operating and renovating real estate assets and my team
at Angelo, Gordon & Co. has those same skills. I've kept our organization
flat—we have lots of informal communication but few meetings. I'm

comfortable making quick decisions, and we get answers to our partners promptly and stick by our commitments. I push accountability down into the organization and give people responsibility at an early age. We have regional teams around the world who run their businesses. I also don't believe in separating acquisitions and asset management. Our acquisitions people must live with the deals they buy, and I believe that the best people are attracted to a business model in which they are accountable and responsible for their investments.

As a leader, you have to know what to look for in people and your partners. I want people who are smart, entrepreneurial, and driven. They need to have a passion for real estate and need to be motivated to excel. I like a self-made person, one who demonstrates commitment. Those who can't move quickly and make decisions aren't the right ones for this organization. The same is true for our operating partners. I am not interested in an empire builder with a map of the United States with pins in every major city. I like operating partners who are focused on making money by adding value to real estate, not by collecting management fees.

Success is about intensely studying and understanding the facts and then making a decision based on what you know, not what others tell you. You have to have conviction to make your own decisions even if they are contrary to the herd.

BRYCE BLAIR
CHAIRMAN, PRESIDENT, AND CEO
AVALONBAY COMMUNITIES, INC.

"My approach is to be clear on our direction, and remain laser-focused on our execution."

AvalonBay Communities, Inc., is in the business of developing, redeveloping, acquiring, and managing high-quality apartment communities in the high-barrier-to-entry markets of the United States. Bryce Blair oversees the

development, construction, acquisition, and management of more than $10 billion
of multifamily assets.

From my perspective, there are two leadership styles. One is a dominant or autocratic leader, where the CEO perseveres through sheer will. The other would be what Jim Collins in his book Good to Great calls "level 5 leadership." Collins describes level 5 leaders as leaders who, while incredibly ambitious, are focused on the company's success, not their own directly. They try to approach these goals with a sense of personal humility and try to give as much credit to others as possible. While I certainly have work to do, I try to emulate the latter leadership style.

My approach is to be clear on our direction and remain laser-focused on our execution. I strongly believe that with focus comes results. Being an engineer by training and having started my career in management consulting, where a framework is first established and then a solution is determined, I have always taken a disciplined approach to business. I try not to be directive in style, but my approach is to gain selective input and then reach a decision. I would much rather have a poor strategy and execute it well then have a great strategy poorly executed.

I have always been a competitive person, and I challenge the organization to perform at a very high level. I tend to be an individual who is never satisfied and always encourage our people to not become complacent. I find that good people perform better when the bar is always raised. During my early part of my career with Trammell Crow Residential, I saw firsthand the power of a highly decentralized organization. It empowered the individuals to run the regions in the manner they saw best. It was very low on bureaucracy, and corporate largely stayed out of the way. At AvalonBay, we have tried to take the best of a decentralized culture and combine it with the leverage and power of some specialized centralized functions in order to take advantage of our scale and brand.

We have three core values at Avalon Bay. They are a commitement to integrity, a spirit of caring, and a focus on continuous improvement. Each of these core values is very important to AvalonBay and to me personally, and I try to incorporate them into the way I manage and lead. Integrity is so important in all businesses, particularly in real estate, and our focus on continuous improvement drives us to do better every time we approach something.

Dick Micheaux, who was my mentor and one of the founders of AvalonBay, also taught me the importance of a balanced life. As he was fond of saying, "I love to come to work, and I love going home each night." He also never took himself too seriously. He was constantly the butt of jokes, typically at his own urging.

Our culture at AvalonBay is extraordinarily important to our success. I must admit that early on, I underestimated the value of a strong culture and how important it is in helping us select, train, and motivate our associates. We have built a strong culture and a strong brand, and they support one another. Our associates are proud of our brand; they are proud to wear our company logo and to be called "Avalonians."

In identifying one of the most important attributes for potential new hires, we look at what the traits are of the most successful associates at AvalonBay. We found that competitive spirit is important, as is a strong intellect and problem-solving capabilities. And finally, we hire for attitude—positive attitude.

H. ERIC BOLTON, JR.
CHAIRMAN AND CEO
MID-AMERICA APARTMENT COMMUNITIES, INC.

> *"New leadership needed to provide focus and establish credibility and respect among the company's constituents."*

Mid-America is a multifamily REIT with investments primarily in the South and Southeast. Bolton joined Mid-America in 1994 and was promoted to chief operating officer, and later to chairman and CEO. He spent the earlier part of his career with Trammell Crow.

I focus most of my time on formulating and implementing our strategy, as well as monitoring our current operations. I'm committed to building relationships with our employees and mentoring their development, thus I also work to ensure I am devoting time to building human resource capital for our company.

A very important aspect of our culture as a service organization is to support and serve associates who work on the front lines at our properties. Property management and the service side of what we do are extraordinarily important to the long-term success of our company, and staying in touch with our properties is important. After all, our associates at the properties are the ones affecting our customers on a daily basis. Building and fostering a service-minded culture, with servant leadership principles setting the tone, is very important to our success.

One of the bigger challenges that I believe a new company leader can face is assuming responsibility for a company when its founder retires. That's a high-risk event. Questions surrounding company direction, organizational structure, future opportunities, and the likelihood of future success will all exist, regardless of how carefully the transition is planned. Our company was formed in 1979, and our public offering took place in 1992. Our founder retired in 2001. The organization's culture, track record, and much of our identity was tied up with the company's founder. Our various constituents—shareholders, employees, lenders, and tenants—needed assurance that certain company qualities and attributes would prevail.

However, while providing some assurances of stability during a time of transition, I think it is important that new leadership establishes its own credibility and respect among the company's constituents. It's important to build confidence quickly among the company's constituents when leadership transition occurs. I feel like we've been able to do that but also recognize that confidence in leadership is something that needs to be earned and reinforced continuously.

MICHAEL W. BRENNAN
FORMER PRESIDENT AND CEO
FIRST INDUSTRIAL REALTY TRUST, INC.

> *"If you stay focused on your customer, your strategy falls
> right into place."*

*Starting out as a private real estate investor on the south side of Chicago and then
working as an investment broker for CB Richard Ellis, Mike Brennan moved on
to become a cofounder of First Industrial (NYSE: FR), a publicly traded REIT. In
1998, Brennan was named president and CEO, and the company now owns and
manages more than 100 million square feet of industrial space across the United
States and Canada. In 2008, Brennan left First Industrial.*

I've had a number of mentors in my life. Jay Shidler, First Industrial's chairman, taught me innovative ways to structure complex transactions to satisfy
the particular needs of customers—creating value in the process. Mike
Tomasz, the former CEO of First Industrial, showed me the importance
of being entrepreneurial and how to uncover new investment opportunities.
At First Industrial, I also realized just how critically important it is to recruit
the best talent. Integrity, customer knowledge, investment acumen, and
market experience are the primary attributes we look for when hiring
new employees.

   We had an open, candid, and supportive culture at First Industrial, and
we wanted employees who have the courage of their convictions. "Robust
dialogue" was encouraged because it created new ideas—and you can never
have enough good ideas. We motivated our employees to be entrepreneurial
by giving investment officers a percentage of the profits that they produced.
And very importantly, a significant percentage of their incentive compensation was paid in restricted stock, which vested over three years just like it did
for senior management. So our employees' compensation was directly tied
with shareholders' interests, as well as those of our customers.

Our best new investment opportunity was repeat business or a referral from an existing customer. We prided ourselves on serving customers, and we made it a cornerstone of our company to have the highest customer service scores in our sector.

If you stay focused on your customer, your strategy falls right into place. The first step in establishing the strategic direction of the company was to identify the major factors that were driving customer demand. Since client needs are always changing, you have to stay on top of customer trends to remain at least one step ahead. Next, you need to align the company's resources behind the major factors driving demand. This often involves change within the organization. Managing change is the biggest challenge I've encountered as a leader, because it creates anxiety for employees. The best way I have found to address this challenge is to regularly communicate the strategic direction of the company and the rationale behind our decision making. If your people understand where you want to go and how you plan to get there, they'll be much more receptive to making the necessary changes to achieve the company's objectives.

When you realign and grow the resources of your company to satisfy customer needs, you are simultaneously enhancing the company's franchise value because you are building stronger customer relationships. In doing so, you create a company that can achieve sustainable long-term growth and favorable returns that reward the owners of the company—the ultimate goal for the leader of any company.

ROBERT P. BRENNAN, JR.

MANAGING DIRECTOR–GLOBAL HEAD, REAL ESTATE
    FINANCE SECURITIZATION
CREDIT SUISSE

> *"I go out of my way to promote and acknowledge success in*
> *the business, and we are unwilling to hire professionals that*
> *might disrupt our culture. We focus on doing the right thing*
> *for the client, as well as the firm, and in the process, respecting*
> *each other."*

Rob Brennan is global head of the Real Estate Finance and Securitization Group
at Credit Suisse, overseeing origination, securitization, and distribution of CMBS
and other real estate–related products. He is a member of the Investment Banking
Management Council and the Fixed-Income Operating Committee and sits on the
board of Column Financial, the Bank's commercial mortgage conduit. Brennan
is on the Board of Governors of the Commercial Mortgage Securities Association
and is a member of the Real Estate Roundtable.

I focus the majority of my time on trying to determine how to make money
and drive the profitability of the group. Our capital is allocated to pursue arbitrage opportunities and market inefficiencies across the broad spectrum of
real estate assets all around the world. I have to understand the downside to
pursue these opportunities successfully. I'm very comfortable with the risk
elements of our business; having been a trader and later running trading
desks has been a tremendous help in that regard. I also think it has helped
create significant credibility for me with my people and within the firm.

I get highly involved in the business and try to spend time with borrowers and investors. Increasingly, however, I spend more and more time
internally with my team. I am constantly reviewing performance data and
deciding how to organize our human and financial capital to pursue the
best opportunities. I have come to realize that my best clients are the people

who work for me, and that my highest and best use is in creating an environment in which talented people really believe they can succeed.

Although we had a strong culture at my former firm, DLJ, we've had to work hard to establish a new culture at Credit Suisse that reflected the realities of the merger between DLJ and Credit Suisse. I go out of my way to promote and acknowledge success in the business, and we are unwilling to hire professionals who might disrupt our culture. We focus on doing the right thing for the client, as well as the firm, and in the process, respecting each other. It is important for our people to recognize that there are internal clients who need to be satisfied as well. Now, with the heightened focus on risk management, credit, and a variety of governance issues, our people have to contribute to a cooperative and respectful internal culture. It can no longer be "front line versus back office."

I learned a lot when my former partner, Don McKinnon, left the firm and Steve Kantor asked me to step up and run the entire CMBS business. I assumed additional responsibilities for credit, structuring, and originations. Earlier in my career, I had a reputation as a hotheaded trader, and Steve taught me how to balance all considerations and try to understand everyone's motivation. This was partly a maturation process. I try to listen to a variety of people and treat numerous constituencies fairly. I've learned to be humble and admit that I don't know everything. I try to learn from people's feedback. At the end of the day, I've picked the right people to run the business and have been comfortable in promoting people who have strengths greater than my own. We've also been successful in trimming the dead weight and identifying and promoting high performers.

Ultimately, people have trusted me and bought into my management style. And we've obviously been successful in making Credit Suisse a leader in the league tables. But I measure our real success in two other ways: we have created a highly profitable business that has grown exponentially over the years, and we have built a team of incredible talent that has been together for the better part of a decade—very unusual for Wall Street.

PRESTON BUTCHER
CEO
LEGACY PARTNERS, INC.

> *"High-performing companies live in a constant fear of failure,*
> *and our people are always trying to execute and assess risk.*
> *There is a tenaciousness to the culture."*

Legacy Partners, a real estate development and management firm, specializes in the acquisition, development, and management of commercial and residential real estate in the western United States. Since its inception, Legacy Partners Commercial has acquired or developed more than 60 million square feet of commercial property at a cost of $5.5 billion. Legacy Partners Residential has acquired or developed 66,000 residential housing units at a cost of $4.4 billion. Preston Butcher has led Legacy since it spun off from Lincoln Property Company in 1998.

My leadership style changes depending on where the company stands in its cycle. From 1969 to 1989, I watched the numbers very closely and took a very hands-on approach to the business. From 1990 to 1994, at the height of the recession, I did everything possible to stay alive. And since 1994, I have reinvented the business and have two people running our multifamily and commercial divisions. I delegate to them and focus my energies on our strategic issues, such as where the economy is headed and where the industry is headed by city. I carefully monitor our cash flows, overhead, and the risk profile of each deal. The balance of my time is spent walking the halls and interfacing with various people in our organization. My approach is much more hands off today, and fortunately, I work on whatever I want to.

Our company has been successful because we aggressively seek individuals with positive energy and a positive attitude. High-performing companies live in a constant fear of failure, and our people are always trying to execute and assess risk. There is a tenaciousness to the culture. I want my people to be comfortable making mistakes, because they understand the reality of the deal, both the upside and the downside. We are known as a firm that will step up and take a measurable risk, which is extraordinarily important in the development business. All of our key people have project ownership. We sincerely try to promote a culture in which people like to have fun and they are genuinely nice.

Great leaders learn from their experiences. If anything has taught me the value of relationships and following through on what you promise, it's been the industry cycles. The most difficult time of my life was 1974 and 1975. All of our development projects were highly leveraged, and I had personal guarantees on the loans. The economy was awful, as was the real estate business. Our company survived by restructuring our transactions with the various lenders and equity partners. We survived because of our trustworthiness and the integrity we demonstrated in trying to make our situation a win-win for myself, my lenders, and everyone else involved.

DEBRA A. CAFARO
CHAIRMAN, PRESIDENT, AND CEO
VENTAS, INC.

> *"I try to be honest, do the right thing, work hard, and encourage a team orientation."*

Debra Cafaro joined Ventas, Inc. as CEO and president in March 1999 just as the REIT, an owner of nursing homes and health care facilities, faced a crisis. The company's main tenant, Vencor Inc., a health care provider, was insolvent and on the verge of filing for bankruptcy protection. Ventas' stock was one of the worst-performing REITs. A former real estate, corporate, and finance lawyer, Cafaro took charge and was able to turn the company around.

Success in the seniors' housing and health care business is a long-term game. You need a strong management team in place that has experience in the sector. Compensation must be aligned with investors, using a significant equity component. Given the intensity and passion with which we pursue this business, compensation must provide a strong upside. Our culture is similar to an investment bank but probably more collegial. We run a flat organization with few employees, because we own but do not operate our assets. People make sacrifices, but they feel they are part of a successful enterprise. Of equal importance is maintaining a good balance sheet and not becoming overleveraged. Our cost of capital, whether it is debt or equity, needs to be continuously competitive.

While leadership priorities constantly change depending where a business is in its evolution, I focus my time in a few critical areas. When I joined Ventas, I had to restructure the business and recapitalize the balance sheet. Next, I focused on growth, put a strategy in place, and hired a management team. Now I am focused on developing a performance-based culture and leading by example. I find that people like to see the path, so I set clear objectives and constantly repeat them. I try to be honest, do the right thing, work hard, and encourage a team orientation. In my people, I look for confidence, consistent performance, intelligence, integrity, and a strong work ethic.

I am very proud of the way that our management team has turned around Ventas. I am the first to admit that some luck has played its part, and the REIT bull market has helped. But we have been successful because we benefited from a great team of advisers, including our board members. I also have extraordinary fortitude. There were many people opposed to our restructuring effort, ranging from the banks to our debt holders, tenants, and even the U.S. government. But my legal and personal background gave me the inner toughness and negotiating skills to get through. Through the pressure, we always carefully evaluated our options, made decisions, and stuck by them.

While I am always involved in analyzing deals and acquiring assets, I spend a lot of time studying trends and understanding where investment opportunities reside. I involve my board and my management team in strategic decision making, and then we agree on goals and monitor our achievement.

TIMOTHY H. CALLAHAN
PARTNER
CALLAHAN CAPITAL PARTNERS

> *"I don't run the company as a democracy. I like to hear other*
> *people's insights, and then formulate my own conclusions.*
> *But it is important that I have a management team to whom*
> *I can delegate."*

Tim Callahan headed Trizec Properties from 2002 until 2006, when it was
acquired by Brookfield Properties and The Blackstone Group. Trizec Properties
ranked behind Equity Office as the nation's second largest office REIT, with more
than 50 properties totaling 37 million square feet. From 1996 through 2002, Cal-
lahan served as president and CEO of Equity Office Properties. After the acquisi-
tion by Trizec, he formed a private investment firm, Callahan Capital Partners.

I pull the senior management team from across the country together on
at least a quarterly basis and communicate where the company is today
and where it needs to be. I put a premium on communication, whether it's
through a regular newsletter to employees, a national employee conference
call, or a specific group or one-on-one meeting. My style is collaborative,
but I don't run the company as a democracy. I like to hear other people's
insights and then formulate my own conclusions. But it is important that
I have a management team to whom I can delegate. Consequently, I have
high expectations as that relates to accountability. I want to be viewed as
accessible and fostering an open culture. I spend a lot of time in one-on-
one conversations.

CEOs have to be adaptable and flexible, not only due to changing
business environments but also as their companies grow and evolve. I
believe very strongly that cycles of change will happen much more quickly
in the future. And as the economy becomes more global, the U.S. economy
will be affected, and this will have a domino effect relative to our business.

These incidents may range from terrorist attacks to financial crises in various parts of the world. These global challenges bring a wider variety of risks and change. Managing risk will be extraordinarily important.

TIMOTHY R. ELLER
FORMER CHAIRMAN AND CEO
CENTEX CORPORATION

> *"I strongly believe in the value of encouraging focus and collaboration. These attributes are at the heart of leading a successful business enterprise."*

Centex Corporation, founded in 1950, is one of the nation's leading homebuilding companies. Centex operates in major U.S. markets in 25 states. Tim Eller joined Centex in 1973 and was appointed chairman, president, and CEO of the NYSE-listed company in 2004. Pulte and Centex announced their intention to merge in April 2009.

My role was to ensure that the organization knew where to focus its energies. I spent quite a bit of time keeping my executive leaders and division presidents informed and aligned. Part of that effort included crisp messaging to keep everyone on point. It also involved plenty of listening. Building homes is, after all, a very local enterprise. It pays to listen closely to the field. Along with focus, we placed a heightened importance on collaboration—across functions and geographies—to ensure we shared information and best practices. Combined, focus and collaboration are key levers to leading performance.

I have been through six housing cycles in my career, so I've seen the value that leadership can bring to not only excelling during the good times, but also gaining ground when the markets are.

JOHN P. FOWLER
VICE CHAIRMAN OF THE BOARD OF DIRECTORS
HFF INC.
EXECUTIVE MANAGING DIRECTOR
HOLLIDAY FENOGLIO FOWLER LP

> *"We have a culture in place where people work together to*
> *determine the best solutions for clients. This culture of trust*
> *and teamwork is unique in the brokerage business."*

Holliday Fenoglio Fowler L.P. is a leading national commercial real estate and
capital markets services firm and a wholly owned subsidiary of HFF Inc. John
Fowler, one of the founding partners, oversees the company's New York, Boston,
and Chicago offices, working on major commercial financing, equity, and sales
transactions, and heads up the firm's exploratory international expansion initia-
tive. In the past 20 years, he has successfully completed close to 700 real estate
transactions valued at well over $15 billion, in all property types.

High-performing firms in our space are client oriented and try to do everything with integrity. An adviser can never run the risk of abusing the trust
of a client. We present the facts objectively, so that everyone involved can
make an informed decision. High-performing companies also have a broad
leadership platform and ideally represent the different constituencies within
a firm. In addition, high performers keep their talent. Most of our people
have been with us for 15 to 25 years. They started as analysts and work their
way up. We have a culture in place where people work together to determine the best solutions for clients. This culture of trust and teamwork is
unique in the brokerage business. What's even more remarkable, we have
held onto people even though our company experienced four ownership
changes in five years.

I split my time between thinking strategically about how to grow the
business, recruiting high-quality people, and cultivating clients. The stra-

tegic process is inclusive by nature. I believe in collaborating with our senior management team. I try to spend time talking with people throughout the organization and encourage our team orientation, putting the client's interest ahead of everyone else's.

DANIEL S. FULTON
PRESIDENT
WEYERHAEUSER COMPANY

> *"The reason we've been successful is that we've allowed each*
> *of these firms to remain relatively entrepreneurial, after we've*
> *purchased them. They have a high emotional attachment to what*
> *they do, and we don't require a significant amount of conformity*
> *across our homebuilding companies."*

Weyerhaeuser Company is involved in real estate development, homebuilding, industrial and rural land sales, and financial services. Dan Fulton was appointed president and CEO of Weyerhaeuser Real Estate Company, a wholly owned subsidiary of Weyerhaeuser, in May 2001 and named to the Weyerhaeuser Company's senior management team in April 2003. He was appointed president of the parent company in 2008. His long-term tenure with the organization began when he joined Weyerhaeuser in 1976.

Within the real estate group at Weyerhaeuser, we own and operate five homebuilding businesses, as well as a finance organization. I've always believed that homebuilding is a local business, where the day-to-day operations of the business must be run by local operators. These entrepreneurs clearly understand the value proposition and what must be done strategically. In contrast, our corporate team at Weyerhaeuser provides sponsorship and the infrastructure for these leaders to run and build their businesses. For example, we have the capacity to buy land, which over the longer term will allow them to make money.

The reason we've been successful is that we've allowed each of these firms to remain relatively entrepreneurial after we've purchased them. They have a high emotional attachment to what they do, and we don't require a significant amount of conformity across our homebuilding companies. The homebuilding business is a competitive one. Entrepreneurs want the flexibility and autonomy to run and grow their businesses. Unlike many big companies, we allow them to do that.

We don't attract people for whom compensation is the primary driver. People who become part of our organization—and most of the senior management teams have been here for 30 years—are attracted by our culture. We tell our people that it's okay to make mistakes. Our senior managers are called "principals," reflecting my respect for their contribution and acknowledgment of what I view to be our peer relationship.

My successor will face different challenges in the business than I have. Because Wall Street always likes to understand how the real estate business at Weyerhaeuser is faring, my successor will have to spend much more time interfacing with investors. This requires a special expertise. And homebuilding will change in the future. It will become more like a manufacturing business. Public companies will continue to consolidate, and issues such as supply chain management, construction efficiencies, customer service, operational excellence, and sales/cycle times will make the homebuilding business much more homogenized. It will be about a process, delivering homes. With this push toward conformity, my successor can't destroy the entrepreneurial spirit now established in our homebuilding businesses; otherwise, my guess is that you'll see a marked change in the performance of these entrepreneurial businesses.

THOMAS GARBUTT
MANAGING DIRECTOR AND HEAD
TIAA-CREF GLOBAL REAL ESTATE

"It is extraordinarily important to define one's culture. At TIAA-CREF, client-centric is the culture."

As a seller, purchaser, shareholder, and lender, the TIAA-CREF organization is one of the most active real estate investors; its professionals have an extensive network of real estate relationships. TIAA-CREF is the largest U.S. tax-exempt real estate manager, with more than $69 billion in assets under management as of March 31, 2008, including all five property types for broad diversification. Thomas Garbutt is responsible for the firm's global real estate activities, including acquisitions, sales, research, business development, product development, and portfolio and asset management. He has more than of 25 years of experience in the real estate finance and investment industry.

As I assumed responsibility for the real estate business at TIAA-CREF, I moved forward according to a couple of important tenets. First of all, I always assume that change is constant, and those who remain stagnant are not successful. I'm also convinced that the successful leaders hire smart, dedicated people and then delegate to them. The traditional patriarchal approach to management in the real estate business doesn't work any more for large-scale operations. Your people's goals need to be aligned with the overarching enterprise goals, and then you need to let your leadership team move ahead, with periodic direction and feedback.

To be successful over the long term, it is important to define one's culture. At TIAA-CREF, client-centric is the culture. We built the business around serving our clients, and we know we must exceed their investment objectives and service expectations. Our professional team members understand that they serve multiple masters and that they must serve all clients in an equally outstanding manner. We've structured our platform to

accomplish just that. And we've raised the bar for everyone. We've selected people to move into senior roles who understand the importance of
performance and service, and who have extensive experience and relationships across geographic markets and property types. We've also hired junior
people into the firm who have come out of strong client service–oriented
organizations.

Even our compensation programs are client focused. We pay people
relative to fund investment performance, as well as client satisfaction. In
building the TIAA-CREF real estate platform, I've tried to learn from a variety of competing firms by deploying aspects of their business models which
I believe represent best in class into ours.

We also look to lead in how we manage the properties in our portfolio. We announced an energy efficiency initiative in 2008, through which
we are working to implement no- and low-cost ways to reduce our energy
use—thereby creating additional value for our tenants, as well as our clients,
through reduced operating costs and improved quality of life.

The challenge for me and my peers in the industry today is building a
true global platform. That requires having the right leadership team in place
that can manage a multicultural team spread across many time zones. It's
also crucial to make the organization feel global and not like an aggregation of field offices. We are seeing more commitment to this goal and a few
firms, along with TIAA-CREF, are creatively approaching this challenge. For
example, one of the major U.S.-based real estate asset management firms
has its CEO residing in its U.K. office, and a major REIT moves its executive
team to one of its non-U.S. locations each summer. These are terrific ways
to build a global culture that is sensitized to clients and local staff.

RON HAVNER
VICE CHAIRMAN, PRESIDENT, AND CEO
PUBLIC STORAGE

> *"I keep an eye on the operating side of the business. I'm fond of*
> *saying, 'What gets inspected, gets respected.' In short, an analysis*
> *of our existing business creates other opportunities."*

Public Storage, a REIT which is the largest self-storage company in the United
States, owns more than 2,200 storage facilities in 38 states and seven European
nations. Public Storage recently acquired Shurgard Storage Centers, Inc., a REIT
about half its size. Ron Havner has served as CEO since 2002.

I tend to prioritize my time on the high-value projects, whether it's an
acquisition candidate or raising capital. These are areas where I can truly
add value. I also keep an eye on the operating side of the business. I'm fond
of saying, "What gets inspected, gets respected." In short, an analysis of our
existing business creates other opportunities. I go out of my way to communicate with our various constituencies including investors, our board,
and our people. I depend on our senior management team to focus on the
strategic issues affecting our business, and I constantly ask, "Why are we
doing this?" At the end of the day, the strategy has to be complemented by
a value system, and in our case, there is a focus on quality. We are a team
that works together.

As CEO, you need to take responsibility for what happens. I can
remember a situation where we experienced material corporate underper-
formance. I took responsibility for the problems on our various investor
conference calls. It didn't make any sense to make excuses, and I needed
to take responsibility. I'm a big Warren Buffet fan, and I learned from him;
when Salomon Brothers had their problems, he offered to make the whole
situation right. When things go wrong and you're the CEO, you have to
show humility and vulnerability. That takes strength.

STEVEN J. HILTON
CHAIRMAN AND CEO
MERITAGE HOMES CORPORATION

"I recognize I can't run this business alone, and I've built a team around me that complements my strengths and weaknesses."

Steve Hilton cofounded Arizona-based Monterey Homes in 1985. Under Hilton's leadership, Monterey became publicly traded and merged with Legacy Homes in 1997. The combined organization rebranded as Meritage Homes Corporation (NYSE: MTH). The company designs, builds, and sells attached and detached homes in the southern and western United States.

In the homebuilding industry, success means having a vision. Actually, it's true in any business. As Wayne Gretzky said, "You need to know where the puck's going to be, not where it is." A successful leader needs to be a risk taker and think ahead. Consolidation in any industry, including home-building, will not create the barriers to entry that many think. Smaller firms will still be able to compete quite effectively in selective niches. The bigger question in homebuilding is whether technology will change. We've been building houses the same way for 30 years. Will someone figure out how to build houses off site? And if so, our true competition in the future won't be other homebuilders but rather manufacturers with foresight.

Even though I'm fairly conservative, I've always been an entrepre-neur, and that's stood me in good stead. A tailwind has helped build this business, over the last 13 years, from a standstill to $3 billion—we've been good, but we've also been lucky. Now we have to take it to $6 billion. To help us, I set a goal to change our culture by developing a new mission and value statement. I am embarking on a 14-city roadshow to share this with our people. Like most homebuilders, we've had a lot of business success focused on short-term results. From listening to feedback from our employ-ees, it is clear we need to be more sensitive to their needs and wants. Our middle-management level especially has not benefited economically nearly as much as members of the senior team. We need to breed more loyalty through training and development, and ensure that middle managers understand that customer satisfaction is critical to the success of our business.

I've never been a rock star CEO—the company is not all about me. I like to operate more behind the scenes and pride myself on being decisive yet pragmatic. I'm a blend of aggressive and conservative. I recognize I can't run this business by myself and built a team around me that complements my strengths and weaknesses. As we have grown, we have been challenged to maintain our entrepreneurial, decentralized management structure—and at the same time to grow our centralized corporate infrastructure in finance, legal, and human resources to support our operations.

All entrepreneurs think of times when they could have lost control of their business. I can remember the spring of 1991, when the United States was involved in the first Persian Gulf War. I was out one weekend having bagels and coffee with my father. I told him if we didn't sell some homes this month, we'd be out of business. And then the war ended very quickly, the country was jubilant, consumer confidence returned, and we began selling houses. The point of the story is that you need perseverance as well as a little luck.

JOHN B. JOHNSON
PRESIDENT AND CEO
MORTGAGEAMERICA, INC.

> *"I try to allow my people to run their businesses on a decentralized and autonomous basis. It's not always easy, however, since I'm an entrepreneur by background."*

MortgageAmerica is a mortgage banking firm engaged in the origination and servicing of residential real estate loans in the Southeast. Founded by John Johnson and his good friend and mentor, Dr. Harry L. Phillips, in 1978, MortgageAmerica prides itself on delivering "outrageous customer service."

I've tried to create a culture in which people actively participate in business decisions. We've enjoyed tremendous continuity in the business, but I get concerned that we can occasionally become too complacent and may need to be rejuvenated by outside blood.

I'm constantly thinking about new products and customer needs. For example, in the late 1970s when I founded this company, we were the first mortgage business in Alabama to offer adjustable rate mortgages. It's important to have an aggressive firm that does the right thing by consumers. I try to allow my people to run their businesses on a decentralized and autonomous basis. It's not always easy, however, since I'm an entrepreneur by background. I'm also keenly focused on controlling expenses.

As for other innovations for customers, I can remember a reengineering exercise of ours in the early 1990s. Following the refinancing boom in 1986, the business went flat from 1989 to 1991. We continued business as usual, but it wasn't working that well. The loan approval process in the days before automated underwriting was taking much longer than 15 days. We were trying to be perfect in the process, asking for too much information, and everyone was irritated, including borrowers, real estate agents, and brokers. We made a strategic decision to move underwriting to the branch offices to speed up reviews. It took a new branch manager one week to make the transformation, while other veteran managers took up to three years. Nonetheless, I was persistent and pushed people to make decisions in hours and minutes, rather than in days and weeks. Ultimately, everyone made the transition. The cultural transformation allowed the company not only to handle more business, but also to deal with all parties in a much more satisfactory fashion. The change paid big dividends, given the huge increase of volumes achieved in 2001, 2002, and 2003. We, in essence, doubled our volume without adding a significant number of people.

MICHAEL J. KULA

SENIOR VICE PRESIDENT, CONSUMER REAL ESTATE

BANK OF AMERICA

> *"In the residential mortgage business, leaders of successful*
> *organizations need to have passion. They must stay committed*
> *to a strategy and manage through the cycles, which can be quite*
> *severe in our business. I call it controlled chaos."*

Bank of America's Consumer Real Estate and Insurance Services Group has two
primary businesses: first mortgages and home equity. The first-mortgage business in-
cludes origination, fulfillment, and servicing of first-mortgage loan products. The home
equity business includes lines of credit and second mortgages. Before joining Bank of
America in 2004, Kula had worked for Washington Mutual and PNC Mortgage.

In the residential mortgage business, leaders of successful organizations
need to have passion. They must stay committed to a strategy and manage
through cycles, which can be quite severe in our business. I call it controlled
chaos. Sometimes the market imposes chaos, and other times, the leadership team pushes chaos. Typically, success in our business is about one's
ability to get to the market quickly. You need to have a management team
that is balanced with technical talent as well as with general management
talent. They complement each other, and both are necessary for success.

Micromanagement is unacceptable. You need to set the rules of
engagement and then do an incredible job at communicating. I do believe
strongly that a business only gets better if people are hired who are superior
to the current management team.

From a cultural perspective, we try to blend accountability with a human touch. Balance is both important and necessary. Any business franchise
is fragile, and especially one in a very cyclical industry such as mortgage
banking. This business requires an experienced leadership team. Regardless of
what others have said, there's too much risk and volatility to learn on the job.

BENJAMIN V. LAMBERT
CHAIRMAN
EASTDIL SECURED LLC

> *"Our professionals always put the clients first and don't allow
> any territorial or other jealousies to get in the way of doing what's
> best for the client. Everyone is encouraged to be team players—
> not only by nurturing the younger professionals but also by
> protecting the Eastdil Secured brand."*

*Headquartered in New York, Eastdil Secured (formerly Eastdil Realty) special-
izes in the sale and financing of investment-grade properties for institutional
and private investors. Eastdil Realty was established in 1967; in 1999, the firm
was purchased by Wells Fargo Bank. In early 2006, Eastdil acquired the Secured
Capital firm, forming Eastdil Secured. Eastdil has closed more than $266 billion
of transactions. Ben Lambert is chairman of the firm and its founder. Lambert and
the other Executive Committee members—Roy March, CEO; Mike Van Konynen-
burg, president; and Jay Borzi, senior managing director—manage the day-to-day
operations of the firm.*

We've always believed in a lean management structure at Eastdil and have
traditionally outsourced many of the administrative functions. I still spend
the majority of my time on transactions, as well as mentoring our younger
people to create a strong culture. The average tenure per professional is 16
years. We have been able to retain people because we ask them to serve as
generalists, both originating and executing transactions. Our professionals
always put the client first and don't allow any territorial or other jealousies
to get in the way of doing what's best for the client. Everyone is encouraged to be a team player—not only by nurturing the younger professionals
in the firm but also by protecting the Eastdil Secured brand, by providing
our clients with the highest level of service, and by holding ourselves to the
highest ethical standards.

I put a high premium on perpetuating the firm's culture, which is integrity-based. Our people are trained to listen to clients. "We" is much more important than "I." We don't tend to have a lot of meetings and prefer to approach strategic issues in a hands-on fashion in the context of our day-to-day operations.

Roy March has been my partner in running the business for over 25 years, and I think our success comes from combining both deal-making and leadership instincts. Even though neither of us went to business school, I think we have positioned the firm well for the future by learning on the job.

ALAN M. LEVENTHAL
CHAIRMAN AND CEO
BEACON CAPITAL PARTNERS

"I set high expectations for the organization and myself. While Beacon is a demanding place, I believe it is viewed as a place people like to work."

Beacon Capital Partners, a Boston-based real estate investment firm, has a skilled team of real estate professionals experienced in acquisitions/dispositions, asset management, development, finance, and accounting. Alan Leventhal, Beacon's founder, was awarded the Realty Stock Review's Outstanding CEO Award for 1996 and 1997, and named the Commercial Property News Office Property Executive of the Year for 1996. In 2004 he received Ernst & Young's New England Entrepreneur of the Year award.

Historically, the real estate business started off as an entrepreneurial, project-by-project business. Today, much of this has been transformed, as many real estate companies have become national and global companies, and issues such as strategy and culture have become much more important. Beacon dates its history back more than 63 years to 1945. Today we run it as a business, with a disciplined approach to issues such as compliance and risk management. This is critical if we want to become a self-sustaining enterprise and ensure our long-term success.

I have always viewed real estate as a business that is not complicated. We don't have to develop a new product every year or run the risk of being underpriced through outsourcing to India and China. I have always believed that any company, especially one in the real estate business, should have a very clear and straightforward strategy. Our strategy is to buy the best buildings in the leading cities, where there is a concentration of intellectual capital and significant barriers to entry.

We have a great company because of our people and culture. If I could point to a single factor that has been the reason for our success, it's the people we have been able to attract and keep at Beacon. That will remain the key to our continued success.

STUART A. MILLER
PRESIDENT AND CEO
LENNAR CORPORATION

> *"Predicting ahead three months can be difficult enough. So, I run this business with one foot on the brake and the other on the accelerator."*

Lennar Corporation is a leading homebuilder and provider of financial services. As of 2004, Lennar had built more than 500,000 houses, and its annual revenues exceeded $6 billion. Lennar builds about 36,200 homes annually for first-time buyers and move-up buyers. It also develops age-restricted active adult communities for retirees and empty nesters and provides financial services (residential mortgage, title, and closing services). During his tenure at Lennar, Stuart Miller has led the company through a series of acquisitions that resulted in rapid growth and profitability.

I run this business in 24-hour increments. Anyone who says they can look out strategically over 24 months or even a year is kidding themselves. Predicting ahead three months can be difficult enough. So, I run this business with one foot on the brake and the other on the accelerator. My focus is to make sure that our balance sheet is always in shape, and that the firm is in a liquid position with low leverage. Conversely, my foot can be on the accelerator in either a slow-growth or high-growth mode, depending upon the opportunities that the markets afford.

As an example, whoever would have guessed that 9/11, after its initial negative impact, could positively affect the homebuilding industry? People decided to invest in their homes because they offered them a sense of security, and the low interest rate environment added fuel to the trend.

CONSTANCE B. MOORE
PRESIDENT AND CEO
BRE PROPERTIES, INC.

> *"We stick to our knitting, and we get things done as promised.*
> *Like a pilot, we constantly watch the altimeter and ensure we stay*
> *as close to cruising altitude as possible. Deviating from that can*
> *be a recipe for disaster."*

BRE Properties, an NYSE-traded REIT, owns, acquires, develops, refurbishes, and manages apartment complexes in the western United States. Connie Moore joined BRE as chief operating officer in 2002, after serving as a managing director at Security Capital Group, and became president and CEO in 2005.

In my opinion, successful companies in our industry stick to what they know. They stay with a strategy and have extraordinary internal conviction, even though it may not be the most popular approach. This is especially important in a cyclical industry like real estate.

I've had a number of mentors in my life, who taught me two fundamental things. One is the importance of being strategic, and the second is never resting on one's laurels. Successes are short lived, and one needs to continue to work hard, be smart, and have some luck along the way.

I would describe my style as fair and demanding—and I'm probably too much of a perfectionist. I move ahead with a sense of urgency, and I'm effusive in praising people when they do well. But I'm not always great in confronting issues. Within BRE, we have something called "from your point of view." Associates, shareholders, and residents are encouraged to share their perspectives on any issue whether it involves another person, a property, or something the company is doing. The correspondence can either be signed or written anonymously. It's our promise as a company that we put ourselves in others' shoes and try to understand their positions. These perspectives are shared with a wide variety of people.

I believe the culture at BRE has changed markedly since I became CEO. We have a renewed urgency and sense of energy. People are proud of our accomplishments. We've moved to a new space and developed in essence a new corporate persona. While change is hard, it's given the company a breath of fresh air and we've begun to see the fruits of successfully implementing our strategy. People like being part of a winner—the stock doubled in price. And they also know that my style is to listen and respond. I'm approachable. They may not always like my response, but associates know they can e-mail me about a whole host of issues.

I think investors invest with us for a number of different reasons. First of all, we're a "California-centric company," which is attractive to many, given the demographics and opportunities in California. Second, we have a development pipeline of more than $1 billion, providing growth for many years. And finally, they know we're disciplined. We stick to our knitting, and we get things done as promised.

Deviating can be a recipe for disaster. Interestingly, our culture is reflective of what I look for in people. I like to understand what drives people.

If I believe they're passionate about making a contribution, they will make a difference to our company.

My important leadership moment happened when I was only 29 and working at Consolidated Capital. I was told to fire half my staff and did not know the company was about to be sold—the real motivating force behind the layoffs. I had to fire six people in one day, including someone on medical leave. I had no idea what to expect, but I conducted each of the sessions with empathy and heard each person out. I gave them a bit more financial cushion than I was told to, and to this day, all of those people are still friends. Firing colleagues is never an easy chore, but having never done it before, I was proud of how I instinctively handled it.

RICHARD M. ROSAN
PRESIDENT, WORLDWIDE
URBAN LAND INSTITUTE (ULI)

> *"In short, besides some luck—which we all need—what differentiates the successful global firms today are the leadership qualities at the top."*

The Urban Land Institute is a 501(c)(3) nonprofit research and education organization supported by its members. Founded in 1936, the institute now has around 38,000 members worldwide, representing the entire spectrum of land use and real estate development disciplines, working in private enterprise and public service. Rosan served as executive vice president and chief operating officer of ULI for seven years and as president thereafter.

My experience in working with developers—and this dates back many years ago, when I was working for the Real Estate Board of New York—is that the big, global firms today have someone at the helm who has a huge vision. Whether it's Jerry Speyer, Jerry Hines, or the Ratner family at Forest City, they are hugely capable people who are able to attract great management teams. This is in contrast to many of the New York–centric real estate families, who are total entrepreneurs and are primarily deal oriented.

The firms that have morphed into global enterprises have successfully developed and implemented a corporate structure and run their firms as a business. Today, they are global fund managers and truly appreciate that access to capital is the key to success. This is also true in the REITs, such as Mike Fascitelli at Vornado.

In addition, these firms all know how to communicate well, even though the styles of their leaders are quite different. For example, Jerry Speyer and Jerry Hines are reasonably quiet and self-effacing, but they've both built organizations where communication is a key priority. Each of these successful leaders also knows his strengths and acknowledges them. And they hire teams to complement them. In short, besides some luck—which we all need—what differentiates the successful global firms today are the leadership qualities at the top.

GLENN J. RUFRANO
CHIEF EXECUTIVE OFFICER
CENTRO PROPERTIES

> *"There were times when the task appeared almost overwhelming,*
> *but I ultimately rationalized it by saying, if I can't do it, who can?"*

A publicly traded REIT, New Plan Excel Realty Trust was one of the nation's largest owners of strip shopping centers, owning and managing 467 retail properties (more than 68 million square feet) in about 35 states. Glenn Rufrano served as CEO from 2000 to 2007. When Rufrano joined New Plan, the company had just completed an ill-conceived merger. Its long-standing reputation had been tarnished and its stock price halved. Within five years, a successful business plan was implemented and the balance sheet recapitalized, helping increase enterprise value by more than $2 billion. New Plan was sold to Australia-based Centro Properties in 2007, and Rufrano became chief executive officer of Centro in January 2008.

My leadership style tries to be rational, adhering to the strategic plan. It's totally nonproductive to change course in an arbitrary fashion, and it's vitally important for everyone to understand what they need to accomplish. I do everything possible to avoid surprises, because productivity is optimized when there is virtually no uncertainty. My role is to steady the ship, keep it on course, and plot its direction. I also believe in delegating, because good people want accountability and appreciate my setting high performance expectations.

My greatest leadership challenge was in turning around New Plan Excel. New Plan and Excel were two companies with radically different cultures and assets that had been merged. When I accepted the CEO's role, the company had poor transparency and very few people on whom I could rely. There were times when the task appeared almost overwhelming, but I ultimately rationalized it by saying, "If I can't do it who can?" I strained to my limits, but I guess I proved the theory that "if it doesn't kill you, it will make you stronger." I was able to get my arms around the business plan and decided to sell our multifamily portfolio and keep the retail business. There were 23 development deals in process, and I immediately attended to those. I worked hard to communicate a plan to Wall Street, which was ultimately very well received in the public markets. I also recognized that I needed to make a lot of tough decisions, including keeping the $1.65 dividend, with many retail shareholders depending on it. It was an extraordinarily difficult and challenging time.

RICHARD B. SALTZMAN
PRESIDENT
COLONY CAPITAL, LLC

> *"Today, the most successful real estate investment firms represent a balanced middle ground. Our senior leaders are still creative, willing to think outside the box. But they also recognize the importance of governance and risk management."*

Colony Capital is one of the world's leading real estate investment management firms, founded by Thomas J. Barrack, Jr., in 1991. With 14 offices in ten countries, the firm has invested globally in properties, real estate intensive operating companies, and securities having an aggregate value in excess of $20 billion. Before joining Colony in 2003, Richard Saltzman spent 24 years in investment banking. He ran Merrill Lynch's real estate investment banking business and helped drive the opportunity fund and securitization wave, including the creation of the modern REIT industry.

Successful leaders in the real estate industry straddle a culture between entrepreneurial and institutional. Neither should be overweighted. Historically, our industry has been very entrepreneurial and investors very institutional in their behavior. In short, we made strange bedfellows. Today the most successful real estate investment firms represent a balanced middle ground. Our senior leaders are still creative, willing to think outside the box. But they also recognize the importance of governance and risk management.

You attract and retain the best people if you're able to create and maintain an entrepreneurial culture. That's, in part, why the investment banks are a good training ground for real estate investment professionals. They attract entrepreneurial talent but provide them with an institutional footprint. Much of what we witness in our space today is a function of having integrated real estate into the mainstream of capital markets during the 1990s. Increased transparency and liquidity, better information flow, and better governance are all byproducts of the institutionalization of property ownership. This has occurred through securitization (i.e., CMBS and REITs) and private equity formation (i.e., real estate opportunity funds).

However, it is critical to retain an entrepreneurial spirit and philosophy. Without it, the ability to generate "alpha" or positively distinguish one's investment performance is close to impossible. Too much of either trait can be fatal—too much institutionalization leading to bureaucracy and stagnation, and too much entrepreneurialism leading to careless and poor risk management. The genesis of many of these ideas occurred at the investment banks, and I am proud to have played a leadership role at Merrill Lynch in both their conception and their execution.

I also learned a great deal about managing organizations, having worked with a myriad of clients who have different styles and are superb at what they do. This puts me in a favorable position to amalgamate what I consider to be best practices at these various organizations. At Colony, I help try to foster an environment which is a meritocracy, free of politics and biases. It's very entrepreneurial, meaning we give our people as much autonomy as they can responsibly handle, albeit with our senior leadership always available to provide advice and counsel. And while this is always easy to say, we never compromise our integrity—it's axiomatic to our culture.

As much as possible, I try to be proactive and not reactive. But in managing and running any business, a leader spends a fair amount of time putting out fires. To stay proactive, you need to surround yourself with an organization that can manage the day-to-day affairs of the business, while you focus on identifying and pursuing strategic opportunities.

I believe I have made a limited number of mistakes in my career, and admittedly I have probably taken fewer risks in order to make fewer mistakes—but not at the expense of shying from bold business decisions. You need to possess instincts and common sense that allow you to accurately assess risk.

It's vitally important for a leader to stay close to employees and clients. Only if you're willing to be in the trenches does a leader truly appreciate what's happening at the ground level, what emotions are being experienced, and what opportunities and challenges exist in the market. The great leaders never take their high performers for granted and are terrific at communicating with them. And the high performers are ones that have the right attitude. They figure out a way to get things done and blend a sense of individualism with a team orientation.

DWIGHT C. SCHAR
CHAIRMAN
NVR, INC.

> *"The best homebuilders have simple and straightforward objectives that they want to accomplish. They focus and stay away from experimenting with nonessential issues."*

NVR, Inc., operates in two business segments: homebuilding and mortgage banking. Dwight Schar brought NVR, Inc., from bankruptcy in the early 1990s and turned it into one of the top five U.S. building companies.

At NVR, we have enjoyed extraordinarily low turnover, because our senior team has built their net worth in the business and the business has grown largely due to their efforts. Homebuilders that don't invest in their people make a huge mistake. To be cheap is the kiss of death. But our people only make money when shareholders make money. In other words, our collective interests are aligned.

The best homebuilders have simple and straightforward objectives that they want to accomplish. They stay away from experimenting with nonessential issues. In our case, we are totally focused on earnings per share, and the growth in earnings per share from year to year.

Consequently, we establish our priorities by what initiatives can yield the greatest profitability for the company. The homebuilding business is about leveraging existing resources and economies of scale, and a good homebuilder appreciates where it makes money and where it can't. Adding one new house to an existing community or building a new community contiguous to one of your existing communities allows for better leverage and greater profitability.

In order to be successful, every homebuilder needs to establish goals for each of its operating businesses, and as a corollary, for the senior people running those businesses. You must always focus on the customer, understanding their needs and preferences, and serving them in an outstanding fashion so they remain loyal. I answer my own phone and respond directly to customer complaints. My secretary doesn't screen my calls, and if a customer calls in and can't reach me, my people know to provide that person with my cell number.

Culture is critical to success in any company, but particularly to in homebuilding, which is so labor-intensive and customer-centric. Your people must have fundamental values such as honesty. Of equal importance is creating a culture that is not too insular. We constantly look at bringing people in from the outside who will question how we are performing and why the company is doing things in a certain way. Fortunately, over the last ten years, NVR has produced a compounded 50 percent growth in earnings per share. How have we accomplished this? It's all about bringing people into the company who think strategically and create value as they move across the company's various business lines.

JOHN SCHLIFSKE
PRESIDENT
NORTHWESTERN MUTUAL

> *"We pay our people reasonably well and have developed a culture that is committed to the real estate market over the longer term, giving them some security."*

A privately held mutual firm, specializing in life insurance and retirement products, Northwestern Mutual is a highly regarded commercial real estate lender and investor, and Schlifske managed Northwestern Mutual's real estate investment activities. He became president of the company in March 2009.

At Northwestern Mutual, we have been blessed by modest turnover. Our field organization stays very close to the assets, and the corporate office focuses on strategic issues. We pay our people reasonably well and have developed a culture that is committed to the real estate market over the longer term, giving them some security.

Unlike many lending organizations, whether banks or insurance companies, Northwestern Mutual has been successful in the real estate business over the longer term. We concentrate on achieving total return—our people are not paid on how much they invest, so we tend to avoid doing bad deals. Our real estate field offices know their local markets and establish relationships with high-quality developers. They adopt a long-term investment strategy, not a production mentality.

I like to set definitive objectives and hold people accountable. That allows me to wander the halls and encourage a team approach in running the business. Northwestern Mutual's philosophy is to hire at entry level and grow people into management. First, they must demonstrate technical competence and good judgment, then show leadership and strategic capabilities. I spend a tremendous amount of time on succession planning, so the right people will follow behind me.

LANCE T. SHANER
CHAIRMAN AND CEO
SHANER HOTEL GROUP, L.P.

"I operate the company with substantial transparency, fostering communications, and when issues arise we address and resolve them, not letting them fester."

Shaner Hotel Group owns and operates 23 hotels with 4,000 rooms in the eastern and southern United States. The hotels have an asset value of more than $250 million. Shaner launched the company with his brother, Fred, in 1983.

I establish five to six priorities annually and then make sure they happen. These are typically major issues that affect the company financially. I have never strayed too far from our strategy: Marriott is our partner, and we build and buy properties in high-barrier-to-entry markets. My style is to be analytical and decisive, and I remain highly visible in the company, constantly visiting our properties. I operate the company with substantial transparency, fostering communications, and when issues arise, we address and resolve them, not letting them fester.

September 11 tested leadership skills. We own a lot of convention center hotels, with significant overhead, and revenue dropped by 30 percent. In conjunction with the senior management team, I developed a plan, communicated it to employees as well as investors and lenders, and successfully implemented it. I was honest about the state of affairs and did everything that I promised to do. We hosted numerous meetings with our people in the field and were proactive in communicating with our various equity and debt sources. Our ability to manage through the crisis was driven by putting a plan together quickly and being decisive about its implementation.

WILLIAM J. SHAW
PRESIDENT, CHIEF OPERATING OFFICER, AND DIRECTOR
MARRIOTT INTERNATIONAL, INC.

> *"I always emphasize that success is never final. Culture is*
> *all about hard work, taking pride in what you're doing, and*
> *constantly being evaluated relative to the competition."*

Marriott International is a leading worldwide hospitality company with more
than 2,800 lodging properties in the United States and 69 other countries and ter-
ritories. (The company reported sales of more than $11 billion for fiscal year 2005
and has more than 140,000 employees.) Bill Shaw is responsible for Marriott's
lodging, information technology systems, architecture and construction, strategic
planning, and human resources.

Marriott's culture is all about service and taking care of customers. We feel
it's incredibly important to anticipate people's needs. The senior team here
operates as a partnership, in which individuals are collaborating together
and no one is looking for credit per se. I always emphasize that success is
never final. Culture is all about hard work, taking pride in what you're doing, and constantly being evaluated relative to the competition.

Bill Marriott has been an extraordinary mentor. He taught me how to
deal with people with integrity and ensure that the company is caring and
responsive, while still being demanding. He taught me to see the big picture,
while remaining extremely detail oriented. It's all about having good people
on your team and setting an example to show what you're willing to do.

Strong leadership requires one to stand by his or her convictions. In
the late 1980s and early 1990s, the world underwent a difficult financial crisis. The United States was involved in the Gulf War and the Japanese economy nosedived. Japan had been the largest provider of capital. We were in
the process of building new hotels and had about $700 million of deals on
the market. We had approximately $2 billion of real estate that we couldn't

sell and another $3.5 billion of debt we needed to source. Concurrently, our stock price dropped from $40 per share to $10. Sellers predicted we would run out of money. But we successfully renegotiated with the banks and convinced outsiders that we could deliver on our financial obligations. While a significant crisis for me at a young age, it taught me a tremendous amount about fortitude, staying the course, and doing the right thing.

JIM C. SNYDER
CHAIRMAN
KENNEDY ASSOCIATES REAL ESTATE COUNSEL, LP

> *"I encourage our people to be honest and straightforward with our investors when we make mistakes. I may be too blunt when we stray, but a forthright approach with investors usually works."*

A real estate investment manager, Kennedy Associates Real Estate Counsel has approximately $7.5 billion under management for 250 institutional investors. Jim Snyder is the founding principal and has served as president and CEO from 1978 through 2007. He became chairman in 2008.

Leaders often must make decisions when they are not fully informed but have no alternative. A strong earthquake in California severely damaged one of our 800,000-square-foot office properties, which was less than a mile from the epicenter. Fortunately, no one was hurt because it occurred in the early morning hours. While the property management firm had a contingency plan in place, we needed to move quickly regardless of insurance carrier reimbursements. It was simply the right thing to do for our tenants. I dispatched helicopters on location to quickly assess the damage. We spent the money necessary to protect our tenants and investors, and were repaid by our insurance company after a two-year battle.

High-performing firms, run by partners who are real estate entrepreneurs, understand what is important to tenants, ultimately benefiting investors. I encourage our people to be honest and straightforward with our investors when we make mistakes. I may be too blunt when we stray, but a forthright approach usually works. I also ask our people to stay very close to our tenants because they drive the value we're trying to create. And I have no patience if our people don't know the facts.

JAY SUGARMAN
CHAIRMAN AND CEO
ISTAR FINANCIAL

> *"We're a learning company, where information is shared.*
> *Our culture is a differentiating point. I would describe it as a*
> *meritocracy where smart people are self-motivated."*

Since 1997, Jay Sugarman has headed iStar Financial, the leading provider of structured loans to high-end private and corporate owners of real estate in the United States. He also was responsible for the formation of Starwood Capital Group, in conjunction with Barry Sternlicht.

I focus on reviewing investments, because I never want to lose sight of the portfolio and the performance of the assets. I feel this would be a fundamental disservice to both the investors and the borrowers. I also spend a fair amount of time on strategic issues and various relationships in the firm. And finally, I focus on hiring great people. We set the bar quite high. Since I prefer not to spend time cracking the whip, it's better to have outstanding individuals and give them tremendous latitude.

We're a learning company where information is shared. Our culture is a differentiating point. I would describe it as a meritocracy where smart people are self-motivated. As the company grows, greater information flow has been increasingly difficult to assimilate. So we are reengineering and utilizing visual maps, instead of pushing a tremendous amount of text at people. It's the only way to stay close to the business and manage it effectively.

LYNN C. THURBER
CHAIRMAN
LASALLE INVESTMENT MANAGEMENT, INC.

"My role is to establish the corporate culture, starting with the way I conduct myself. I make decisions after I listen to input from a variety of sources. What I've learned about leadership is that integrity is critically important, and successful firms put their clients first."

LaSalle Investment Management, a member of the Jones Lang LaSalle group (NYSE:JLL), is a leading global real estate manager with over $30 billion of real estate investments in Europe, North America, and Asia Pacific. More than $6 billion is invested in publicly traded real estate companies worldwide. Lynn Thurber served as CEO from 2002 to 2007, having earlier worked for Alex Brown Kleinwort Benson Realty Advisors Corporation and Morgan Stanley.

I have three priorities. First of all, I create a vision and strategy for our clients, shareholders, and employees. The vision must be clear, and I constantly reinforce it in everything we do. Second, we must determine client needs and understand whether we are meeting, exceeding, or underperforming their expectations. Investment performance and client service are the important markers. Last, I focus the organization on retaining and hiring the most capable people. All of my direct reports have succession plans in place.

My role is to establish corporate culture, starting with the way that I conduct myself. I make decisions after listening to input from a variety of sources. What I've learned about leadership is that integrity is critically important, and successful firms put their clients first.

Many organizations fail to realize that the tough part of running a business is implementing strategic initiatives. When LaSalle Partners and my former firm, ABKB Realty Advisors, were combined, the new firm was on less than stable footing. We committed ourselves to becoming a leading

global investment manager and decided what initiatives had to be prioritized and achieved. I put a global policy committee together that constantly
assessed whether initiatives needed readjustment. Articulating and implementing the strategic vision were critically important to turning around the
merged company.

Now that we are part of a much larger global platform at Jones Lang
LaSalle, I spend a tremendous amount of time visiting various offices and
communicating at all levels with employees. I also establish performance
checkpoints for myself throughout the year. I convene our global senior
management team to discuss strategy, and we're all accountable for successful implementation. I avoid getting drawn into deals, which can be a
problem for any CEO running a real estate company.

CHAPTER SEVEN

BUILD A LEGACY, NOT A REPUTATION

Building a legacy depends upon leaders putting together a winning team of complementary executives and determining a reasoned succession strategy. CEOs need to guard against overly inflated egos and against catering to "superstar" subordinates. High-performing CEOs recognize that gaining the confidence and loyalty of all employees is one of their most important objectives—they need to show a firm command of issues and develop a strategy that works. These CEOs understand that time spent creating a high-profile public persona can often be distracting and counterproductive. Jeff Furber of AEW Capital Management, one of the global investment managers, proffers "My goal is to become dispensable." In fact, many of Furber's successful peers steer clear of the spotlight, avoiding regal trappings and attention. They win subordinates over by hard work, incisive decision making, and concern for others. Effective leadership styles lean on modest, self-effacing, and understated qualities as well as the confidence to credit success to others.

Recognize the Need for a Team

No one person can run a company. The chief executive is responsible for providing a vision and strategy, then identifying the executives best suited to carrying out the objectives. "Collective leadership has the best potential to yield desirable results," says Bob Larson of Lazard. "The strategic process needs to involve senior management—that way you can collectively develop the best ideas while enhancing buy-in, bonding, and teamwork," says Tom Szydlowski, formerly of Reilly Mortgage, which was purchased by Wells Fargo. "The process commits everyone to doing things better." But people at all levels need to be recognized and encouraged for their contributions. Stuart Scott, now retired from Jones Lang LaSalle adopted a "cheerleader" role over "the policeman." People want and "need to be reinforced," he says.

Respect Everyone

At the root of building a team is treating all employees well. Compensation is only part of the equation. The work environment needs to be stimulating and nourishing—a company that takes care of its people will have its people take care of its customers. "I believe very strongly in respecting everyone," says Steve Marcus of The Marcus Corporation, a leading hospitality player. "You can't run buildings without good janitors, and you can't run your office without good secretaries."

Provide Compassion and Demand Accountability

Building an accountable yet compassionate culture is a powerful platform for successful leaders. If people get sick or have family problems they need to be helped through the difficult times. But when the company needs that extra effort, employees need to be held accountable for stepping up and delivering. As Lance Anderson of Novastar Financial stated, "I want people committed with both their heads and their hearts."

Success Is Never Final

Leaders can never be satisfied. Steven Furnary of ING Clarion challenges himself to accomplish at least two major projects a year to boost company results. "This puts pressure on me and inspires the troops by example," he says. To leave a legacy, you "always need to be a driver," says Adam Aron, former CEO of Vail Resorts, "never the passenger."

The message in this chapter is about perpetuating the success of the organization and downplaying the reputation and ego of the CEO. Great leaders are acknowledged as just that. They build great organizations that will self-perpetuate. That is their hallmark: giving the credit to others, not to themselves. At the end of the day, great CEOs make themselves expendable, as Jeff Furber of AEW Capital implies. The organization behind the CEO must take the business to the next level.

As Joe Azrack of Apollo emphasizes, CEOs build legacies by engendering trust and then being successful through genuine effort: "To turn around AEW Capital Management, we had to regain everyone's trust and reshape the firm's reputation, through genuine and sincere efforts and results." Milt Cooper of Kimco summarizes the message well: Leaders need to acknowledge the requirement for great partners. "The greatest form of punishment is solitary confinement." This issue of being accountable is clearly critical to a CEO's legacy, as Steve Furnary articulated. An organization needs to perceive its leader as someone who holds himself accountable. Hamid Moghadam of AMB talks about the company's goal as perpetuating "enduring excellence." This is all about his legacy.

W. LANCE ANDERSON
PRESIDENT AND CEO
NOVASTAR FINANCIAL, INC.

> *"I want people committed to the business with both their head
> and their heart."*

*Lance Anderson is cofounder of NovaStar Financial, a REIT that originates, pur-
chases, invests in, and services residential nonconforming loans in the United States.*

I very much like thinking outside the box. At most residential mortgage
companies, account executives interface with brokers in the community. I
created a system of affiliated brokers on our payroll who function much like
a franchise. Other firms haven't done this because they are unable to manage the effort, but there is much to be gained if you are willing to commit
the time and this approach has worked extraordinarily well for us.

Great companies focus on the long term. During the 1998 hedge
fund crisis, eight of my ten competitors blew up. It's extraordinarily important that Novastar understands credit risk better than our peer group. We
need to be good at process, as well as understanding how to manage costs.
Technological sophistication is also important for any high-performing
company—for example, we pursue the Internet as another retail origination
channel. This will allow us to lessen our focus on wholesale originations
and reduce the need for an expensive local presence in markets.

Ultimately, leadership is about communication and being forthright
with your people. My partner and I started the company in December 1996,
we took it public in October 1997, and then the hedge fund crisis occurred
in October 1998. We had negotiated a $50 million line of credit with one of
the major investment banks. When the liquidity crunch ensued, the investment bank reneged on its commitment. My partner and I were forced to
sell some assets but finally renegotiated a line of credit with another lender.
Throughout, we communicated with employees regularly. We were honest

and told them we were unsure about whether we could survive but would do everything in our power. We shared information and never gave up. Most of our competitors went out of business, but we were lucky enough to manage through, and I think our people appreciated our open and honest approach. Ever since, we communicate with everyone in the company once a quarter to share performance information and any other important issues.

ADAM M. ARON
FORMER CEO
VAIL RESORTS

> *"Outstanding CEOs embody a drive for innovation and leave*
> *their footprints. They must be change agents, not implementers;*
> *drivers, not passengers."*

Vail Resorts, a public company traded on the NYSE (MTN), operates the moun-tain resorts of Vail, Beaver Creek, Breckenridge, and Keystone in Colorado; Heav-enly Resort in California and Nevada; and the Grand Teton Lodge Company in Jackson Hole, Wyoming; as well as ten resort hotels located throughout the United States. Previously, Adam Aron was president and CEO of Norwegian Cruise Line, the fourth largest cruise company in the world; senior vice president of market-ing for United Airlines; and senior vice president for Hyatt Hotels Corporation in Chicago. He left Vail Resorts in 2006.

Successful CEOs must be passionate about their business. They must have impeccable integrity, and they must be humble with their financial reach. Years ago, I was about to be paid a substantial, performance-based equity award. The local newspapers got wind of it and, to save the company a lot of agony, I communicated the facts to all employees—so that they heard the whole story from me, not some outside source.

Outstanding CEOs embody a drive for innovation and leave their footprints. They must be change agents, not implementers; drivers, not passengers. They must appreciate the need for change, even though they may not know exactly where they are going. The personification of my leadership style would be a cartoon character with a big mouth and big ears. I try to be a good listener, but I'm not afraid to state my opinion.

JOSEPH F. AZRACK
MANAGING PARTNER, REAL ESTATE GROUP
APOLLO GLOBAL REAL ESTATE

> *"In short, we had to regain everyone's trust and reshape the firm's reputation through genuine and sincere effort and results."*

Joe Azrack was recruited in 2008 to launch a global real estate investment management business for Apollo Global Real Estate. Earlier, he had been CEO of Citigroup Property Investors (CPI), a unit of Citigroup Alternative Investments He was previously CEO and chairman of AEW Capital Management, L.P., and the founder of AEW Partners Funds, a director of Curzon Global Partners, and founder and chairman of IXIS AEW Europe. Combined assets under management of these companies exceeded $18 billion.

I try to prioritize my time between interfacing with clients, managing people and the firm, acting as a missionary for the industry, and thinking strategically about investing and the business. It's difficult for a CEO to manage a global business because you can't be around day to day, but you need to work closely with the organization—especially with your partners. In investment management, a chief executive must also be visible to his clients. I try to constantly communicate with clients through meetings, calls, and e-mail. I also try to empower my people to cultivate client relationships as much as possible.

One of my greatest leadership accomplishments was turning around AEW Capital Management when I became CEO in the early 1990s. Not unexpectedly when entrepreneurs run a company, there were unclear lines

of authority. It took several years to reposition the business. We had to reinvent ourselves—the platform was too complicated. We also had to rebuild
trust with clients—our performance had weakened, partially due to market
conditions. We had to convince pension funds and their consultants that we
were a firm that would survive and act in their best interests. We had to formulate and communicate a compelling new strategy, convincing to both the
outside world and our own people, and our fees had to be restructured and
made more performance based. It was essential to align the interests of our
clients and our firm. In short, we had to regain everyone's trust and reshape
the firm's reputation, through genuine and sincere effort and results.

Leadership is all about listening, motivating your people, and action—whether it is to clients, your people, or the markets. There is seldom
an obviously "right" course of action. A chief executive has to follow his
instincts and trust his gut in making the right decision. Given the cyclicality
of the business, real estate CEOs must have extraordinary perseverance. It
can be lonely at the top, and it may take years to prove out a strategic decision. One needs to endure to be successful.

DAVID R. BINSWANGER
PRESIDENT AND CEO
BINSWANGER CORPORATION

> *"Whenever my grandfather walked into a property, he would
> go into the bathroom first. He'd say that's where you are most
> exposed and where you had to be most comfortable. If you weren't
> comfortable there, you wouldn't be comfortable anywhere else in
> the building."*

*Binswanger has grown from a single Philadelphia office to an international real
estate leader with 160 offices worldwide. Its two operating divisions provide real
estate consulting services as well as brokerage services. Having recently established a presence in Warsaw, San Juan, and Taipei, Binswanger serves corporate*

clients such as Motorola, Comcast, Wal-Mart, Shell, Intel, and ExxonMobil. David Binswanger became president and CEO of the Binswanger Companies in 1997. The firm was founded in 1931 by his grandfather, Frank Binswanger, Sr., in the midst of the Great Depression. Frank Binswanger's energy and vision have characterized the company throughout its history.

My grandfather always contended that to run a real estate firm a leader needed a psychology degree, not a business degree. You have to be dedicated to your people, as well as to your tenants. It's all about creating relationships. If the organization treats its customers well and its employees well, and the employees are treating each other well, you should have a successful real estate business. Whenever my grandfather walked into a property, he would go into the bathroom first. He'd always say that's where you are most exposed and where you had to be most comfortable. If you weren't comfortable there, you wouldn't be comfortable anywhere else in the building. Your people need to be excited about taking care of their customers and doing a great job on their behalf.

I learned a lot from my grandfather and have tried to perpetuate that in the business today. I truly lead by example and get in the trenches with our people. They rely on me to help them win and manage the business. I try to give our people a lot of flexibility and encourage them not to be afraid to make mistakes. I communicate what's important, I tell them I'll be there for them, and I encourage them to try to figure it out on their own. They enjoy the independence, and their solutions are often quite creative.

I try to spend about 50 percent of my time with our clients, 30 percent with our people, and then 20 percent ensuring that the business is performing financially. I want clients to know that they have access to me and that I'm here to help them. As the business becomes bigger and there are more issues to address, I get increasingly concerned that I'm running from point to point and being less productive and not staying as closely in touch with our people and clients as I should be.

Recently, I traveled to Brazil because a multinational Fortune 50 client was looking to make a $150 million investment there. When we arrived, our local partners unfortunately had no clue how to consummate a deal this size. Despite language barriers, in 48 hours, my team and I mapped out every piece of land in the area and developed the market knowledge so important for our client to make the right decision. At the end of this fire drill, we had a good idea of what our client needed to do, and he had no idea of what we truly didn't know. But we served him well, and all pitched in as a team to make it happen.

JON E. BORTZ
CEO
LASALLE HOTEL PROPERTIES

"[I]t's important for people to recognize that I am just like them. I lead by example and don't ask anyone in an organization to do something I wouldn't do."

LaSalle Hotel Properties, a leading REIT headquartered in Bethesda, Maryland, primarily operates luxury and upscale full-service hotels. LaSalle owns interests in about 30 upscale and luxury full-service hotels, totaling approximately 8,500 guest rooms in 15 markets, in 11 states and the District of Columbia. Jon Bortz has headed the company since 1998. Bortz's conservative financial philosophy has helped propel company results to be consistently ahead of those of its peers. Bortz has also overseen an expansion of the REIT's property portfolio.

We work as a team, and I lead by example. I constantly communicate with our management team and other associates about everything from strategy to performance. I also spend considerable time communicating with our board. Since our company has only 28 people, advancement opportunities are limited. So I need to make sure people want to stay with us for other reasons. I want everyone to own stock, and I try to personalize the business by knowing our employees and their families well. We have several team-building exercises out of the office every year. In short, our culture is an important mechanism to retain people.

My style is best described as casual, firm, and professional. I am probably viewed to be pretty serious, which is true in the sense that I like to get things done. But it's important for people to recognize that I am just like them. I lead by example and don't ask anyone in an organization to do something I wouldn't do. At the end of the day, integrity and a strong work ethic are critical to success in our business.

Since the hospitality industry is cyclical, leadership is often about re-sponding in difficult times. When the planes hit the towers on 9/11, we real-ized the business had to be run much differently than before. We put a crisis management plan into place and worked with our operators to diligently cut costs and virtually halted all capital spending. We cut the dividend to protect the long-term value of the company. In short, we circled the wagons to protect the company's balance sheet. We had an integrated, corporate-wide reorganization plan approved by the board in a week's time, while keeping the troops calm throughout the process. We did this by constantly communicating with them and soliciting their ideas. Ultimately, we were successful because our people believed in the plan and our leadership.

MARTIN "MARTY" COHEN
CO-CHAIRMAN AND CO-CEO
COHEN & STEERS CAPITAL MANAGEMENT

> *"The culture at Cohen & Steers is about values, integrity, and an environment focused on excellence. I am not after perfection, but I want to see passion."*

Established in 1986, Cohen & Steers, Inc. is a leading global investment manager specializing in REITs, large-cap value, and utility portfolios. It serves individual and institutional investors through a wide range of open-end funds, closed-end funds, and separate accounts. An NYSE-listed company with offices in New York, Seattle, Brussels, London, and Hong Kong, Cohen is considered one of the nation's leading experts in real estate securities investment. In 1980, while a vice president at Citibank, Marty Cohen organized and managed the Citibank Real Estate Stock Fund for that bank's pension clients. In 1985, while a senior vice president at National Securities and Research Corporation, he and Robert Steers organized and managed the nation's first real estate securities mutual fund.

I try to make sure that I am fully informed on everything that is going on in the public markets—that means voraciously reading all types of newspapers and reports before the business day starts. Once at work, I spend time communicating directly with people on the front lines—our traders, analysts, marketing professionals, and portfolio managers. I talk to them throughout the day. I'm not a big fan of e-mail, simply because it depersonalizes communication and important messages. In between, I talk to investors and people at REIT companies. At the end of the day, I try to think strategically about investments and what has changed. The challenge of the business is that things change so quickly, and you always have to be prepared.

We focus on excellence at the company. I am not after perfection but want to see passion. It's been hard to learn to delegate, but the overload of issues has stretched my capacity. Fortunately, I have a great partner and talented staff. I pay extraordinary attention to detail, including noticing the dirty carpets. I look to empower strong people and hope they rise to the occasion.

I try to learn from my mistakes, study what went wrong, and try not to replicate them. Being a good listener is very important. You have to pay attention to details, have disciplined execution, and try to be flexible. In the investment business, if you cannot embrace change, it will dim your future prospects.

WILLIAM E. COLSON
FORMER PRESIDENT AND CEO
HOLIDAY RETIREMENT CORPORATION

> *"Unlike any other seniors' housing company, we have two*
> *couples on site at each facility. They live, eat, and sleep there,*
> *interacting with and assisting our customers. It's been a*
> *wonderful formula that has stood us in good stead."*

Holiday Retirement Corp., with its related entities, is one of the largest owners
and operators of retirement housing in the world, with locations in the United
States, Canada, and the United Kingdom. Bill Colson was also the president and
CEO of Colson & Colson Construction, founded in 1963, which has built more
than 275 retirement communities in North America and is also one of the largest
multifamily builders. Colson & Colson Construction was sold to Fortress Invest-
ment Group in 2007. Tragically, Colson passed away in 2007. He was a "true
giant" in the seniors' housing industry.

Our success in the seniors' housing business is all about our philosophy
of treating our customers well. I tell our people that they need to be accountable to our customers. We discuss our "Touch in Holiday" approach,
where we go out of our way to recognize that each customer, who on average is 84 years old, deserves to be treated nicely and with respect. We've
believed in this for all 35 years that we've been in business. If you analyze each of our 13,000 employees, we try to hire for attitude. If somebody
comes to work with a smile and believes that the glass is half full versus half
empty, they'll go a long way in our organization. Attitude plus brains is our
simple prescription.

My mentor in the seniors' living business is Carl Campbell, who
built the first senior living facilities in this country. I partnered with him
to build his sixth to his 29th facilities, before we started Colson & Colson.
These were all facilities that had somewhere between 60 and 70 units. Carl

taught me to be fiscally conservative and always understand the numbers, but more important, that we needed to offer outstanding service—and especially good food. Unlike any other seniors' housing company, we have two couples on site at each facility. They live, eat, and sleep there, interacting with and assisting our customers. It's been a wonderful formula that has stood us in good stead.

I'm hands on, but I delegate. I stay very close to the financial performance of all of our facilities and review the 300 financial statements on a monthly basis. But I hire people who are self-motivated and who don't want to be micromanaged. So I let them have a lot of latitude in making decisions. Prior to my recent bout with cancer, I traveled 65 percent of the time. Our plane was nicknamed the "Midnight Express," because I always wanted to be at our last destination the night before, so that we could start fresh first thing next morning. We've had wonderful continuity in the business, in that virtually none of our people leave. In fact, the first person that I hired in 1971 is just retiring. I view our people to be largely irreplaceable.

One of the great things about being an entrepreneur is that you learn the importance of perseverance. Whether you look at our seniors' housing business or our construction company, it took us a long time to start making money in those businesses. In fact, that really didn't occur until the mid-1980s, about 15 years after we started the business. I can remember my father asking me whether we were "going to make it." There were numerous times when I thought we'd have to declare bankruptcy, and it just didn't seem like we could get it right. Nonetheless, we stuck with it and ultimately figured it out. Today, we have one of the largest and most profitable businesses of its kind nationally.

MILTON COOPER

CHAIRMAN AND CEO

KIMCO REALTY CORPORATION

> *"A person makes two partnership decisions in his life. The first*
> *is whom you marry and the second is the career you pick, and*
> *ultimately with whom you partner. This partnership concept*
> *is extraordinarily important to the human animal. One needs*
> *only to remember the greatest form of punishment is solitary*
> *confinement. "*

Kimco Realty, one of the oldest REITs, was cofounded by Milton Cooper. The
company specializes in developing, owning, and managing neighborhood and
community shopping centers.

I spend a lot of my time working with our business unit leaders, coaching
and brainstorming with them, and I meet frequently with our retailers, who
in essence are our customers. I try to support a team orientation, promoting
an absence of sibling rivalry. Each person must enhance the others and treat
them as each would like to be treated. They should clearly be drawing upon
each other's strengths. And integrity is a fundamental criterion for everyone;
it starts with the hiring process.

To achieve success, a person needs to be capable of three things. First
of all, you have to enjoy your work, even though you don't love it every day.
Second, you have to be capable of loving others. And third, you have to
make the time to do nothing because you are entitled to leisure and taking
care of yourself. These three principles kept me focused in 1991 when I was
in the process of trying to take Kimco public. Investors—who thought that
the real estate industry nearly brought down the thrifts, as well as the commercial banking and insurance industries—wanted nothing to do with the
real estate business. The whole road show process was quite demeaning.
On the other hand, I knew that going public was the right answer, not only

to create liquidity for my partners but also to provide capital for growth. Once I decided to do it, there was no turning back, and we made our IPO by the skin of our teeth—one order literally put us over the top.

ROBERT F. COTTER
FORMER PRESIDENT
KERZNER INTERNATIONAL LTD.

> *"My responsibility has been to develop one organization that works well together."*

Robert Cotter most recently served a president of Kerzner, and before that was president and COO of Starwood Hotels & Resorts, one of the leading hotel and leisure companies in the world, with properties in more than 80 countries. Kerzner International Ltd., through its subsidiaries, is a leading international developer and operator of destination resorts, casinos, and luxury hotels. Cotter was Barry Sternlicht's partner in successfully building Starwood Hotels & Resorts World- wide. He became chief operating officer in 2000 and president in 2004.

Barry Sternlicht and I had a wonderful partnership. It takes a team to run a company successfully. Barry innovated tremendously in hotel design and utilized Starwood's balance sheet incredibly well in order to grow, assimilat- ing five organizations through mergers and acquisitions. My responsibility was to mold disparate companies into one organization that works well together. I concentrated my efforts on the people side of the company and developed a world-class human resource capability. In 2004, we conducted 60,000 360-degree performance assessments. Amazingly, they were all Web based. After conducting an employee survey, we discovered that the general managers in our company were much less happy than either our associ- ates or our guests. We instituted a leadership training program for general managers, who clearly are key to future success.

In a cyclical business like the hospitality industry, you often have to make difficult and unpopular decisions. In 1992 when I headed marketing at Sheraton, the company reported performance numbers that were way off projection. ITT (Sheraton's parent) demanded that overhead be cut from $60 million to $30 million. The head of one of our largest divisions refused to agree, and the head of human resources and I had to find a solution. We had to deliver pink slips to employees with 15 to 20 years of tenure. It taught me to say goodbye based on fairness, not cronyism. Acting objectively with integrity, honesty, and compassion is always the right answer.

CURT S. CULVER
CHAIRMAN AND CEO
MGIC INVESTMENT CORP.

> *"High-performing companies are straightforward in dealing with their people, even if they're making unpopular decisions."*

Curt Culver's career spans more than 28 years in the mortgage insurance business, including 22 years at MGIC. In 1996, he became president and chief operating officer and from 2000 to 2007, served as CEO of MGIC Investment Corporation, a member of the Standard & Poor's 500. Before joining MGIC, Culver worked at Verex, a private mortgage insurer.

I focus on our people and culture, hosting many of our employee meetings to communicate the firm's performance and direction. I view myself as a cheerleader and motivating force. Of course, strategic issues, investors, and customers take up a lot of time. Staying visible with customers is extraordinarily important—whether the large, residential mortgage banking firms or agencies like Fannie Mae and Freddie Mac.

I try to emulate the high-performing companies in our business. First of all, they have a reputation for being honest and develop longstanding relationships with customers, vendors, etc. Next, high-performing companies are known to be straightforward in that they are upfront with how they deal with their people, even if they are making unpopular decisions. Furthermore, high-performing companies are known for their customer service, especially in industries where customers can choose a multitude of service providers, as is typical of a commodity business. And finally, high-performing companies have a backbone. In other words, they are willing to make unpopular but nevertheless the right decisions.

MGIC's culture is its greatest strength. The firm pays fairly, offers good benefits and flexible work hours, and pushes employee wellness through a high-quality fitness center. That is all part of the culture, which is family-oriented, open door, and not high pressure. MGIC also has the advantage of being in Milwaukee, which is an affordable community and offers a good quality of life. In short, like other high-performing companies, we're honest, straightforward, care about customer service, and can make tough decisions.

BRUCE W. DUNCAN
PRESIDENT
BLAKELY CAPITAL

> "Everyone had concluded that bigger is better. While that was
> the appropriate strategy at the time, it was now time to change
> our strategy. I tried to communicate that better is better, and top
> quarterly performance is the objective. I wanted accountability
> and measurability."

Bruce Duncan was CEO of Equity Residential, the largest publicly traded apartment company in the United States, for three years beginning in 2002. Duncan had served as chairman, president and CEO of the Cadillac Fairview Corporation Ltd., a real estate operating company. He is chairman of Starwood Hotels and Resorts Worldwide, Inc., and launched a real estate investment platform, Blakely Capital, in 2006.

A good CEO needs to be a good listener and be open to the opinions of employees, customers, and shareholders. The CEO needs to figure out the company's strengths and weaknesses and formulate his or her game plan accordingly. Then it is critical to communicate the plan to the organization and make sure everyone understands what their role is in the mission. Since my experience is that behavior follows compensation, it is critical that the compensation system encourages behaviors that match what is expected from the business plan.

When I joined Equity Residential, the company had spent the last ten years on an acquisition binge that had grown our portfolio from 25,000 apartments to 225,000. Everyone had concluded that bigger is better. While that was the appropriate strategy at the time, it was time to change our strategy. I tried to communicate that better is better, and top-quartile performance is the objective. I wanted accountability and measurability. We needed to use our size and scale to drive operational excellence and reposition our portfolio out of the slower-growing Midwestern markets and into higher-barrier-to-entry markets.

I became CEO of Cadillac Fairview, Canada's largest real estate company, based in Toronto, when it was just emerging from bankruptcy. The organization had a proud history, but unfortunately almost everyone still possessed a sense of arrogance and entitlement despite the bankruptcy. As a first step, I met with people at all levels of the company and spoke with a variety of customers and outside advisers. The company had been run on a centralized basis, and the cost structure was way out of line. For example, we had 110 company cars—I felt like Hertz. I needed to change the culture quickly. I replaced all but one of the senior management team. I also let go 35 percent of the head office. I decentralized the organization and installed a compensation plan in which we eliminated perks but the management team got well rewarded if we reached our aggressive financial goals. I communicated that people needed to be part of the solution and everyone had to commit to budgets and goals. You need to make the tough decisions quickly and set the tone and goals for the organization.

T. PATRICK DUNCAN
PRESIDENT AND CEO
USAA REAL ESTATE COMPANY

> *"Great leaders tend to be humble, but they are also strong-willed, determined, and focused on what they need to accomplish."*

USAA Real Estate Company is the real estate acquisition, development, and investment arm of USAA, an insurance and financial services association with 5.6 million members worldwide. USAA Real Estate operates in 21 states and manages more than 36 million square feet of commercial property. Pat Duncan oversees a portfolio of real estate projects that exceeds $3 billion, including office buildings, land holdings, shopping centers, hotels, and industrial projects.

Over the years, I have had the privilege of working with a number of people, each of whom have been recognized as great leaders n their respective fields. These include Trammell Crow, Byron Nelson, and at USAA, General Robert McDermott and Robert Davis. I was always impressed by their clear vision of what they were trying to accomplish. They weren't always particularly charismatic, but they knew what needed to be done and they kept their vision simple. All understood their company's competitive advantages and used those advantages wisely in growing their business…often putting the company's interest ahead of their own. They all have tended to be humble leaders—at least during their highly productive years—and were strong-willed, determined, and focused on what they needed to accomplish.

Through our company's ownership of the Four Seasons at Las Colinas, I had the honor of getting to know golfing legend Byron Nelson. After each tournament he would go back to his hotel room and study every hole and ponder any mistakes he made, while his peers would generally be out partying. The results of his efforts and focus were that he won 11 straight PGA tournaments and 18 tournaments in that same year—a record still not broken. In fact, at a banquet shortly after that famous year, it has been said that golf legend Sam Snead told the audience that Byron doesn't drink, swear, or party and therefore doesn't have any fun. Upon reaching the podium, Byron noted that this is not true. He said winning 18 tournaments in one year was a lot of fun. Byron was all about humility, focus, and determination. He was truly a gentleman.

Another very focused individual that I had the privilege of working for was Trammell Crow, who, from his modest beginnings of building a warehouse real estate development company in 1948, grew his company to one of the largest real estate empires in the world. Trammell had a simple, clear vision for the company, and the lesson to be learned from Trammell was the power of creating value by partnering with outstanding local developers.

At USAA, I also have had the good fortune of working with great leaders, many of whom were leaders in the military and carried many of those disciplines into the financial services business. General Robert McDermott was a true visionary, clearly ahead of his time. He transformed USAA from a small auto insurance company into a full-service financial services company. His vision too was simple. He looked at a military person's life as a whole and put into place products to serve not only their insurance needs but also all their financial services needs through their entire life. Today, Robert Davis is transforming USAA again, to meet modern-day challenges. Bob Davis's vision is very clear and, simply stated, is for USAA to be the provider of choice for the military community when it comes to financial products. Bob is very focused and is one of the most engaged leaders I have encountered. He devotes 100 percent of his time and efforts to making USAA operate as one association with multiple financial products for military personnel. He continually works to further understand all the individual and family needs of our military. He unrelentingly demands the highest level of customer focus and speed of execution from employees.

At USAA Real Estate we continue this tradition of being customer-oriented, and we strive daily to be the real estate services provider of choice. As CEO, I stay very involved in all aspects of the business, raising institutional capital for coinvestments, overseeing all aspects of our development business, acquisitions, etc. By providing solutions that cover the entire development spectrum from site analysis to move-in, over the years USAA Real Estate has become recognized as one of the leading developers for the Fortune 500, the U.S. General Services Administration, and other institutional owners and investors.

An important part of our success is our great people. We give our people the required resources and expect them to deliver in a very goal-oriented and fun culture. We've had virtually no turnover and strongly believe in offering performance incentives even to our most junior and administrative support people. This encourages everyone to perform at their highest levels. We've also had a lot of success in hiring and developing people with high emotional intelligence skills. We expect our employees, at all levels, to be engaged, highly focused, results-oriented, and easy to deal with, as well as trustworthy and honest. Everyone is expected to be a role model.

JEFFREY D. FURBER
CEO AND MANAGING PARTNER
AEW CAPITAL MANAGEMENT, L.P.

"My objective is to build a legacy, not a short-term reputation. I don't believe in the rock star CEO. In fact, my goal is to become dispensable."

AEW Capital Management is one of the largest real estate investment managers, serving as a fiduciary to pension funds. Operating globally, the firm employs a range of risk/return strategies in private real estate portfolios and REIT securities. Jeff Furber joined AEW in 1997.

My objective is to build a legacy, not a short-term reputation. I don't believe in the rock star CEO. In fact, my goal is to become dispensable. I would characterize myself as a good listener who is quite comfortable making decisions. I like to walk the halls, preferring to meet people in their offices, not my own.

Our success at AEW has been driven by a couple of factors. While performance is important to investors and consultants, the key issue is trust. Our clients have confidence that AEW will do the right thing. The growth of our platform has been critical to our ability to compete. We have grown from $6 billion in assets under management to more than $30 billion. And my biggest challenge, by far, today is managing growth. We must be continuously responsive to clients, provide our people with autonomy to run their businesses, and ensure the firm is making money. Meeting these combined demands can be a daunting task.

When I was named CEO, I chose not to use that title but instead chose managing partner. I wanted to instill a culture of partnership within the firm. I also had a number of important objectives, and I didn't want titles and hierarchy to impede my message. I established four goals across the firm that people could understand and focus on:

- Think as one firm (especially at the senior management level).
- Embrace change (even though change is not perceived as a good thing in the investment management business).
- Be proud of yourself and AEW.
- Work hard and have fun.

We had a lot to accomplish, including integrating two cultures (AEW and Copley), changing title structures, and implementing an equity compensation plan. While the firm was well perceived by various external constituencies, we needed to bond people together internally while implementing change. It's been a long road, but we are definitely seeing the results of our efforts.

STEPHEN J. FURNARY
CHAIRMAN AND CEO
ING CLARION/ING CLARION PARTNERS

"Every year, I tell our people that I will do two meaningful things, but I never know what they will be. This puts pressure on me and inspires the troops. And these tasks inevitably are challenging accomplishments."

In 1983, Steve Furnary cofounded ING Clarion Partners, a global real estate investment management firm with more than $40 billion in investments. The company is now part of the ING Real Estate Group, headquartered in the Netherlands. Furnary previously worked at Lazard Realty and Citibank.

Strong CEOs recognize what they need to accomplish and prioritize, and don't deviate. I've learned over my career what to do and, just as important, what not to do. Great leaders learn through their environment and benefit from their genetics. Leadership is a blend of the professional and entrepreneurial. Management is overrated, and leadership is underrated. It is much more difficult to inspire people through leadership. I'm firmly convinced that the great leaders give all the credit to the people who work for them. My goal is to help others do their job better.

At ING Clarion, we have an operating committee that runs the business day to day. It reports to an executive committee. The people who serve on these committees represent the next generation of leadership at the company. These opportunities allow our people to learn and contribute, and I can see them in action. I encourage our people to take on new responsibilities across the firm. The best way for people to learn is to push them into the water and allow them to swim. For example, I recently asked our head of investments to assume responsibility for research.

As a leader, I also need to be accountable to our organization and drive business performance. Every year, I tell our people that I will do two meaningful things, but I never know what they will be. This puts pressure on me and inspires the troops. And these tasks inevitably lead to challenging accomplishments. In 2002, I felt the firm needed to make a major investment in industrial properties. One of my younger acquisitions professionals identified an opportunity to buy Trammell Crow Industrial, and I totally focused on leading the team to get the deal done, raising $800 million in equity from clients with no distractions. I didn't take the easy way out, to admit one or two public funds that wanted to do the whole deal, but did the right thing by structuring an open-ended fund. The stakes were high, and I worked hard to accomplish it, taking only one week of vacation during that year.

In 1998, we sold Clarion. ING was an attractive buyer with a global platform and everyone internally supported the deal, although I had to work hard to make sure that everyone committed to remaining with the firm. Throughout the process, I had to negotiate with ING effectively to the benefit of our clients and staff, and keep our team on board—either they needed to leave immediately or work hard to manage the business and stay with it. For a variety of fortuitous reasons, we retained virtually the entire senior management team and have grown from $6.8 billion in assets then to in excess of $40 billion today.

DOUGLAS G. GEOGA
PRINCIPAL
GEOGA GROUP, LLC

"No one person can run an operating company effectively. It's much too complicated and requires a team. In my opinion, the rock star CEO is out of favor, and the great CEOs are talented at selecting and motivating strong management teams."

Doug Geoga served as president of Global Hyatt from 2002 until July 2006, following which he formed a hospitality and advisory firm. Geoga had been with

*Hyatt for 22 years, serving as president of its Hospitality Investment Fund, presi-
dent of Hyatt Hotels Corporation, and executive vice president of development for
Hyatt Development Corporation, among other executive positions.*

The culture at Hyatt was derivative of its family ownership, and so was
both entrepreneurial and, to some extent, nurturing. Most of our talent was
home grown, with a number of people who had very extended tenure with
the company. One of our challenges in such a situation was to ensure that
the company did not become too inbred. Although our employees had a
tremendous amount of pride in being associated with the company, they
were ambitious for the company to become all that it could be and very
much wanted to be part of something larger and even more successful. To
accomplish that, we had to develop a more capable and dedicated team
than our competitors, which meant that while we wanted to maintain the
good elements of our family-based culture, we also had to become more
street smart and effective.

I believe that our people respected the disciplined approach to business that we tried to establish. We hoped that our employees would feel
that our senior management team was highly capable, so that they would
feel confident and comfortable following our leadership, while recognizing
that in many cases the successful accomplishment of their jobs involved
experiences and talents unique to each employee. I think we were successful in articulating where the company was going and how it would get
there. An effective leader needs to embody and evolve the culture, including establishing the self-image of the organization. I tried to set the tone
for how people in the company would deal with each other, as well as how
they would relate to customers and third parties. It's very important to have
a moral standard and to set an example of a high level of dedication to the
company. A leader needs to set the agenda for what the company aspires to
be in terms of future growth and achievement and to be the spokesperson
or cheerleader for that direction.

No one person can run an operating company effectively. It's much too complicated and requires a team. In my opinion, the rock star CEO is out of favor, and the great CEOs are talented at selecting and motivating strong management teams. Today, micromanagement is rightly out of favor; instead, great CEOs give credit to their people and allow them to have visibility. I always aspired to be a great coach, getting people to work together toward a common goal.

THOMAS H. GRAPE
CHAIRMAN AND CEO
BENCHMARK ASSISTED LIVING

"I'm more comfortable spending time internally, motivating our people by being a thoughtful leader."

Privately held Benchmark Assisted Living develops, owns, and manages senior living communities. With more than 20 years of experience in the seniors' housing industry, Tom Grape is a leader in lobbying for the industry at state and federal levels.

I prioritize my time by focusing on strategy, culture, and, when necessary, raising capital. I'm more comfortable spending time internally and motivating our people by being a thoughtful leader.

We have a value-based culture, which is widely understood throughout the company. Early in our history, we invested a tremendous amount of time in training people. We knew the only governor on growth would be our ability to attract and retain people. And in fact, I would describe my greatest leadership moment as initiating an organizational development function in 2000. As a young company, it signaled that we were willing to invest in our people. Organizational development was unknown in the seniors' housing business. But I knew that companies could expand and then blow up. At one time, the industry had 16 public companies. Today, there are only four.

We differentiate from the competition by setting a high bar and demanding a lot from our people. People who want to be challenged join our company. They appreciate they will be well trained but understand performance expectations are substantial. If they are unable to contribute, they have to move on.

The high performers in seniors' housing share attributes common among high-performing firms in any industry. They are clear in their mission and have a singular focus. They are committed to their organization and their people. They communicate clearly what they're intending to accomplish. And finally, they have a long-term mission, and don't pursue the "flavor of the day."

WILLIAM P. HANKOWSKY
CHAIRMAN, PRESIDENT, AND CEO
LIBERTY PROPERTY TRUST

"You can lead through fear or respect, and people will follow you.
I prefer to empower people so that they don't need to follow me."

Liberty Property Trust, an office/industrial REIT with more than 450 employees serving markets throughout the eastern and midwestern United States, was founded by Bill Rouse in 1972. In 1994, the company went public and today has a market capitalization of over $6.5 billion. Bill Hankowsky joined Liberty in 2001 as chief investment officer and was appointed president and CEO in 2003.

Ours is definitely a different business than it was 15 years ago. Back then, it was entrepreneurial, privately held, fragmented, and the land of the sharpshooter. Local market intelligence was king, and project finance was the rule of the day. We had great entrepreneurs such as Bill Rouse and Mel Simon. Today, you've got 185 public REITs; global, publicly traded brokerage companies; and national, public homebuilders. While the majority of our industry is still privately held, larger aggregators dominate the landscape.

Corporate governance at public companies is now one of the key watch-words. In contrast to before, we now have a healthy tension between the entrepreneurial spirit driving our real estate companies and the infrastruc-ture required to run these bigger businesses.

Unlike many of my peers, I grew up in the public sector and worked for five mayors, including Ed Rendell, who is now the governor of Pennsylvania. I learned to be a quick study and take risk, which is just the antithesis of how many people perceive the public sector. I knew Bill Rouse for 15 years, before joining Liberty, and Bill was one of the great business and civic leaders. He per-sonified integrity and was a great listener. He was never overly zealous about his positions on any subject. These were important lessons for me to learn.

I'm a big believer in culture. And our culture really hasn't changed since I took over as CEO from Bill Rouse in 2003. We have an open-door policy, where anyone can join any meeting. I want people to be comfortable that they can go to anyone and ask for help on any subject. We tend to run a very family-oriented business. And we give people a lot of autonomy in a decentralized environment. We operate 20 offices, and when analysts come to visit the company, I encourage them to visit any office—and no one from corporate accompanies them. Our people are truly empowered. When you talk to someone who has joined our firm from a competitor, they will say that the reality matches the perception. Our values are critical to us. I always remind our people that, while they have to pursue life with a passion, it's better to lose a deal than lose your reputation.

My style is to stay out of the way. I tend to be very analytical and want to know the facts. These two tendencies sometimes come into conflict. But I view my job as one where I share the vision of where we're going and also take seriously the welfare of our constituents, who include employees, tenants, and brokers. I try to lead by example. You can lead through fear or through respect, and people will follow you. I prefer to empower people so that they don't need to follow me.

I can remember when Bill Rouse told me that his cancer had reoccurred, and he wanted to make me CEO. I suggested that he wait until the next annual meeting. He said no, he wanted me to take over as soon as possible. Ironically, he died a day before the annual meeting, which I then considered postponing. But I knew that Bill would have wanted me to plow ahead. And as a board member reminded me that day, Bill Rouse wants you to do what you want to do and not what he would have done. I went ahead with the meeting because life is all about showing up, and I needed to show up.

STEPHEN P. HOLMES
CHAIRMAN AND CEO
WYNDHAM WORLDWIDE CORPORATION

> *"I try to know as many people in the organization as possible,*
> *including the person ringing the cash register in the cafeteria."*

Wyndham Worldwide is one of the world's largest hospitality companies, offering individual consumers and business customers across six continents a broad array of hospitality products and services. Holmes has served as chairman of the board of directors and as CEO since the separation from Cendant in August 2006.

As I assumed responsibility for managing this business, I worked hard to create a strong culture for our new company. My style is collaborative, and I push for feedback from my management team. While I recognize that I may need to make the ultimate decision, I value the input from the team. As I moved into the role of chairman and CEO, I spent a fair amount of time creating a values statement which, much to my amazement, the team appreciated and supported. We have five core values that define our culture:

- Act with integrity.
- Respect everyone everywhere.
- Provide individual opportunity and accountability.
- Improve our customers' lives.
- Support our communities.

My approach is to be open and respectful. I try to know as many people in the organization as possible, including the person ringing the cash
register in the cafeteria. I believe in all our core values, including treating
our customers with respect. If we do that, we earn their loyalty and build a
viable, long-term business. Treating my management team with respect is
equally as important. Working together as one team, we can accomplish a
lot more, and celebrating our collective victories is so important relative to
who we are as a company.

I've always had a tremendous amount of respect for Bill Marriott and
his organization. He represents what I call "consistent leadership" in that
he continues to drive the business, and yet, my perception is that he also
gives credit to others for the business's success.

MICHAEL P. KERCHEVAL
PRESIDENT AND CEO
INTERNATIONAL COUNCIL OF SHOPPING CENTERS

> *"A common leadership thread in our industry is extraordinary*
> *passion for the product. Not only do leaders like to be creative*
> *with the physical product, but they also constantly interact with*
> *the customers and retailers in order to think outside the box."*

Founded in 1957, the International Council of Shopping Centers (ICSC) today is
the global trade association of the shopping center industry. Its more than 65,000
members in the United States, Canada, and more than 80 other countries include
shopping center owners, investors, and retailers. He joined the ICSC in 2000 as
executive vice president, was later named chief operating officer, and was named
president and CEO in 2001. Earlier, he was associated with Lend Lease, the
Australia-based global real estate investment management firm, and prior to that
with Equitable Real Estate, largely in research and portfolio management roles.

In the retail real estate industry, a wide range of leadership styles and corporate cultures can be successful. Even across the largest five or six players, there are great contrasts. They range from very nurturing, employee-centric cultures to the sort of high-productivity, leading-edge, produce-or-perish culture more typically expected at perhaps a hedge fund. The clues are often subtle: windowed executive offices versus putting the administrative staff along the sight lines; time off for community service versus hefty bonuses for overtime. Much has to do, frankly, with the personality and management style of the firm's leadership. I see absolutely no downside to this. The vast style spread creates meaningful opportunities to attract and retain top talent, while the industry's leaders (and their respective firms) have thrived within their own comfort zones.

But a common leadership thread is the extraordinary passion for the product. Not only do leaders like to be creative with the physical product, but they also constantly interact with the customers and retailers, helping them to think outside the box. I can only imagine that very few office-building landlords spend significant time chatting with the office workers employed by their tenants. Within our industry, even the biggest names— the Taubmans, Coopers, Bucksbaums, Simons, and so on—incorporate a blend of self-confidence and humility as they recognize and get to know their vertically integrated constituency: employees, consumers, tenants, retailers, community leaders, and investors.

I have also observed that the most successful in our industry are not glad handers, operating with a mere "grip and grin." They prefer to be often just out of the limelight, appreciating the importance of having a strong management team, typically with a quite extraordinary "number two." Almost without exception, the most notable firms have a Bob Michaels, a Rick Sokolov, a Billy Taubman, or a Dave Henry. It may be simply style, as the legacy of these companies often involved a close power-sharing partnership, or more likely, the firm's success has stemmed from this successful model.

Finally, I find that the current generation of leadership in the industry recognizes the importance of work-life balance. Many of their fathers worked seven days a week, 24 hours a day, often out of necessity, pulled from their families. Their businesses were sole proprietorships that were their total responsibility. I note that 50 years ago these industry founders would meet for ICSC purposes only on Saturdays and Sundays, because they didn't feel they could leave their businesses during the week. In contrast, today our industry's leadership wants to meet on Thursday and Friday—same passion for the industry, but with weekend time for the family. Clearly, each generation has been successful in its own skin at different points in the industry's evolution.

JEFFREY P. KRASNOFF
FORMER PRESIDENT AND CEO
LNR PROPERTY CORPORATION

> *"We give people enough rope to make mistakes and time to correct them. We push teamwork and espouse a tough, but fair culture."*

LNR Property Corporation, which recently went private, owns and manages a portfolio of real estate properties and real estate finance investments. Jeffrey Krasnoff served as CEO from 2002 to 2007, and its president since 1997. He earlier worked for LNR's former parent, the public homebuilder, Lennar Corporation.

I spent a lot of my time focusing on the direction of the business. In collaboration with the LNR senior management team, I tried to look at all decisions in relation to longer-term objectives. Day-to-day operations were delegated to the senior management team, subject to approved business plans for their respective areas of responsibility. We also exerted a fair amount of corporate control. For example, every new investment required five signatures, including mine. In addition, because we all have worked together so long, our folks knew when to communicate with me and each other, so there were no surprises.

From a cultural perspective, our passion was to create value and have fun doing it. We tried to offer an intellectually stimulating environment in which people were focused on building value and making money for our investors. There clearly was a Wall Street flavor. We gave people enough rope to make mistakes and time to correct them. We pushed teamwork and espoused a tough but fair culture. We worked hard on building relationships, both internally and externally, and followed through on what we've committed.

As a leader, one often ventures into the unknown and has to figure it out. Stuart Miller, Lennar's CEO, asked me to leave the corporate staff at the homebuilder and start a workout business in 1990, leveraging our expertise in the commercial property development and management business. Our challenge was to create a business that really did not exist previously: making money from nonperforming commercial real estate loans. Fortunately, through prudent balance-sheet management, we also had capital to invest—which was a very rare commodity at that time. Meanwhile, forward thinkers like Morgan Stanley and Sam Zell were raising their first opportunity funds, even though the federal government had not yet begun proactively selling the assets from failed thrifts. Not only were we looking to partner with these new opportunity funds, pitching no more than a concept, but we also were intending to invest in high-risk, nonperforming assets in the middle of an unprecedented downturn.

Partnering with the Morgan Stanley Real Estate Fund in its first investment, in 1992 we closed on our first billion-dollar portfolio through the now defunct RTC (Resolution Trust Corp.), from what used to be Florida's largest saving and loan. From those beginnings, we built a separate company with its own infrastructure, which we grew and then spun off from the homebuilder as an independent public company in 1997. Along the way, we utilized those same underwriting and workout skills to help develop the CMBS "B-piece" investing business alongside our property development and management businesses. As with our hands-on approach to our property business, we were able to manage our risk and create value in CMBS and loans through our special servicing operation, which is now responsible for more than $200 billion of commercial real estate loans in the United States and Europe.

JOHN Z. KUKRAL
PRESIDENT
NORTHWOODS INVESTORS

> *"This is a people business. We are not operating machines or manufacturing widgets. That means the best-performing companies need to attract and retain talent, providing their people opportunity to take on responsibility at all levels, ranging from negotiating to due diligence."*

John Kukral retired in 2006 as president and CEO of Blackstone Real Estate Advisors. Kukral cofounded the real estate business at Blackstone, joining the firm in 1994. During his tenure, he completed more than $13 billion of real estate investments, financings, and restructurings, while building a global organization with more than 70 people. He recently started his own investment firm.

The best performers in the real estate investment management business tend to specialize in one aspect of our industry. They may specialize in debt investing, opportunistic investing, development, or core properties—it does not matter. It's hard to be all things to all people and to offer all products to your investors. The people who try won't be in the top ten percent of any of their endeavors.

Real estate is very much a people business. We are not operating machines or manufacturing widgets. That means the best-performing companies must attract and retain talent, providing their people opportunity to take on responsibility at all levels, ranging from negotiating to due diligence.

My priorities as a leader of the group transition as the environment changes. When we are finding great investment opportunities, the team can complete transactions with little oversight by me. They get great satisfaction in negotiating and closing transactions and experience the highs of the deal business. But in a difficult investing environment it is a different story. Nobody likes to spend significant time working on a transaction to just get it shot down. I need to spend the time agonizing with the team. As the leader, you simply can't say "no" to doing deals. That's extremely bad for morale. We need together to reach the right conclusion, so it becomes basically their decision to stick at a lower price or just let the transaction go.

In the groups that I have led, we prided ourselves on an open and hard-working culture. Questions are never too basic or simplistic to ask, and we made all decisions by consensus so there's no assigning blame if a deal sours. Leadership is about making incremental progress toward your goals—it's a series of small pushes in the right direction for the organization and the funds. You want to be able to achieve outstanding results for investors and at the same time have the admiration of competitors for how you've conducted yourself in the market and for the team that you have built. That's what's important to me.

THOMAS C. LEPPERT
FORMER CHAIRMAN AND CEO
THE TURNER CORPORATION

> *"I like to be inclusive and engage my people, even to the point of conflict. Debate can be healthy."*

Turner Construction ranks among the leading general builders in the United States, performing work on about 1,500 projects annually. Turner's international subsidiary operates in Asia, the Middle East, Europe, and Latin America. In 1998, Tom Leppert joined the Turner Corporation from the Estate of James Campbell, where he was trustee of the Bank of Hawaii and Pacific Century Financial Corp., where he had been vice chairman. He previously served as president and CEO of Castle & Cooke Hawaii, as well as a partner with McKinsey & Co.

Twenty-five years ago, the construction services industry was about blocking and tackling well. The United States was rapidly growing, business was good, and deficiencies were reasonably easy to hide. Information was not nearly as transparent. Today, our business has become more of a commodity and disintermediation has occurred, causing compression within our distribution channels. Our industry will continue to bifurcate into either big firms or boutiques, without advantage to public companies since most of these organizations manage elevator assets. In the future, winners will understand how to create competitive advantages by adding value in unique ways to their business, as well as for their clients. For example, we started a logistics company to leverage our procurement economies of scale, to provide a new, differentiated service to our clients.

I am an anomaly in the construction business—I didn't grow up in it. I started in management consulting at McKinsey looking at many different businesses in different industries in different ways. As a result, I actually enjoy dealing with change, which is not true of all CEOs. At Turner, we tried to look at things differently, whether it's implementing new technology solutions, applying our green building initiative, or starting businesses in facilities management and insurance.

Turner has an extraordinarily strong culture. We have three fundamental values—integrity, commitment to prioritizing our clients' interests, and teamwork. We're famous for doing things "the Turner way." Beginning with our college recruiting program, we mold our people in a fashion that makes sense to us. We fight becoming too inbred and insular by exposing our senior people to ways in which businesses are constantly changing, including sending them to seminars at Harvard Business School. Companies that don't invest in educating their people ultimately will not compete successfully.

I put a premium on building teams. Stylistically, I'm results oriented, intense, driving—and can be impatient. But I also have a sense of humor and am very fair in my dealings. I like to be inclusive and engage my people, even to the point of conflict. Debate can be healthy.

CHARLES F. LOWREY
PRESIDENT AND CEO
PRUDENTIAL INVESTMENT MANAGEMENT

> *"Leadership is a tapestry woven from a myriad of small and large decisions. All decisions can be important within their own context, and it's a significant task to make more correct ones than wrong ones."*

Prudential Investment Management, Inc., a subsidiary of Prudential Financial, Inc., is one of the world's largest institutional asset managers. It serves more than 2,000 clients, including corporations, endowments, foundations, insurance companies, and public funds. Charlie Lowrey was named president and CEO of Prudential Investment Management in 2008. He earlier headed Prudential Real Estate Investors. This business division of Prudential Investment Management has approximately $33 billion in gross assets under management worldwide. An architect by training, Lowrey had been managing director and head of the Americas for J.P. Morgan's Real Estate and Lodging Investment Banking group, where he began his investment banking career.

Having worked in real estate investment banking and now serving as a fiduciary in real estate investment management, I have developed a strong bias for what makes organizations successful. It's all about people. The management teams of successful organizations inevitably are constituted by high-quality people, who thrive in a team-oriented culture. They have the ability to offer speed of execution, making things happen quickly while not compromising quality. And since ours is a local business, they all recognize the importance of having local expertise and drive that into their cultures.

I have tried to learn from these "best-in-class organizations," as I build and shape my organization. I also try to listen to clients. Their feedback can be very helpful in formulating the appropriate strategy for the firm, my top priority. Then you try to make sure we have the right people in the right chairs. Our culture is based on client service—everything we do revolves around a team approach to understanding and serving clients. We live in an extraordinarily competitive environment today, given the amount of capital attracted into real estate. In order to serve our clients well, we have built a truly global operation with local offices in Latin America, Asia, Europe, and the United States, combined with a range of products that span the risk spectrum.

Leadership is really a tapestry woven from a myriad of small and large decisions. All of them are important within their own context, and it's a significant task to make more correct ones than wrong ones. If I'm doing my job properly and have established the appropriate strategy and culture, and put the right people in the right positions, the firm should theoretically succeed and grow well beyond my tenure. I'll judge my accomplishments on whether I had a significant and positive influence on the firm and how it prospers without me.

DAN B. MADSEN
PRESIDENT AND CEO
LEISURE CARE, LLC

"So, I focus on inspiring, not requiring."

Headquartered in Seattle, Washington, Leisure Care provides upscale housing and hospitality-based lifestyle services for people age 55 and older. The company owns and manages more than 40 communities with more than 7,000 units throughout the United States and Canada. Dan Madsen began his tenure at Leisure Care in 1988, holding various executive positions and serving as its CEO from 1999 to 2003. He purchased the company from original owners Chuck and Karen Lytle in 2003.

I believe that great firms have CEOs who constantly repeat their vision. They overcommunicate with people, telling both the good news and the bad news. They create a high-energy environment where people can have fun. I always like to do the parking lot check. When people come to work with a spring in their step, that means they're happy and inspired and looking forward to their day. I try to teach people they have an opportunity to positively affect every person with whom they come in contact. This type of attitude and leadership translates into results.

I strongly believe in measuring quality. I'm convinced that if it doesn't get measured, it doesn't get done. After hours, I call residents directly and test the quality of their experience. I also spend time calling our leaders at our communities to get a better idea of what works well and what doesn't.

Much of our culture is driven by what I learned as I moved into a leadership role. When I became CEO, there was no training manual. It took me a while to acknowledge that I didn't know everything and to realize it was okay. I needed to communicate to people that I wasn't perfect. I became vulnerable to them, I became real, and I became approachable. Learning to share my mistakes in public—and, in some ways, acknowledge my own mortality—not only made me a better leader but influenced the rest of management to behave similarly. It helped create trust.

STEPHEN H. MARCUS
CHAIRMAN AND CEO
THE MARCUS CORPORATION

"I believe very strongly in respecting everyone in the company."

Publicly traded on the NYSE, the Marcus Corporation operates movie theatres and hotels, primarily in the Midwest. Steve Marcus joined the company in 1962, became president and chief operating officer in 1980, and became CEO in 1988.

Culture is very important to our mission. I believe very strongly in respecting everyone in the company. As my father told me, janitors need to be respected just like executives—you cannot run theatres, hotels, or restaurants without good janitors. Respect is also about involving your management team in strategic decision making. I believe in a ground-up approach to set a road map. New ideas need to percolate up. Division general managers need to think about a whole host of issues affecting their businesses, ranging from profitability to human resources and marketing. Developing a strategy together helps communicate the mission and adds to the morale of the organization.

I'm hands-on, but I allow our division presidents to run their businesses. I interact with them on a regular basis, primarily to kick around ideas and issues as well as to discuss capital allocations. We have been in business for 70 years. Our people are comfortable in a supportive environment where they can have tenure and develop their careers. But loyalty is a two-way street. I am cognizant of not having anyone become too complacent, because everyone needs to contribute.

This business is all about taking educated risks for the right long-term reasons. Your people respect you for this. We decided to change the Budgetel name to Baymont Inns. Budgetel had been our successful limited-service brand, but new competition like Hampton Inns and Comfort Inns offered a slightly more upscale experience in the limited-service sector. Budgetel sounded cheap. While it was very expensive to change the name, it ultimately was the right answer to preserve and enhance the brand.

HAMID R. MOGHADAM
CHAIRMAN AND CEO
AMB PROPERTY CORPORATION

> *"Our goal as a company is to perpetuate 'enduring excellence.'*
> *We encourage people to grow into leadership roles, much as a*
> *novice matures into a champion."*

*A REIT headquartered in San Francisco, AMB Property Corporation invests in
and manages industrial properties in North America, Europe, and Asia. The U.S.*

government and FedEx are among the REIT's largest tenants. Hamid Moghadam
is a founder of the predecessor to AMB Property Corporation, launched in 1993.

In our culture, integrity and professionalism are extraordinarily important. It's
dangerous for any leader to take things too seriously, and it's productive to
have a variety of personalities in the company. Everybody in the company is
watching me, and it's important for me to do the right thing. Everyone sits in
cubicles, and the concept of acceptability is important. I prefer a flatter organization which is prone to action, where I can give responsibility earlier on.

There is no star system at AMB, and I feel the CEO role can be over-
exaggerated and is overrated. Simply too many CEOs use the opportunity to
become a Hollywood performer. While I recognize it's important to attend to
investors and ensure the public message is not confused, most CEOs confuse
the organization's capabilities and success with their own accomplishments.

Strategy and change management are highly interrelated. A number of
difficult decisions faced my management team in taking AMB public. The firm
had just enjoyed its best year ever as an investment manager, but the landscape
was changing and we couldn't afford to be complacent. Public, integrated operating companies were the wave of the future, but we had to recognize there
could be some potential of failure in going public. We faced a decision of doing
nothing, selling the investment manager, recapitalizing it, or transforming it
into a public operating vehicle. In retrospect, we made the right decision.

We also made a strategic decision to get out of the retail business and
sold more than $1 billion in assets. We had a successful business owning
the highest-quality shopping centers, and we knew that ongoing growth
would require us to acquire properties of lesser quality. I was also concerned
about how the Internet would affect the retail business. In the final analysis,
we thought the company would prosper more to focus strictly on industrial,
as it does today. Later, we decided to go global.

Our company wants to perpetuate enduring excellence. People should
grow into leadership roles, much as a novice matures into a champion.
There is a dependent phase, and then with knowledge, people become

more responsible. Once they buy into the goals of AMB, they become accountable and initiate actions that are in the best interests of the company
and their partners. And then with wisdom, they ultimately become independent and true leaders. But without goal buy-in and wisdom, they can
achieve no higher level than responsibility for carrying out a function.

DANIEL M. NEIDICH
CO-CEO AND CHAIRMAN
DUNE CAPITAL MANAGEMENT LP

> *"I always supported people's decisions and ran interference*
> *where I could be helpful. I shared credit for our successes and*
> *responsibility for our failures."*

Dune Capital Management LP manages approximately $2.3 billion in two funds:
Dune Capital, a broad-based credit opportunity hedge fund, and Dune Real Estate,
a real estate private equity fund. Dan Neidich launched Dune in 2004 with Steven
Mnuchin and Chip Seeling, two of his former Goldman Sachs partners. At Gold-
man Sachs, Neidich has served as a managing director, a member of the firm's
Management Committee, cohead of the Merchant Banking Division, and chairman
of the Whitehall Fund Investment Committee. In 1991, Goldman Sachs, under
Neidich's direction, raised the first Whitehall Fund to invest in real estate opportu-
nities. When he left Goldman, the Whitehall Funds had raised total equity of $12
billion and had purchased more than $60 billion of real estate interests worldwide.

A CEO should focus on important responsibilities that no one else can bear.
Acknowledging that perfection is probably not attainable, the key issue is
leveraging an organization to make money. In private equity, the stakes are
much higher, since the risk of losing capital is of much greater concern than
winning or losing an agency assignment.

At Goldman, the culture was so well defined that I didn't have to
focus much on instilling a strong culture. Also, I had co-chief operating of-

ficers who were outstanding culture carriers. As a result, I could concentrate on how to manage the business model and on investment opportunities. Unlike many of my peers, my time spent interfacing with investors was modest, since Goldman raised third-party capital through its high-net-worth sales force. Within Whitehall, we focused on teamwork and excellence. Gang-tackling problems and opportunities was the routine of the day, and we ran the real estate business on a very integrated basis.

My style has always been to try to lead by example. I think I was thought of as demanding but fair. I tried to be genuine—there were no secrets when I was either pleased or dissatisfied. My people knew I cared about them, and I never leveraged them for my own benefit.

I'm very proud of the fact that we built one of the largest and most successful real estate private equity businesses in the world. I successfully recruited partners into the business who had enormous potential, and they have been integral to our success. I assembled the right team, and our growth was outstanding. Ultimately, I recognized that we had to make money for our client, Goldman Sachs. I always supported our people's decisions and ran interference where I could be helpful. I shared credit for our successes and responsibility for our failures.

DAVID REILLY

PRESIDENT AND CEO

CORNERSTONE REAL ESTATE ADVISERS LLC

"If you touch it, you own it."

Cornerstone's mission is to actively represent its clients' interests in ways that help them create value through real estate investments. David Reilly is responsible for all facets of Cornerstone's operations, including chairing its Strategy and Investment Committees. His career in real estate spans more than 30 years, with extensive experience in asset and portfolio management, acquisitions, dispositions, and operations.

At its core, the real estate investment business is about working efficiently and cooperatively with people—whether with joint venture partners or firms that provide brokerage, property management and leasing expertise, legal, accounting, and other services. Strong industry relationships inure to Cornerstone's and our client's benefits. Hence, my leadership style and Cornerstone's culture demands respect and balance. I like to approach issues with a blend of immediacy, thoughtfulness, integrity, and, importantly, a sense of humor. While the decisions we make are not "life or death," they can often be very stressful—thus, a sense of humor helps bring things into perspective and often takes the edge off difficult negotiations. In addition, having a sense of humor is very important to creating a culture in which people like to work and in forming long-term, industry relationships.

People also know me as very hands-on, demanding, and focused on high quality. I pay attention to details and want things "done right the first time," strongly believing in accountability. I have a saying within Cornerstone, "If you touch it, you own it." What this means is that whenever any employee "touches" (writes, reads, reviews, prints, etc.) any client report, investment brief, or other company-generated information, I expect that person to be alert to inadvertent errors and either correct them or bring them to someone's attention. Simultaneously, I go out of my way to show respect for everyone in the organization and have encouraged a culture which is team oriented, fair, and interactive. For example, all of our employees from the receptionist to my senior team attend an annual offsite meeting to reinforce the team concept and share knowledge and skills that characterize Cornerstone. Why? A business like ours simply cannot be run by one individual.

One of the things that I respect most about any leader is foresight and synthesizing imperfect information in order to make good decisions, albeit sometimes unpopular ones, if the circumstances so warrant. I emphasize individual responsibility within a collaborative team environment. In the broader context of leadership, the image of an organization is established at the top, since the operation ultimately takes on the style of its leaders, both the good and the bad. We are fortunate at Cornerstone in that our parent company (MassMutual) allows our investment management business to run autonomously, so my management team sets the tone, not the parent company. We have developed a culture that works; we are responsible for our own business directives and profit and loss statements; and we have a compensation program that rewards us for performance.

As the real estate investment management business matures, successful businesses will blend consistency and innovation. This seems somewhat dichotomous. However, consistency is all about generating expected returns to investors, maintaining relationships, and avoiding turnover in staff. Innovation is critical because new products need to provide "the alpha." Without it, all businesses fail. All this loops back to the basics of leadership: developing strategic foresight, making informed decisions, and establishing the style and culture of the organization.

JOSEPH E. ROBERT, JR.
CHAIRMAN AND CEO
J.E. ROBERT COMPANIES

> *"At our company, we like to think about our IRR, and I don't mean internal rate of return. It stands for integrity, results, and relationships. Integrity is the foundation for everything we do. Results are all about performing for your investors. Relationships signify trust, and it's impossible for a firm to be successful in the real estate business without strong relationships."*

J.E. Robert Companies is a global real estate investment management company with more than 25 years of experience in sourcing, underwriting, and managing a broad spectrum of real estate equity investments and debt products in North America and Europe and has recently expanded into the emerging markets. Joe Robert founded the company in 1981.

Organizations with institutional longevity are ones that reinforce integrity as the key component of their culture. Unfortunately, not all firms in our industry view integrity to be inviolate. Supreme Court Justice Potter Stewart defined integrity as the difference between knowing what you have a right to do and what is right to do. At our company we like to think about our IRR, and I don't mean internal rate of return. It stands for integrity, results, and relationships. Results are all about performing for your investors. Relationships signify trust, and it's impossible for a firm to be successful in the real estate business without strong relationships. Otherwise, how can you source off-market transactions?

While I've worked hard all of my life, I must say that luck has also played a significant role. And my guess is that I'm not alone in this regard. I started but did not finish my first year of college and then became a condominium salesman. With plenty of downtime waiting for customers, I think I read every real estate text book ever printed. A couple of years later, in 1974, the real estate market collapsed, and a lot of properties went into foreclosure. Many, if not most, lenders were focused on working out their owned real estate. I became good friends with Tom Malone, who at the time was the CEO of First Virginia Bank. First Virginia had lent on a number of condominium projects, and even though I was a young kid, he trusted my instincts and mentored me as I tried to help First Virginia work out of its problems. Thank God for good mentors!

My other mentor was John Horne, who was the chairman of the Federal Home Loan Bank Board during the Johnson administration. I went to a Board of Trade breakfast in 1976, and there was this elderly man with an empty seat next to him. Since there was no other seat available, I sat down next to John and we struck up a conversation. I assumed no one else wanted to sit next to him because he was way past his prime and didn't look like a mover and shaker. How wrong they were! John was a very thoughtful person, and he in fact predicted the ultimate collapse of the FSLIC under the crushing weight of nonperforming loans.

My experience from working with First Virginia and others told me that the market would completely misprice the risk associated with these complex and troubled assets. I wanted to find a way to arbitrage that mispricing of risk. Further, I believed that most institutions did a fairly mediocre job of managing their troubled assets, giving me a chance to arbitrage mediocrity as well. John took me to lunch at the Metropolitan Club once a month, and we talked about this opportunity and how to capitalize on it. Our talks became the very foundation of the new company (JER) that I would start a couple of years later. I was saddened when John died a year after I started my investment business.

From a cultural perspective, we have built this organization based upon integrity and trust. We always try to do the right thing and incorporate respect for everyone. I acknowledge that ours hasn't always been an easy place to work. Some called it a sweat shop early on, which offends me to this day. I've always worked hard, and maybe some people who are no longer here didn't share that work ethic. However, two months after we hired our now president and chief investment officer, Debbie Harmon, she became pregnant, and I built her a nursery at the office in order to allow her to balance her work and family life. In that regard, we have always been a progressive company. Diversity is the hallmark of our senior executive management team. In fact, more than 50 percent of the team's makeup reflects gender and cultural diversity.

My style is to lead by example. Leadership is about having the vision to see what others cannot—convincing others to follow you, developing relationships beyond the confines of the real estate industry, taking on new talent, seizing opportunities, and making the right choices. I do not believe that work ends at the close of the business day. There is no separation for me between work and pleasure or work and home. Business is integrated into all aspects of my life. And that extends far beyond the traditional real estate industry. Real estate houses the economy. I have focused my time on developing relationships with those who are the demand generators for real estate. I have always gotten on an airplane and gone anywhere to pursue a relationship that I felt had long-term potential.

I've also always encouraged our people to be an intellectual and financial asset to their communities. It is a very important part of our culture. Eighteen years ago I founded Fight For Children to support heath care and K–12 education for underprivileged children in the Washington, D.C., area. Since then, Fight For Children has contributed in excess of $190 million to support these causes. Everyone in the company supports Fight For Children in some way.

I've always pushed to eliminate the sharp elbows in the firm and foster teamwork. In the past we've hired some of the wrong people at the senior levels, who have been out more for themselves than for the good of the company. My experience is that if you hire people at an early stage in their careers, it can be easier to mold them into team players who share the company's values.

Leadership is all about making the tough decisions. Throughout the 1980s, we were making a ton of money managing nonperforming real estate portfolios for organizations such as the FSLIC and the FDIC. Later we became the largest contractor for the RTC. I believed that the RTC would be forced to conduct large bulk sales and that these real estate and loan portfolios could be purchased at a huge discount. Also, I predicted that profit margins on new RTC management contracts would quickly disappear. Against the wishes of virtually every senior person in our organization, I decided to pour every nickel I had into creating a separate principal investment group. I convinced Steve Schwarzman at the Blackstone Group that the coming opportunities would be enormous. And so we formed a partnership and called it the Blackstone Robert Group. Later I hired Debbie Harmon, a 29-year-old commercial banker, for three times the amount of money I was paying any of my other senior people. She was a cultural anomaly for the firm, and most of the senior management team initially rejected her. Nonetheless, I was firmly convinced that she had the skill set to play a leading role in our new partnership with Blackstone. Today she is the best partner I could ever have.

So we stopped bidding on contracts, and I poured $15 million of my own cash into the business before I saw a penny returned. Blackstone Robert was incredibly successful, but we needed more money, fast. Debbie led us to Goldman Sachs. I can remember sitting with Goldman partners Dan Neidich and Mike Fascitelli, who viewed the risk to be huge but recognized the potential for tremendous upside. During our negotiations they asked me how much I thought we could acquire over the next few years. My answer was at least $3 billion. Everyone thought I was nuts. Well, as it turned out, we bought approximately $7 billion in sellers' book value with equity from Goldman Sachs Whitehall Street Funds! Leadership is all about the ability to make a decision and act on it.

THOMAS J. SAYLAK
FORMER PRESIDENT
MERRILL LYNCH COMMERCIAL GLOBAL REAL ESTATE,
   MERRILL LYNCH & COMPANY

> *"We wanted to differentiate the firm as totally reliable. We delivered on what we've promised to our clients as well as to ourselves. So we built our strategy and culture around the concept of 'real commitment.'"*

As president of Merrill Lynch Global Commercial Real Estate, Tom Saylak was responsible for all of Merrill's real estate investment banking, commercial mortgage lending, and principal investing activities worldwide. For nine years before that, Saylak served as cohead of Blackstone Real Estate Advisors, building the firm into one of the powerhouses in the real estate private equity business.

High-performing firms do what they say and do it on time. They're not afraid to say no. They have the ability to make a commitment and stick by it. The commercial real estate industry can be quite volatile, and there are plenty of opportunities to retrade a deal and take advantage of circumstances. But the outstanding firms stay the course with their commitments. They are led by people whom the community genuinely likes, people of integrity whose handshake can be relied upon.

At Merrill Lynch, we undertook a strategic and cultural transformation. This was a great franchise that had lost a bit of its luster, and we were in the process of regaining a dominant market position. As we thought about how to reposition and differentiate the firm, we settled on the concept of "real commitment." In an industry known for fast talkers and over-promising, we wanted to hold ourselves out as totally reliable. We wanted the market to understand that we delivered on what we promised, and we did not promise what we could not deliver. Beyond a rallying point for an ad campaign, real commitment was also the keystone for our team culture. Commercial Global Real Estate was conceived as a fully integrated, all-encompassing partnership that combined investment banking, lending, and private equity. In order for the partnership to be successful, we had to build a culture of mutual support, where no one felt obligated to protect his own turf. In fact, we referred to each other as partners, and we paid everybody out of a common bonus pool driven by the profits of the overall business.

People who know me well would say that my leadership style is focused and determined—I like to set a strategy and a vision that everyone can understand and then stick by it. Being a "change agent" was difficult, and you had to become comfortable in making unpopular decisions. While I can be a bit combative, I also tried to be constructive. The key task in any turnaround situation is to project an intolerance for mediocrity. The team first had to embrace and accept the possibility of being a winner, and then begin behaving like they expected to win every mandate, every pitch, every deal.

One of my fondest leadership memories was on November 6, 1997, when I was at Blackstone's limited partners' meeting in Florida. We had just closed our second fund, and our returns to date were in excess of 40 percent. On that morning, we took Cadillac Fairview public at a huge premium to our investment. And on the front page of Section C of the *New York Times* there was a terrific story explaining what Steve Schwarzman, John Schreiber, John Kukral, and I had created at Blackstone. In fact, it was the first color picture that the *New York Times* business section had ever printed. The photograph was of Steve, Kuks, and I standing on the top of an office building that we had acquired, and the article talked about the successes that we had experienced as a group. I was enormously proud at the time. On the following Monday, we gathered the team together, ranging from the administrative assistants to the senior executives. We thanked them for their contributions, because the whole organization contributed to our great results. We wanted them to be proud of being part of the best real estate shop in the industry. I remember saying, "All of us will enjoy many moments of success in our future careers. But right now, this morning, all of you play for the best team in the industry. Enjoy it, because it won't last forever."

I've been blessed with two great mentors during my career. The first was Sid Smith, my first boss at The Horne Company in Houston. Sid taught me the art of listening before talking, and the importance of leading by example. The other important mentor in my career has to be John Schreiber. While John is a tremendously successful investor and a savvy negotiator, he is also a man of principle who is relationship-driven and constantly thinks about the long term. He's the epitome of professionalism and personal integrity. You would be hard pressed to ever find anyone willing to say an unflattering thing about either Sid or John. They both taught me that great leaders combine success with principles.

STUART L. SCOTT
FORMER CHAIRMAN
JONES LANG LASALLE

> *"I was a cheerleader, not a policeman, and reinforced people versus being critical of them. I communicated that flexibility and openness were essential to success."*

Publicly traded, Jones Lang LaSalle is one of the largest real estate corporate services and investment management firms in the world. Stuart Scott served as

*chairman of the board of directors and CEO of Jones Lang LaSalle, and chair-
man of the board of directors and CEO of LaSalle Partners from December 1992
through 2001. He then served as chairman of Jones Lang LaSalle from 2002
through 2004.*

High-performing firms will focus on major markets to win significant market
share. When Bill Sanders and I and our other partners started LaSalle Partners, we used the investment banks as a model. We chose to focus on serving
clients in businesses with good margins. We also wanted to promote a team
orientation. Too many real estate services firms were focused on deals, not
clients. In fact, we were so focused on doing business as a team that, if there
were stars who disrupted the system, we ultimately let them go.

I twice served as the firm's CEO: once before the acquisition of
Jones Lang Wootton and the second time after the acquisition, when I
moved to London to head the aggregated businesses. It was extraordinarily
important to put in place consistent values and a common culture. And
the best way to do this was to focus on helping people be successful in running their businesses properly. I was a cheerleader, not a policeman, and reinforced people versus being critical of them. I communicated that flexibility
and openness were essential to success. And today, our firm attracts and
retains great people because our strong culture enables people to enjoy
working together.

R. SCOT SELLERS
CHAIRMAN AND CEO
ARCHSTONE-SMITH

"Leadership comes from serving those around you."

*Formerly a leading apartment REIT, Archstone-Smith is a major landlord in
Boston, New York City, San Francisco, coastal southern California, Seattle,
and Washington, D.C. It was taken private in a transaction involving Lehman
Brothers and Tishman Speyer Properties. Scot Sellers has been CEO since 1997,*

overseeing the firm's organic growth as well as its acquisition of several large
apartment companies, including Charles E. Smith Residential, one of the largest
high-rise apartment owners and developers in the country.

Above all else that a leader does, I believe that creating and nurturing the
right culture is the most important responsibility. Within our company,
we have worked hard to build a strong culture through two pivotal areas
of focus: First, we believe that it is a leader's responsibility to serve those
around him or her. As we focus on serving our customers, shareholders, and
associates, we create loyalty, engagement, and significant long-term value.
Second, the most important factor in decision making is to do what we
believe is right, even when it is unpopular.

Let's face it: running a public company, especially in the current
environment, is not an easy thing. Management frequently confronts the
pressure to make decisions that produce short-term results at the expense
of significant potential long-term gains. We made a challenging decision to
pursue the industry's first dilutive, multibillion-dollar merger with our acquisition of Charles E. Smith Residential in 2001. It has been a tremendous
success for us, because it allowed us to reposition the entire company into
stronger markets with better long-term growth. However, if we had not had
the courage of our convictions that pursuing this dilutive merger was right,
even in the face of tremendous criticism, we would have never had the opportunity to build the high-performing company we have today.

Building a strong culture means giving associates a vision of what all
of us at the company are working together to achieve and then empowering
them to pursue this vision together. As managers, we must take the time to
understand the dreams and goals of each of our associates as individuals.
Working together to help our people pursue their dreams, in the context
of their careers, creates a powerful commitment to excellence and a shared
vision. Strong, connected teams that work together can achieve far more
than talented individuals. It is a leader's responsibility to build and maintain
such a team.

Capital allocation is also one of senior management's most important responsibilities. Ours is a very capital-intensive business; a single asset can cost hundreds of millions of dollars. Ensuring that our capital is deployed into locations and assets with optimal fundamentals for long-term growth and value creation is essential to our success. Our team works closely together to make forward-looking capital allocation decisions that have created tremendous long-term value for our shareholders.

Finally, I don't believe you can be an effective corporate leader today without an extensive familiarity with business, political, and economic issues across the international spectrum. As a result, I am an avid reader and have cultivated relationships with leaders in other companies and countries, in an effort to better understand current trends around the world. As a result of some of the insights gained through this process, we recently expanded our operations to include Germany and now have close to a billion dollars of capital invested there, which adds an exciting dimension to our long-term growth platform. Intelligent capital allocation decisions and an informed global perspective are important ingredients to long-term success, but it is only when these are combined with a strong culture and a willingness to make decisions based on principle, rather than popularity, that a company will truly achieve excellence. The achievement of excellence has been, and continues to be, our goal year in and year out.

GLENN A. SHANNON
PRESIDENT
SHORENSTEIN PROPERTIES LLC

"Too many companies are held back because they tend to 'manage around' people problems."

Shorenstein Properties now owns and manages some 18 million square feet of Class A office space throughout the United States. Its closed-end real estate funds have acquired and developed more than 28 million square feet of properties.

Glenn Shannon oversees all operating activities, including strategic planning and asset management of the company's investments. He has helped transition Shorenstein from a local San Francisco office developer and owner into a nationwide investment manager.

The office property business can clearly be a roller coaster, affected by a range of factors from unemployment to the economy, interest rates, and capital flows. Since opportunities present themselves over time in such a dynamic context, to make money consistently you need to have an organization that can make innumerable discrete investment and operating decisions quickly and correctly

I focus my time on choosing and developing our leaders and creating a positive environment that encourages our leaders to work together. We have a demanding culture but expect people to be collegial and respectful. I also spend a lot of time determining the company's mission and direction and communicating it so that everyone can understand the company's strategic advantages over the competition. Finally, I am focused on the company's performance relative to benchmarks. It's important to have feedback loops so that everyone understands how well we are performing relative to our mission and goals.

As a lawyer by training, I appreciate the importance of building successful relationships—both outside and inside the company. Too many companies are held back because they tend to "manage around" people problems. I find the best people are ones who recognize the importance of attitude and integrity. Commitment, respectfulness, and humility are also important attributes. The best people can manage as well as be managed. I try to set the same standards for everyone. While I'm hands-on in orientation, I believe our people feel good about my interest in what they are doing. And I pride myself on asking good questions. Ours is a complicated business, so I think the right model for leadership is not to try to provide all the answers but rather to encourage a process from which good, solid decisions emerge that reflect the expertise and experience of the whole organization. When people are included in formulating the company strategy, setting performance objectives, and establishing a compensation program that rewards performance and behavior, it's truly incredible how their behavior can change.

In the late 1990s, as the scale of our closed-end fund business was growing, I felt we needed to interact with our investors differently—provide them with more information and engage them in a more regular dialogue about our business. But a number of my colleagues disagreed. So, I decided to bring investors and consultants to our offices to meet with our team and talk through our strengths and weaknesses. Rather than just try to convince others of my view of the situation, I set up a process that would create a common context for our people and an open forum to address the issue. Ultimately, we came to a consensus that a more active and robust investor relations plan made sense, given the evolution and development of our overall business strategy.

RICHARD A. SMITH
PRESIDENT, CEO, AND DIRECTOR
FELCOR LODGING TRUST INC.

> *"I do feel strongly that it is the leader's responsibility to set
> a vision, and to communicate it well."*

FelCor is a public REIT that today owns 85 consolidated hotels and resorts, in 23 states and Canada. FelCor's portfolio consists primarily of upscale hotels, which are flagged under global brands such as Embassy Suites Hotels, Doubletree, Hilton, Renaissance, Sheraton, Westin, and Holiday Inn. Richard A. Smith joined FelCor in November 2004 as executive vice president and chief financial officer.

I do see myself as a "change agent," where I bring a sense of urgency to get to the end game as quickly as possible. However, I don't change things needlessly. When I arrived at FelCor, I found a wonderful culture here created by Tom, and it is something that we have tried to further enhance. However, I do feel strongly that it is the leader's responsibility to set a vision and to communicate it well. Strong senior management teams are self-motivated and will execute as part of their mandate. They are also motivated by a leader who has a work ethic and who will roll up his sleeves and get things done.

I have had the good fortune to work in a number of different cultures for a variety of personalities. I have learned the value of vision and work ethic from Barry Sternlicht. From Tom Corcoran here at FelCor, I've learned how important it is to create a fun and supportive culture. Starwood under Barry was a very entrepreneurial company, where I was given a lot of opportunity and exposed to every facet of the financial discipline. And then when I went to Wyndham as chief financial officer, I became exposed to field operations and the marketing side of the business. Most important, I learned the value of spending time with our people, especially those in the field. Today, I spend a lot more time walking the halls and talking to our people than sending e-mails. And in fact, I sometimes surprise our general managers in the field when I tell them that it's more important for me to meet our people there, than to immediately analyze the financial performance of the property.

ROBERT E. SULENTIC
GROUP PRESIDENT
CB RICHARD ELLIS

> *"The goal is for the team to win and our people to feel good being a part of the team. I try to lead by example and personify the customer-centric team orientation that is so critical to our company."*

Before its recent acquisition by CB Richard Ellis, Trammell Crow Company was publicly traded on the NYSE and was one of the leading real estate services firms in the United States and Canada. Bob Sulentic served as president and

CEO from 2000 to 2006. He joined Trammell Crow in 1984. He now oversees all international activities for CB Richard Ellis as well as the firm's domestic investment business.

Trammell Crow serves three primary constituencies: customers, employees, and investors. In my capacity, I regularly called on customers, tried to visit all 30 offices at least once a year, and stayed close to our investors.

One of our goals was to build a much less cyclical business. We focused on driving specific annual initiatives to guide and drive our business. We wanted to create an environment in which our people are excited. And I really wanted the team to win. I try to lead by example and personify the customer-centric team orientation that is so critical to our company.

The high performers in our industry do three things particularly well. They put the customer first, cooperate internally to serve the customer, and provide tools and infrastructure for their people to serve their customers. We have a national platform, with technology, human resources, and accounting capabilities to support all our offices. We have a culture that puts the customer first. Our senior people have driven the importance of being customer focused and team oriented broadly throughout the organization.

THOMAS C. SZYDLOWSKI
FORMER EXECUTIVE VICE PRESIDENT
WELLS FARGO MULTIFAMILY CAPITAL

> *"The strategic process involves the senior management team, which enhances bonding and teamwork. It helps break down the silos and improves communication. And it requires everyone to commit to doing things better."*

Reilly Mortgage provides acquisition, refinancing, and new construction loans primarily for apartments and health care facilities. In 2001, Tom Szydlowski left Berkshire Mortgage, and his mentor, Peter Donovan, to position Reilly Mortgage Group for a sale to an institutional owner. In 2006, Wells Fargo acquired Reilly.

CEOs can spend too much time reacting versus planning. I liked to balance the short term and long term. I also tended to focus on those issues that can have the biggest impact on the business. Following our strategic planning sessions, each department had the road map for what they needed to accomplish in order for the firm to be successful overall. I delegated that responsibility to them and clearly held them accountable. The strategic process involved the entire senior management team, which enhanced bonding and teamwork. It helped break down silos and improved communication. And it required everyone to commit to doing things better. An organization must prioritize three or four objectives and then get them done.

In the mortgage business, successful firms are extraordinarily creative and innovative about deal structures, and they focus on customer service. To meet commitments, they push people hard and stress the accomplishment of results.

I am a serious and direct person and can be perceived as intimidating. But CEOs are only successful if they are open to meaningful feedback. Growing up in the business, I disagreed with senior management when appropriate, but I was always a supportive team member. Communicating honestly has always been a priority for me. I wanted it to be equally important for my team.

ROBERT TAUBMAN
PRESIDENT AND CEO
THE TAUBMAN COMPANY

> *"I've been successful in setting a strategy for the company, and creating a strong value system by developing a matrix that measures performance. Holding everyone accountable, including myself, is extraordinarily important."*

Taubman Centers Inc. is a REIT that owns, develops, and operates regional shopping centers nationally. Robert Taubman joined the company in 1976, was elected *chairman in 2001, and has led an aggressive growth strategy. After successfully thwarting an unsolicited hostile takeover bid, Taubman presided over a total return to shareholders of more than 51 percent. In addition, the company raised $1.3 billion in debt financing, completed a $103 million share repurchase program, began plans for Asian expansion, and engaged in several other development, acquisition, leasing, and renovation projects.*

Leadership is all about communication and expending endless energy. People want to know their leaders are committed, and blind faith doesn't fly anymore. While compensation needs to be competitive, people join companies and enjoy working for them because they are part of a team where a culture is strong and the value system is material. People like working for a winner. Part of being a winner is demonstrating successful growth. People want to feel that there is a sound strategy in place, which needs to be communicated through the organization and bought into. There must be an alignment of interests between people, the company, and investors.

The hostile takeover bid by Simon was something that we successfully persevered through. I literally communicated with our people every two weeks, made sure they were aware of our strategy, and provided an update on the "battle." Interestingly, I didn't even implement change-of-control provisions until the end and lost nobody from either senior or middle management. In addition to communicating well, I've been successful in setting a strategy for the company and creating a strong value system by developing a matrix that measures performance. Holding everyone accountable, including myself, is extraordinarily important.

STAN THURSTON

RETIRED CHAIRMAN

LIFE CARE SERVICES LLC

"We have a supportive culture, where longevity is promoted and encouraged."

In 1995, the management and employees of Life Care Services split off from The Weitz Corporation, becoming the largest employee-owned, privately held company servicing the retirement living industry. Stan Thurston became chairman of Life Care Services in 2006, after serving as president and CEO. Thurston joined The Weitz Corporation in 1977 as project development manager. He was promoted to president and chief operating officer in 1990, and CEO in 1995.

Everyone in the company needs to be focused on the care of our residents. We have a supportive culture in which longevity is promoted and encouraged. We look for people who have a passion for seniors and who want to make a difference in their lives. I believe in fostering a team-oriented culture. People are empowered, but I'm there if they need me. I stay close to the challenges and problems we face and am comfortable stepping up to meet the pressures. That's what leadership is all about.

When I took over as chief operating officer, the company had consummated a number of development projects. Unfortunately, the economy had become troubled. We had significant investments in these assets, and interest rates increased as home sales declined. Conventional construction financing became very expensive and difficult. I didn't panic but came up with a plan to convert some of the continuing care retirement communities to not-for-profit status and utilized tax-exempt bond financing. We found joint venture equity with another CCRC so Life Care Services could maintain its ownership and profit potential. Throughout the process, we didn't lose sight of our residents.

ROBERT I. TOLL
CHAIRMAN AND CEO
TOLL BROTHERS, INC.

"In our Monday night meetings, I always have pitchforks available. I tell my team that they have two options. They can listen and try to understand what is happening, or they can take a pitchfork out of their rear ends if they get themselves in some type of serious trouble."

Toll Brothers is the leading builder of luxury homes in the United States. Bob Toll has led the company since he founded it in 1967. In the 1990s, he transformed the firm from a regional builder in five mid-Atlantic and northeastern states into a nationwide builder with operations in 20 states and six regions.

I encourage my peers in the industry to describe themselves as homebuilding companies, not homebuilders. Our industry suffers from too much of an image of the journeyman homebuilder in his pickup truck. The successful homebuilding companies have CEOs who have built strong cultures. They are sensitive and aware, spread their leadership philosophy through the ranks, and are nimble.

Our organization focuses on the performance details. Every Monday night, our people work until 11:00 p.m., including myself. Each of the operating division's management teams, including project managers, reviews performance. Virtually every professional in the company receives a weekly status report on all projects across the country, including ones in which they are not involved. I like my people to focus on the details, work hard, and contribute to the company's performance. Our environment encourages everyone to question what's going on in the business. Three times a year, we do a thorough analysis of the entire business. And in our Monday night meetings, I always have pitchforks available. I tell my team that they have two options. They can listen and try to understand what is happening, or they can take a pitchfork out of their rear ends if they get themselves in some type of serious trouble.

Being a lawyer by training, I tend to hire lawyers and investment bankers rather than hiring out of the homebuilding industry. I put them through a year-and-a-half training program, and then give them a project to run. I subscribe to the aphorism that the wise man recognizes what he doesn't know.

And I recognize that as the company grows, our management structure will have to change. Our senior people will be called upon to run their own businesses and report to the senior management team and me on their performance. Nonetheless, I will utilize the same reporting process that has characterized the company and made us successful. While our compensation system has been more subjectively dependent on the company's performance, I recognize that it must become more formulaic, especially as the organization becomes more decentralized.

While everyone in the company works extraordinarily hard, it is important to have a culture in which people enjoy being here and benefit from our success. Over time, we have built guesthouses at various destination resorts around the country, and we allow our employees to stay at these guesthouses free of charge. These houses are usually booked a year in advance. It's a way for the company to express its appreciation for the time commitment and passion that our people show for the business.

JON VACCARO
MANAGING DIRECTOR
DEUTSCHE BANK

> *"It's extraordinarily important to have our people share in the success of the business. They need to feel like they have skin in the game."*

After starting his career at CitiGroup, Jon Vaccaro went on to build and manage Deutsche Bank's Global Commercial Real Estate business, among the largest and most respected in the industry. Over the past ten years, he built the business through a combination of bolt-on acquisitions and organic growth into new countries and products.

One of my greatest accomplishments has been going from a small team of two dozen people to over 500 people around the world in less than a decade. Those original people represented a mosaic of complementary skills and experiences, and most of them are still with me today. We've been successful because we harnessed an entrepreneurial spirit early on and have kept it going. It's extraordinarily important to have our people share in the success of the business. They need to feel like they have skin the game and are rewarded on the results of the entire business, not just their individual contribution; that's the only way to drive real teamwork and turn senior managers into business owners.

As entrepreneurs and owners, my senior team and I are constantly evaluating the market and developing strategies that we believe in for both short-term and longer-term success. On occasion we have stayed committed to initiatives that we felt had potential, even if they didn't generate immediate returns. Sometimes you have to make a bet based on where you think the market is going, but—without exception—staying the course has paid off for us.

One of the best examples of this is our effort to expand the business globally. Branching out around the world has been one of the most challenging parts of building this business. We run the business globally from New York, but having leaders in each country that are empowered, capable, and connected to the local market is as important as it is difficult. By partnering with several of our global clients in emerging markets, we've placed a bet that real estate is going to be securitized around the world. Now, we're well positioned for that opportunity.

MATTHEW M. WALSH
CHAIRMAN
THE WALSH GROUP/WALSH CONSTRUCTION GROUP/
  ARCHER WESTERN CONTRACTORS

> *"People enjoy working together to create a great end product and*
> *take comfort that character is part of our standard—and we never*
> *cross the line. You can never lose that entrepreneurial spirit. You*
> *must thrive on making deals, hire great people, and pick your*
> *partners well."*

Recognized as one of the nation's most successful builders and developers, the
Walsh Group manages an annual volume of work in excess of $2 billion. Head-
quartered in Chicago, it has regional offices across the country. It counts Chicago's
Millennium Park among its more high-profile recent projects. Founded in 1898,
the Walsh Group is still owned by the Walsh family, with Matt and his brother,
Dan, representing the firm's third generation of leadership.

In the construction/engineering space, successful firms embody three characteristics: entrepreneurial spirit, high energy level, and character. Our firm
was founded in 1898, and we're now the 18th largest construction company
in the United States, with 13 offices doing business in 37 states. When you
dissect our industry, 90 percent of what we do is driven by human capital
and 10 percent by monetary capital. You have to create a working environment with more benefits than just compensation. At Walsh, people enjoy
working together to create a great end product and take comfort that
character is part of our standard—and we never cross the line. You can never
lose that entrepreneurial spirit. You must thrive on making deals, hire great
people, and pick your partners well. As my father used to say, if you go to
bed with dogs, you wake up with fleas.

My grandfather started this business building the World's Fair that
was hosted in Chicago, and my brother, Dan, and I inherited the business

from my father. I was an English major in undergraduate school and earned my law degree at night. I had no technical training. When we entered the business, we were young, and we needed to bring in others who could help us manage and grow it. Today, we're among the leading construction firms in building transit systems, roadways, and water management facilities. My father always preached that you need to know two things, your costs and your clients. You never can forget you're in a service business and need to deliver on budget, on time, and in a quality fashion. You must build every project as if you're building someone's home.

My style is to lead with vision, establish the strategic direction for the business, put the right people in the right spots, and monitor their progress. While we've created a supportive culture, we do have incentive programs in place for virtually everyone, so that they know how they have contributed to the financial successes within the company. The trendy word today is "balanced scorecard," but in reality, we've been doing this for 30 years.

I also like to have regular contact with our people. I enjoy when we are proposing on major projects, and I can sit with our people and brainstorm the best way to solve a particular client's requirements. I remember when we were bidding for the reconstruction of the Dan Ryan Expressway in Chicago. We couldn't figure out how to move our trucks through the construction zones safely without taking an inordinate amount of time. I recommended that we build some ramps between the Dan Ryan and some dormant bridges in order for our trucks to move in and off the site easily. We could reduce costs and increase speed to completion. The idea won the business. There were about 25 of us, seasoned veterans and young people, sitting in a room for a number of days, and we came up with the plan. It's an exhilarating experience.

Our culture is extremely important. When we built our new headquarters on the west side of Chicago, we included a gymnasium so that our people could work out and play basketball. While some thought it was a big waste of space, we felt it was important for our people to exercise and release some energy, and it's been a wonderful benefit for the company. We have always believed in developing strong relationships, whether it's within the business or with outside vendors, such as our bank or surety company, with whom we have been doing business for more than 30 years.

STEVEN A. WECHSLER
PRESIDENT AND CEO
NAREIT

> *"Successful leadership requires an overarching strategic vision grounded in the grasp of significant detail."*

NAREIT is the worldwide representative voice for REITs and publicly traded real estate companies with an interest in U.S. real estate and capital markets. Corporate members include businesses that own, operate, and finance income-producing real estate. Associate members are investors as well as individuals who advise, study, and serve the real estate investment community.

Through my experience working closely with a wide range of eminent leaders in the real estate community, I've come to believe that successful leadership requires an overarching strategic vision grounded in the grasp of significant detail. At the same time, great leaders instill confidence, commitment, loyalty, and trust in the people around them, whether these individuals are employees, investors, partners, shareholders, or stakeholders of some sort. The leaders that I've come to know and admire are both goal-driven and open-minded. Most often, they are seekers of data, opinion, and information of all kinds as part of an ongoing effort to make the best decisions at the most appropriate times.

Leaders also must map boundaries, as well as set and weigh anchors for their organizations. This requires judgment, informed through experience and implemented through discipline. To a significant extent, the recent crisis in the credit markets is a wonderful example of the consequences of leadership deficiencies, now in full view, illustrated by the very absence of boundaries, anchors, and discipline.

It is also important for leaders in a community, such as real estate investment, to look beyond, to see more than just real estate. In this vein, it is worth noting that the real estate community has had outstanding leadership in its ranks for many years, but that there's no doubt the industry can improve over time by embracing the best practices and personnel of the broader business community.

The great leaders of the real estate community with whom I have experience up close certainly fulfill all the criteria mentioned. They also meet one additional important standard: dedication to bringing out the best in others.

W. BRETT WHITE
PRESIDENT AND CEO
CB RICHARD ELLIS

> *"We definitely encourage our people to focus on long-term relationships with our customers. They need to understand that it's okay to leave something on the table, so that they can earn the right to do business with a client over the longer term."*

CB Richard Ellis and its partner and affiliate offices have more than 29,500 employees in 300 offices across 50 countries worldwide. In 2005, the company posted service revenues totaling $2.9 billion. Brett White became president and CEO in 2005.

We definitely encourage our people to focus on long-term relationships with our customers. They need to understand that it's okay to leave something on the table, so that they can earn the right to do business with a client over the longer term.

I spend at least 50 percent of my time mentoring my direct reports, helping them build their businesses. I also involve our senior management team in the strategic planning process, as well as the board. I believe if we collaborate and make decisions in our own collective best interests, we will succeed.

In 1996, Ray Wirta and I sat down and worked out our ten-year plan. But then in 2002, our firm started feeling the impact of an economic downturn. We never violated our loan covenants. Ray and I decided to forsake our bonuses that year. I remember walking down to address an auditorium packed with our 250 most senior managers and asked them if they would be willing to cut their earned bonuses by at least half. Initially, you could have heard a pin drop, but amazingly enough the request was met with a standing ovation. I was stunned and incredibly gratified. Because of our efforts to conserve capital, 2003 to 2005 were good years and allowed us to complete our IPO successfully, which turned out to be enormously rewarding for that same group who made the huge sacrifice.

JAY S. WITZEL
PRESIDENT AND CEO, CARLSON HOTELS WORLDWIDE
CEO, REGENT

> *"Today, my style at Carlson is to be collaborative, open, and relaxed. I tend to listen more than I talk, and I've learned not to make decisions too quickly."*

Jay Witzel, a senior executive in the hospitality businesses of Carlson, leads the global strategies and growth of all of Carlson's hotel operations, which currently include 986 locations in 70 countries.

Leaders incorporate three key attributes. First, they have character; they bring values to the table. Second, every one of them possesses competence. In other words, it's all about what you know and how you grow. And third, they all know how to execute. While all leaders are born with certain personality traits, these don't translate into leadership attributes. These attributes are taught, and in turn, learned.

There are excellent examples of these leadership attributes throughout the hospitality industry. For example, Steve Bollenbach, who started as a finance person at Marriott and later spun the real estate portfolio out of Marriott into Host Marriott, knew how to execute as well as anyone. Later, he restructured Trump's portfolio and then took over at Hilton, not only buying Promus, but also consolidating Hilton and Hilton International. Another great example is Mike Rose, who began his career as a lawyer and not only turned around Promus, but also founded Gaylord Entertainment. Mike has always been regarded as one of the people in our industry with tremendous values. Bill Marriott is yet another example. He took over the company from his father and built it virtually single-handedly. Now, there is competence. Izzy Sharp, at Four Seasons, has been singularly focused on providing each guest the best luxury hotel experience. The performance of his organization has been nothing but extraordinary.

In order to successfully run an organization, a leader has to do four things extraordinarily well. When you tie these in with the three leadership attributes, I call it my seven-digit theory, much like a phone number—you have the three-digit prefix, and the four numbers that follow:

☞ Great leaders clarify the purpose of an organization.

☞ They unleash the talent in an organization, finding the right people and giving them the right tools.

☞ They align systems to remind people what's to be accomplished. People need the right processes and support in order to be successful.

☞ Great leaders inspire trust.

One of the great things I learned while coming up through the ranks at Hyatt was to be an entrepreneur. The Pritzker family were great investors and great mentors. They taught me not to be too introspective but to just do it. Today, my style at Carlson is to be collaborative, open, and relaxed. I tend to listen more than I talk, and I've learned not to make decisions too quickly. In running any company, especially a hospitality company, you learn it's all about the talent in your organization, not the technical aspects in running any particular part of a hotel.

When I arrived at Carlson, there was a culture of mistrust, and I recognized quickly that you don't change this overnight. The principles at Carlson had earlier been abused by mediocre leadership, and inevitably, that mistrust permeated the entire organization. What I've tried to teach everyone is that once you trust yourself, you can begin to trust other people. It takes a long time to effectuate this transformation, but it's worked.

Regarding the future leaders of the industry, unlike many of my peers who are hoteliers, the next generation of leaders will come more from the finance and branding functions. There won't be as many operators running hotel companies in the future. And these new leaders will need to be people who can run global businesses. In fact, the Europeans may be better at this cross-cultural maneuvering than the Americans. I do think that our industry will undergo a period of consolidation and then, once again, blow apart into entrepreneurial pods. And this will fit very well with the goals and desires of the 25-year-old free spirits coming up through the system.

ANDREW D. WOODWARD
RETIRED CHAIRMAN
BANK OF AMERICA MORTGAGE

> *"I would not tolerate grandstanders or prima donnas and drove into the organization that we 'won as a team and lost as a team.' I constantly challenged people to play five feet over their heads. We were quiet and humble, and had a strong work ethic. We executed well: five yards and a cloud of dust."*

As chairman of Bank of America Mortgage, Andy Woodward led the mortgage piece of a banking enterprise serving more than 30 million households. Woodward made it his mission "to make banking work in ways that it's never worked before,"

with the mortgage product being central to a customer's relationship. He also
served as president of the Mortgage Bankers Association of America.

The residential mortgage banking business is a conflict-intensive business. I had functional reports, including sales, operations, capital markets, and servicing. Inevitably, if a decision might benefit one discipline, it could potentially hurt another, so I had to keep everyone focused on what was the optimal total score versus protecting individual fiefdoms. A collaborative management style was critical. Trust was required and decisions were never made in a vacuum. I would not tolerate grandstanders or prima donnas and drove into the organization that we "won as a team and lost as a team." I constantly challenged people to play five feet over their heads. We were quiet and humble, and had a strong work ethic. We executed well: five yards and a cloud of dust.

My job was to draw the road map and ensure the mortgage banking business had the support of corporate. My style was to be collaborative, team oriented, communicative, and motivational. I always looked for people who had common sense, could communicate simply, and had a keen curiosity. Good people never accept a simple answer—they have three more questions for every answer. My Achilles heel is that sometimes my heart can be bigger than my head.

As I think about my career, I realize I was never afraid to climb a mountain. Taking Fleet Mortgage Group public was a turning point in our industry. Our IPO allowed us to obtain almost $2 billion of unsecured debt and, in the process, redefine how large public mortgage banking companies were financed. It gave us the capital needed to continue our strong growth. Over the course of my career, I have been involved in more than 30 mergers and acquisitions transactions.

When I served as the volunteer president of the Mortgage Bankers Association, we had to make course corrections to restore long-term fiscal stability. Much of my term was spent conducting the search for a new executive director while working on rebalancing the financials. The MBA was heavily staffed with very effective, high-profile policy experts who were generally not accustomed to running the association like a business. As a businessman, I was on unfamiliar turf in the complex public policy arena. It took a great deal of compromise and consensus building to balance the conflicts, reset priorities, and find the winning operating formula. We all checked our egos at the door and pulled together as a team. I am exceedingly proud of the staff and the results.

CHAPTER EIGHT

SHARE A SENSE OF VULNERABILITY

Real estate's hard-charging, entrepreneurial image seems to run rough-shod over leadership attributes such as introspection and humility. But real estate is fundamentally about providing desirable shelter, a core human need with strong emotional currents. In fact, most successful real estate businesses build cultures that nurture openness, encourage feedback, and create trust. Running any business requires a partnership among all employees, and the partnership only works if a culture is created in which people's opinions matter. Subordinating individual accolades to team performance is closely allied with strong leaders' willingness to admit they do not have all the answers and to own up to mistakes. Employees bond to a leader's strengths but also appreciate acknowledgement of inevitable weakness. Displays of humility and humanity allow leaders to connect with their organization and bring out the best in employees. Low-ego manage-ment styles form the basis for an open culture that can build trust and a sense of shared goals. But successful chief executives must wrap humility in passion for the company and belief in their vision. Naked vulnerability shat-ters confidence. Ultimately, leaders can rally their troops only if they show unwavering commitment to a well-conceived company mission.

Create a Common Commitment

For a CEO, acknowledging not having all the answers is an essential component of leading by example and rallying the team. It can transform weakness into strength. When you communicate a sense of vulnerability, you connect with people. It helps build a winning low-ego, "we're all in this together" culture, embodying a team orientation over a "me" orientation.

Value Others' Opinions

"The senior management team needs to understand that I want constructive feedback in a culture where people can talk openly without any retribution," says Thilo Best of Horizon Bay Communities, a seniors' housing firm. "The key to my success was that our people decided to trust me." Open communication is a winning formula. "Any CEO who becomes too defensive or gets wrapped up in his own ego will never be successful," says Chuck Ledsinger of Choice Hotels. Attracting and retaining a high-achieving executive team requires "the humility and openness to absorb other people's ideas," says George Chapman of Health Care REIT. "Know-it-all" CEOs— control freaks whose communication style edges toward dogmatic rigidity— can drive organizational opposition underground and grind businesses to a halt as Sidney Finkelstein points out in his book, *Why Smart Executives Fail*. "In diversified firms, chief executives simply can't know everything," says Bob Lowe of Lowe Enterprises.

Openness Matters

Successful businesses don't make many mistakes, but when they do, the mechanisms exist to fix them quickly and limit damage. Chief executives set the tone. If they openly own up to errors, subordinates are more likely to follow suit. "That way you can deal with mistakes before they get out of hand," says Peter Rummell of Nicklaus Companies. "Open communication also allows everyone to learn from the mistakes, so they are not repeated. Acknowledging mistakes is one of a successful company's most important attributes."

Sharing a sense of vulnerability ties into other leadership themes discussed in this book. Vulnerability is all about admitting that a leader is human and that making mistakes is acceptable and, in fact, required, if a company is going to grow and be a winner. Failed leaders are unwilling to admit their mistakes and, all too often, blame others for their failure. This is quite disingenuous and its effects are readily apparent throughout any organization. In fact, many leaders would argue that acknowledging mistakes is the most important attribute or characteristic to emulate in an organization.

This issue of vulnerability is about an organization giving constructive feedback to its leader and that feedback being embraced, resulting in a culture of trust. Bob Lowe said it well: "A CEO simply can't know everything." Peter Rummell attributes leadership success to one's ability to acknowledge mistakes and then fix them. Egotistical CEOs have companies that serve them, as Mark Schulte of Brookdale articulates. He and the senior management team are there to serve their residents and employees. Arne Sorenson of Marriott summarizes the concept best. Because he is open minded and self-critical, his people respect that and in fact emulate it, and the overall business is better for it.

JOSEPH K. AZELBY
MANAGING DIRECTOR
JPMORGAN ASSET MANAGEMENT

> *"I was ultimately successful because I had no biases and spent a lot of time getting to know people, communicating with them, and ultimately doing what I felt was the right thing to do."*

As a part of JPMorgan Chase & Co., JPMorgan Asset Management Real Estate has around $46 billion in real estate assets under management. Joe Azelby has been responsible for globalizing and diversifying the division. While the division's business had been exclusively U.S-centric—investments in multifamily, retail, office, and industrial real estate—today over half of its growth derives from

international or alternative investments ranging from private equity to REIT
securities. Azelby has also expanded capital channels beyond pension funds, foun-
dations, and endowments into the high–net worth market.

Often leadership necessitates moving ahead without being fully informed, as scary as that can seem. When JPMorgan bought O'Connor Realty Advisors in 1998, I had just been given responsibility for the real estate investment management business. But I knew virtually nothing about equity real estate, since I had come from the fixed-income side of our asset management business. There were 28 people in the acquired company, and I was charged with integrating their business into ours. I was ultimately successful because I had no preconceptions and spent a lot of time getting to know people, communicating with them, and ultimately doing what I felt was the right thing to do. I also recognized that I have certain strengths and weaknesses, and built an organization and a leadership team with skills that complemented my own.

THILO D. BEST
CHAIRMAN OF THE BOARD AND CEO
HORIZON BAY SENIOR COMMUNITIES

> *"I needed my senior managers to understand I wanted*
> *constructive feedback to help create a culture in which people*
> *could talk openly without any retribution. The key to my success*
> *was that our people decided to trust me."*

Florida-based Horizon Bay Senior Communities is the largest for-profit manager
of seniors' housing communities, with almost 10,000 units located in 15 states.
Horizon Bay manages several types of communities, including independent living,
assisted living and skilled nursing care.

I needed a senior management team to understand that I wanted constructive feedback in order to help create a culture in which people could talk openly without any retribution. The key to my success was that our people decided to trust me. Interestingly, I never appreciated how lonely it was at the top until I got there. But one of my greatest leadership moments, a real epiphany for me, occurred when a couple of my senior people came into my office and thanked me for my efforts in turning around the business.

My style takes a participatory approach to management, and I want my management team to tell me when they feel I'm heading in the wrong direction. I always want to avoid a culture of management by intimidation. In that type of environment, there is typically very little honest feedback from the management team to the leadership. I have also learned the value and importance of making the hard decisions. As CEO, you realize those decisions are your responsibility and cannot be pawned off.

In refocusing the business, I dug in and tried to learn every aspect of it early on. While I don't view myself as a micromanager, I clearly took a hands-on approach. Initially, I spent a tremendous amount of time focused on getting the right team in place and executing. One and a half years after I assumed leadership of the company, when the company was stabilized, I refocused my attention on strategy, creating value in assets and building a world-class operational team. I found that the key success factors in hiring my operating people were integrity and a sense of urgency.

In order to be a great company in the seniors' housing business, you need to set high standards. Next, you need to hire great people and create a culture that helps retain those people. Today, executives call me asking about opportunities at Horizon Bay. Finally, great companies create cultures of accountability, where good people are constantly challenged and weak performers get weeded out.

GEORGE L. CHAPMAN
CHAIRMAN AND CEO
HEALTH CARE REIT

>*"In order for me to attract the right players, I need to have*
>*sufficient openness to absorb others' ideas."*

George Chapman has headed Health Care REIT since 1996. On December 31,
2006, this REIT had investments in 550 facilities across the full operation of
seniors' housing and health care, leased to some 61 health care operators in 37
states. Under his leadership, the company has become an internally managed
equity REIT, attained investment-grade status, and grown its assets from $472
million to more than $4 billion.

Our success at Health Care REIT stems from selecting the right people and
then letting them perform. Key contributors are rewarded and motivated,
and nonperformers are asked to leave the company. We're in a tough business. Our people are managing a large pool of geographically dispersed
assets. We are like a venture capitalist, constantly seeking new operators to
put into business. As we select and motivate our own people, good operators need to be acknowledged for their performance, and the underperforming ones need to be removed from the system. The cyclicality of the
health care industry compounds our challenges. We try to learn from the
past, so that these cycles won't be so severe in the future.

Our success is also about providing people with the autonomy to
contribute. Yet they need to be team players, because no one individual can
run a company. The team must be built to have complementary skills, especially as the organization grows larger. Even though we have a reasonably
small staff, I involve the management team in strategic planning. We have
a very open dialogue, because I respect the opinions of my colleagues. We
exchange ideas and make certain that the organization is never so rigid that
we can't all think outside the box.

Fortunately, we have assembled a superb management team. In order for me to attract the right players, I need to have sufficient openness to absorb others' ideas. I am always attempting to motivate and recognize people. At the end of the day, a good manager needs to know what to look for in people. I focus on individuals who are smart self-starters, who will challenge all of us on the senior management team. It's okay if these people are occasionally difficult as long as over time they are collaborative, demonstrate courtesy for one another, possess mutual respect, and care for each other.

JAMES F. FLAHERTY III
CHAIRMAN, PRESIDENT, AND CEO
HCP, INC.

> *"I've always tried to keep my ego checked at the door; my picture*
> *will never appear in the annual report, even though the pictures*
> *of our senior management team members will."*

HCP is a REIT that invests directly or through joint ventures in health care facilities. In November 2006, the company's portfolio included 801 properties and consisted of 333 seniors' housing facilities, 265 medical office buildings, 30 hospitals, 144 skilled nursing facilities, and 29 other health care facilities, including facilities recently acquired from CNL Retirement Properties Inc. James Flaherty previously spent 19 years at Merrill Lynch, where he ran the global health care group.

The best companies avoid arrogance and manage their business with humility. They understand what they know and don't know, and are passionate about their expertise. I've always tried to keep my ego checked at the door; my picture will never appear in the annual report, even though the pictures of our senior management team members will. My skill is in hiring good people who will ultimately add value to the enterprise. It's important to accept change, and as a company we try to embrace it. Among health care REITs, reengineering is a reality—given demographic trends, some of these companies should be positioned to become some of the biggest REIT stocks.

Initially, I worried about having the right management team in place. Two weeks into my role as CEO, a crisis convinced me I needed to reevaluate senior management. I terminated a number of long-term employees, and I was conscious of hiring people who complemented me and were willing to speak their piece. Great companies have CEOs who let their people run the business, so they can focus on strategy and building the business.

My biggest challenge has been the transition from investment banker to principal. My people know I am demanding, but I don't ask them to do anything that I wouldn't do myself.

DAVID J. HEGARTY
PRESIDENT AND CHIEF OPERATING OFFICER
SENIOR HOUSING PROPERTIES TRUST

> *"I view myself as understanding and compassionate—while I*
> *want to earn a fair wage, my mission is not about compensation."*

Senior Housing Properties Trust (SNH) is a real estate investment trust, or REIT, which owns independent living and assisted living communities, continuing care retirement communities, nursing homes, wellness centers, and medical office, clinic and biotech laboratory buildings located throughout the United States. Senior Housing Properties Trust has 223 properties that are leased to 11 tenants.

I view much of my compensation as making a contribution to society. Like many leaders in the seniors' housing and health care industry, I came up through the ranks and gained the respect of the rank and file. I view myself as understanding and compassionate—while I want to earn a fair wage, my mission is not about compensation. I tend to look at the business on a long-term basis and believe that success in the industry involves balancing the needs of tenants with required returns to shareholders.

Managing the enterprise is similar. I treat my management team as responsible adults and give them flexibility in accomplishing objectives. I delegate responsibility but in the final analysis expect things to be accomplished. As an example, I was confronted with a major business decision and a difficult one at that. It all got back to people, especially the patients. We owned a number of nursing homes that were being managed by third-party operators that filed bankruptcy in 2000. I decided to manage the properties through the REIT, a huge risk with significant costs attendant to the decision. But the company needed to control its own destiny and care for its properties and patients. If I were to grow the business from here, the portfolio needed to be managed well. With the nursing home industry largely in bankruptcy at that time, my partners looked to me to make this happen. I was able to recruit some outstanding people to form an operating company, and it turned out to be an excellent long-term business decision.

MARK HOPLAMAZIAN
PRESIDENT AND CEO
GLOBAL HYATT CORPORATION

"Integrity is simply the price of entry."

Global Hyatt operates hotels and resorts for travelers in the United States and internationally. It also owns and operates a vacation club and fractional residential properties.

Leadership, whether in a corporate setting or some other environment, revolves around two fundamental tenets. The first is values. These have to be explicit, shared, and constantly promoted. Integrity is simply the price of entry. Next comes mutual respect. We have around 90,000 employees today, and if they don't respect each other, they clearly won't respect our customers or our owners. Then comes intellectual honesty. In order for us to be self-critical and continue to improve, we must have an environment of trust in which our people are comfortable sharing their weaknesses and soliciting help. However, simultaneously, there must be accountability. People need to be held responsible for their performance.

The second critical tenet is that there must be common goals. When I accepted this role, I needed to learn the company, and that required significant travel to meet the people and understand the assets. After that, I started developing a strategy, which our people now own.

I grew up as a transactions person. In my new role, I have come to appreciate that while decisions can be made reasonably quickly, it takes time for them to become engrained in the system. This hasn't been easy for me, because I was more accustomed to immediate gratification. I still like to manage by walking around versus doing most things in e-mails or meetings. It's a little easier now that I've visited our people and properties around the world, and even though it's not the most time efficient, it does allow me to connect with the business in the most fundamental way.

Upon being promoted into this role, I first needed to assemble a management team. I discovered very quickly that people who will be successful are self-aware. They're honest about their strengths and weaknesses, and they work hard to continue to grow. They also aspire to make a difference. I'm not talking about improving earnings in 2009, but making this company one of the best in the industry. Our biggest challenge, as we grow, is that we need to maintain the positive qualities of our field culture. While there are benefits to process and consistency, we have to work hard to maintain our "small big culture." Having that entrepreneurial spirit in the field, where people have autonomy to run their businesses, is critical to our long-term success.

THOMAS W. LATOUR
CEO
LATOUR GROUP

"I call it the tombstone approach—I want to be remembered for allowing my people to achieve their highest potential."

Before founding his own business, LaTour Group, Tom served as CEO of Kimpton Hotel and Restaurant Group which manages boutique hotels across the United States and Canada. Targeting business and leisure travelers, the hotel chain offers smaller, European-style accommodations, often in renovated historic buildings. Bill Kimpton founded the firm in 1981, and Tom LaTour became CEO when Kimpton passed away in 2001. He retired in 2006.

Leadership is all about bold action and conviction. When my partner, Bill Kimpton, passed away, everyone looked to me with confidence. I had been trained well by Bill, in both the principles of the hospitality business and our company cultural ideals. I needed to make important decisions, ranging from capitalizing the company to positioning our assets in the market. While I had some trepidation, making decisions quickly was important and I quickly realized people want to be led.

In running the business, I focused on three priorities. First, our guests and customers part with their dollars in exchange for services and experiences. I was constantly focused on making sure they get value for their spending. I visited our hotels regularly and dined with guests to get feedback, and we e-mail quality surveys to all of our guests. Second, I made sure that we have a skilled and motivated workforce in order to be competitive. We spend a lot of time training staff, and I led orientation/leadership talks throughout the company. Finally, I rigorously tracked our economic performance, for the benefit of our shareholders.

My style is to be honest and compassionate. I feel strongly that a CEO needs to tell the truth and take the truth. I tried to help people get better at what they do. At Kimpton University, our training program, our people are encouraged develop the tools for success; everything from telephone etiquette to food handling is covered, not to mention self-assessment programs. I call it the tombstone approach—I want to be remembered for allowing my people to achieve their highest potential.

People do not join companies because of compensation, benefits, or sabbaticals. They want environments with a commitment to their well-being. They want to be part of a well-run enterprise. People want to be with a company that is committed to their development and personal growth. Growth brings career opportunities, which means more responsibility and enhanced compensation. At the end of the day, our middle management ensures that the company is run well, and our senior management needs to be in the field all the time, caring for and motivating this team. Since employee costs represent 50 cents of every dollar of operating costs in restaurants and 35 cents of every dollar in hotels, nothing is more important for a hospitality company than to attract and retain the best people possible.

CHARLES A. LEDSINGER, JR.
VICE CHAIRMAN
CHOICE HOTELS INTERNATIONAL, INC.

> *"Any CEO who becomes too defensive or who gets wrapped up in his own ego will never be successful. I try to lead with my heart, but people must trust my judgment and feel that the company is a good place to work."*

Choice Hotels International is a franchise system with more than 5,000 hotels in 40 countries. Among the Choice brands are Cambria Suites, Clarion, Quality, Comfort Suites, Comfort Inn, Sleep Inn, MainStay Suites, Suburban Extended Stay Hotels, Econo Lodge, and Rodeway Inn. Charles Ledsinger, who has headed the company since 1998, has directed Choice during a highly volatile period in the hotel industry, one of the most competitive and toughest real estate sectors.

Ledsinger has led the company to an average total annual shareholder return of more than 29 percent. He retired as CEO in 2008.

My style is to set the box and let my people play in it. In other words, I like to delegate and allow my people to execute. I spend the majority of my time on strategy and new business, customer issues, and then overall operations. I am constantly thinking about trends in the sector, where new brands might be appropriate, and how to grow the business. And my people are an important part of this strategic process—I want to hear their challenges and successes so we can constantly adapt in a sector that is increasingly complicated, segmented, and diffused.

A CEO can never underestimate the importance of the people side of the business. Any CEO who becomes too defensive or gets wrapped up in his own ego will never be successful. He needs to reach out and challenge his people to be the best that they can be. I spend a tremendous amount of time interacting with my people, because this is extraordinarily important in a service business. I have brought discipline to the business but also sincerity. Running a business successfully is all about balancing performance with a supportive culture. I try to lead with my heart, but people must trust my judgment and feel that the company is a good place to work.

A CEO can never forget about his value proposition, especially when times are challenging. When I took over Choice Hotels, in 1998, it was in a troubled situation. Our stock was trading at $6.25 a share, and the franchisees were unhappy. I had to rebuild trust. So, I hosted franchisee meetings so they understood how critical I thought they were to our success equation. I then recruited people to my management team who shared this business philosophy and focused on trust, ethics, and taking the high road.

Even though Choice was publicly traded, it still ran like a family business when I joined the company. There were two co-CEOs on the board, as well as two former CEOs. One of the conditions of my employment was changing the board makeup. I focused on what I felt was the right thing to do and focused the company on what it did well. We initially built the company on its strengths and later concentrated on shoring up its weaknesses. We had been trying to do too many things, and I concentrated on basic priorities, in essence leveraging our core business.

FREDERICH LIEBLICH
MANAGING DIRECTOR AND HEAD OF GLOBAL
    REAL ESTATE EQUITY
BLACKROCK REAL ESTATE

> *"I knew what it was like to go through tough times and appreciated the creativity, endurance, and restlessness required to be a business leader."*

Since 1984, Fred Lieblich has served in various positions with Metropolitan Life and SSR Realty (the predecessor to BlackRock) including research, acquisitions, financing, asset management, dispositions, and investment strategy. In 2003, he was appointed head of BlackRock's Real Estate Equity business; by the end of 2006, it approached $21 billion in gross asset value.

Success in our business is derived from attracting and retaining people who fit our culture, as well as speed of execution in implementing corporate and investment strategy. It's one thing to discuss and agree on a strategy, but it's quite another to make it happen.

When I assumed responsibility for this business in 2003, the culture needed changing, and I made a big deal of rewarding new behavior, publicly, privately, and through compensation. We needed to compete at the highest levels, in terms of both attracting capital and investing it. I needed to change some of the current management team and recruit people, like myself, who were energized and had a "can do" attitude. There's a strong team orientation within BlackRock; in fact, the firm's ethos is "One Black-Rock." I want people with low egos and high teaming skills. We are going to have one real estate organization globally that works together toward a common goal, not one with distinct regional and functional silos.

I learned a lot about making something work at an early age. My family was in the homebuilding business, and I always had multiple jobs. In fact, I built my first house as a senior in high school, worked very hard, but still lost money on it—can't fight the market. But I stayed in the business. My father, on at least one occasion, had to declare bankruptcy. I knew what it was like to go through tough times and appreciated the creativity, endurance, and restlessness required to be a business leader.

I try to be participative, ethical, and a genuinely decent human being. Now that we're global, I have 25 members on my senior management team, and we meet regularly to make decisions on the business. I tell them that in order to be good leaders, you need to know this industry so well you feel it in your gut and anticipate what's going to happen. Our organization clearly has better deal makers, asset managers, and client professionals than me. What I enjoy is trying to understand the big picture and setting the vision.

As part of my leadership mandate, I purposely spend a lot of time with our people. I think it's incredibly important to develop a culture of trust. I travel to our offices at least once a quarter and visit with a whole host of people. I can hear the problems, see the opportunities, and most important, address them. I host a company-wide quarterly teleconference, where I can communicate our performance to the entire organization. I also facilitate monthly meetings for each of our functional heads, so that I can understand their goals and what's working—and not working—within the company. I keep a strong hand on the firm's investment strategy, making sure we're thinking about the right markets and pursuing the right types of product. I also closely monitor our portfolio composition to ensure that it's aligned with our clients' investment expectations. I am very proud of our investment process and investment professionals.

When I took over as head of real estate, I had a very small industry footprint. Everyone was wondering, both inside the company and in the marketplace, who I was and what we were going to do. We had a corporate

conference six months after I assumed the top role. I set out some very ambitious goals, including growing the platform from $5 billion in assets under
management to $10 billion with strong investment performance. People
rallied behind me, and we've never looked back.

ROBERT J. LOWE
CHAIRMAN AND CEO
LOWE ENTERPRISES, INC.

> *"My style is to be inclusive, participative, and consensus driven.
> I'm not comfortable with an autocratic, top-down approach. In a
> diversified firm like ours, a CEO simply can't know everything."*

*Lowe Enterprises, founded by Robert Lowe in 1972, has developed, acquired, or
managed more than $6 billion in commercial, hotel, and residential real estate.
The privately held company employs more than 7,000 people in three divisions—
investments, commercial-residential development and property management, and
hotel/resort development and management.*

I spend a lot of time finding and retaining people, using a very hands-on
approach in dealing with problems. Generally, I encourage my direct reports
to run their respective businesses, but when there are issues, I'm comfortable in getting involved.

Our senior management team personifies the company's culture. My
style is to be inclusive, participative, and consensus driven. I'm not comfortable with an autocratic, top-down approach. In a diversified firm like ours, a
CEO simply can't know everything. I also believe strongly in giving back to
the community, as well as to the real estate industry as a whole. This commitment makes us all better at what we do.

Our firm believes strongly in core values. Integrity and ethics are at
the top of our list, and next we pursue quality and excellence in all that we
do. We strongly believe in treating others fairly and with respect, and work

as teams in a collegial environment, where we empower prepared people. We value loyalty and superior performance, and seek balance in our professional and personal lives.

The high-performing companies in our sector take care of their people and understand the importance of accessing competitive capital. Interestingly, these two factors are related, because investors are more willing to align themselves with companies that have low turnover and do quality work. Our culture is strong and we have been able to retain people, allowing us to withstand the various gyrations in the real estate markets. We know what we are good at and don't digress from our focus in commercial property, hotels and resorts, and high-end second-home resort development and investment. Finally, high-performing firms recognize the importance of contributing to their communities, and they build high-quality assets and manage them well. This generates a great reputation, which is the best asset any company can have.

LAWRENCE J. MELODY
CHAIRMAN
CBRE MELODY

> *"I always try to be one of the guys, and we have avoided buying commercial companies full of prima donnas. I have turned over management of the day-to-day business to a competent team. As in automobile racing, one can race the car, drive it, or fix it. I am now the mechanic, advising people on issues where they need help."*

L.J. Melody & Co., a national mortgage banking company, was founded by Larry Melody In 1978; in 1996 it was acquired by CB Richard Ellis and now operates as a wholly owned subsidiary. The integration of CB Commercial Mortgage with L.J. Melody & Co., creating CBRE Melody, has created one of the industry's largest companies. During his career Melody successfully built another mortgage banker, Northland Mortgage.

Since the CB Richard Ellis purchase, we have grown by acquiring other family-owned businesses. I understand from personal experience that the acquired CEO still wants to be involved in running the business, and the best approach is to be a partner with that executive rather than his boss. I started our company 30 years ago with six people. I always try to be one of the guys, and we have avoided buying companies full of prima donnas. Today, I have turned over the management of the day-to-day business to a competent team. As in automobile racing, one can own the car, drive it, or fix it. I am now the mechanic, advising people on issues where they need help.

Since 1996, our success has derived from how CB Richard Ellis has managed us and from my making the right but tough decisions. When I began integrating L.J. Melody and CB's commercial mortgage banking business, they were roughly the same size in production (about $1 billion) and the same size in servicing (about $3 billion). They had different compensation plans, and CB had 25 offices, where L.J. Melody had only seven. CB was unprofitable and we were profitable, so I closed offices and fired some people to right-size the company. This was tough, especially as an outsider, but it was the right thing to do. CB Richard Ellis gave me the freedom to do what I thought was necessary and held me accountable. They provided me the needed funding and always stood by their commitments. They left our compensation program alone and kept the Melody name, even though I didn't require it.

STEVAN D. PORTER
FORMER PRESIDENT OF THE AMERICAS
INTERCONTINENTAL HOTELS GROUP PLC

> *"I try to be approachable, I find ways to engage people through the heart, and I create the right balance of intensity and results with collegiality."*

Intercontinental Hotels Group PLC (IHG) always tries to see the world through the eyes of others. IHG has more guest rooms than any other hotel company in

the world—590,361 rooms in almost 4,000 hotels across nearly 100 countries.
IHG's guests make more than 160 million stays in IHG hotels every year through
seven hotel brands: InterContinental, Crowne Plaza, Hotel Indigo, Holiday Inn,
Holiday Inn Express, Staybridge Suites, and Candlewood Suites. As president
of the Americas, Stevan D. Porter was responsible for the management, growth,
and profitability of the company's largest operating region, spanning the United
States, Canada, Mexico, Central and South America, and the Caribbean. He was
responsible for a portfolio of more than 3,000 hotels and resorts. In 2008, Steve
tragically passed away. He was truly beloved in the hospitality industry.

Regarding my leadership style, I follow three fundamental tenets. I try to be
approachable, I find ways to engage people through the heart, and I create
the right balance of intensity and results with collegiality. In any global
business—and I would argue it's a greater risk in the hospitality industry—
it's too easy to move into an ivory tower and spend all of one's time craft-
ing grand strategies. We are in a business where serving the customer is
most important, and I appreciate that as much as anyone, since I came up
through the system, serving as a general manager and beyond.

It's easy to engage people's intellects, but it's much more challenging to
engage their hearts. Ours is a variation of show business, without the curtain.
We go out of our way to take care of our people and encourage them to open
their minds and embrace diversity. In fact, when I give speeches on leadership
internally, I'm known to quote one of two authors, Dr. Suess or Richard Bode,
who wrote *First You Have to Row a Little Boat.* Their leadership lessons are
simple, but they're powerful: Walk before you run.

Finally, I've tried to create an environment where there's a balance
between results and collegiality. My people know that I understand the
details, and they must do the same. And I will always question them about
various issues, not to embarrass them, but to make sure they're authentic
and willing to debate points where we don't agree. In fact, I look for people
who will push me. They understand the importance of the details, yet they
also see the big picture, embracing it enthusiastically and optimistically. And

in their DNA there is flexibility, because that's the only way to grow successfully in a global firm.

As my own career developed, I had three great mentors, each of
whom taught me something different. Jim Sherwood at Stouffer Hotels
taught me that I needed to know the details, work hard, and people would
follow me only if I had my own skin in the game. Pete Dangerfield, also at
Stouffer Hotels, engrained in me the importance of taking the time to know
people and displaying empathy for them. They in return will follow you
anywhere. And finally, from Mike Rose at Promus, I learned how empowering it was to cut through the noise and ensure that I was focused on the
right stuff in order to effectuate our strategy.

PETER S. RUMMELL
CEO
NICKLAUS COMPANIES LLC

> *"One of the most important attributes of a successful company is
> acknowledging mistakes and then fixing them."*

*In 2008, Peter Rummell was named CEO of Nicklaus Companies LLC, founded
by golf legend Jack Nicklaus and owned by the Nicklaus family. Earlier Rummell
served as chairman and CEO of the St. Joe Company a residential and commercial
real estate development firm in Jacksonville, Florida. Rummell led the company
until 2008. Previously, he served as chairman of Walt Disney Imagineering, the
merged group of Disney Development Company and Walt Disney Engineering. Since 1985, Rummell had served as president of the Disney Development
Company's non–theme park land, directing hotel and related development at the
company's theme park locations in Orlando, Anaheim, Paris, and Tokyo.*

Today, the real estate industry has more sophisticated management and is more
heavily scrutinized than ever. All in all, this creates stability and adds credibility
to the sector but also creates more pressure for the industry's leadership.

I always try to recognize strengths and weaknesses. I spend more time with the board than others in senior management and focus on strategic growth opportunities for the portfolio. Senior management spends much of its time on refining that strategy and on execution of our land development projects, which has to dovetail with our corporate strategy.

As a leader, my style is consensus oriented. I try to hire people smarter than myself—smart people working as a team generate outstanding results. Our culture is creative and team oriented, which is so important in the community development business. When I arrived at St. Joe, there were 60 people in the corporate office. By the time our transformation was complete, I had changed all but four. Over the years I've made my own share of hiring mistakes, but one of the most important attributes of a successful company is acknowledging mistakes and then fixing them.

MARK J. SCHULTE
RETIRED CO-CEO
BROOKDALE SENIOR LIVING INC.

> *"Egotistical CEOs have companies that serve them; in the seniors' housing business, we're here to serve our residents and employees."*

With nearly 550 facilities in 36 states, Brookdale is the largest operator of seniors' living in the United States, with nearly 31,000 employees. Mark Schulte brought 25 years of experience to developing and managing seniors' and assisted living facilities. He joined Brookdale Senior Living's predecessor company in 1991 and was instrumental in the formation of Brookdale in 1995. He oversaw the merger of Brookdale and Alterra Healthcare Corporation in 2005, the combined company's successful IPO later in the year, and the subsequent acquisition of American Retirement Corporation. Schulte retired in 2008.

To be successful in a service-intensive business like seniors' living, a CEO must do a number of things well—resetting priorities, chasing transactions, interfacing with investors and lenders, and addressing the day-to-day issues of caring for our senior residents. I always have to resist the temptation to just react and take the time to listen, strategize, and develop to make sure we are properly utilizing the talent that is here in the company. CEOs need to respond to opportunities when they arise, but a big part of success is keeping the company focused and knowing what not to do.

Successful CEOs in the seniors' living business must keep egos in check or else they can become corrosive to the business and an obstacle to the people around them. Egotistical CEOs have companies that serve them; in the seniors' housing business, we're here to serve our residents and employees. I spend a tremendous amount of time recruiting and mentoring our people. Unfortunately, across American business, there seems to be a constant churning of people. That can't work for us. We rely heavily on building long-term personal relationships with our customers, and the priority is them, not me.

W.E. "BILL" SHERIFF
CO-CEO
BROOKDALE SENIOR LIVING INC.

"A strong culture is reflected in openness and vulnerability."

In 1997, American Retirement Corp. (ARC) became the first seniors' living company to be listed on the NYSE, and in 2006 the company was acquired by Brookdale Senior Living. Starting in 1984, Bill Sheriff led ARC and its predecessors, building the firm into one of the leaders in the seniors' living industry, with more than 82 seniors' living communities in 19 states with 15,350 units.

There are a number of attributes common among high-performing firms in the seniors' housing space, which we tried to emulate at ARC. First of all, integrity is important—people must live by a set of values that are articulated and constantly reinforced. Second, a vision is important; in ARC's case, it's all about serving our residents with respect and humility. Third, courage is critical, encompassing the character traits of confidence, commitment, and dedication. And finally, a strong culture is reflected in openness and vulner-ability. At ARC, there was always an open door policy across the company to address any issue.

In my opinion, no CEO has all the required skills or knowledge. He or she must have a team in place to effectuate a strategy. I view myself as an orchestra leader and allow the rest of the team to focus on the details of executing the business. I spend time on strategic issues and interfacing with the board, but my primary focus is making sure everyone works well together. I bring intensity to my work and expect a tremendous amount of effort from our people. I look for the right people and shape the organiza-tion around them.

ARNE SORENSON
PRESIDENT AND CHIEF OPERATING OFFICER
MARRIOTT INTERNATIONAL, INC.

> *"I empower people and put energy around issues. I take pride in getting a lot out of people, and that's because I'm open minded and self-critical."*

Marriott International is one of the lodging industry's leaders, operating in more than 65 countries. A former partner at Latham & Watkins, Arne Sorenson enjoyed a meteoric career path at Marriott International, joining the company in business development, later being appointed chief financial officer, and later adding responsibility for European businesses. He was promoted to chief operating officer in 2009.

Successful leaders in the hospitality industry need to identify the critical issues facing the business. It's not necessarily the leader's job to solve all of them, but the leader needs to understand them and listen to the organization. It's important to have an open mind and not allow cultural filters to get in the way of identifying important challenges.

Next, it's extraordinarily important for a leader to get the most out of his or her people. You accomplish objectives through people. A leader has to put the right people in the right jobs, ensure they have the appropriate mentoring and management development, and empower them to do their jobs and assume responsibility. Historically, Marriott International has had a somewhat schizophrenic culture—in a positive way. The finance people tend to be fast paced, transactional, and results oriented. In contrast, the operating people have been more conservative and process oriented. My goal is to bridge the gap and pull the two more closely together, because their interaction is critical to the success of our business.

Finally, leaders need to make decisions and make sure that they are the right ones. Unfortunately, decisions often get made with less than perfect information. Then again sometimes too much information can paralyze decision making.

I empower people and put energy around issues. I take pride in getting a lot out of my people, and that's because I'm open-minded and self-critical. It's very important to create an apolitical environment where decisions are made for the right reasons, not influenced by turf battles.

Leadership is about being bold, making the effort, and staying the course through tenacity and perseverance. Prior to joining Marriott, I had been an attorney with a client who was part of a failed Texas thrift. The U.S. Attorney's office informed me that my client was about to be indicted. I hopped on a plane, got to New Orleans, bullied my way into a meeting with the U.S. Attorney, and obtained immunity for my client.

In the hospitality space, long-term success will be driven by strategy and execution. Rock star CEOs won't be effective in running these global companies. Serving the guest is paramount.

INDEX

COMPANIES